MAMMALS

OF THE

NORTHWEST

WASHINGTON, OREGON, IDAHO
AND BRITISH COLUMBIA

By

EARL J. LARRISON

Illustrated by

AMY C. FISHER

THE
TRAILSIDE
SERIES

SEATTLE AUDUBON SOCIETY

1976

CONTENTS

© Copyright: Seattle Audubon Society, 1976

ISBN 0-914516-04-3

Library of Congress Card Number 73-94501

PREFACE

This is the ninth book in the Seattle Audubon Society's *Trailside Series*, a group of guides devoted to interpreting the flora and fauna of the Pacific Northwest. The present volume is an extensive revision of the author's WASHINGTON MAMMALS: THEIR HABITS, IDENTIFICATION, AND DISTRIBUTION, published in 1970 as the sixth number in the series. While some fifty percent of the general text of the earlier volume has been retained, the illustrations are new, the species' descriptions revised, the habitat notes enlarged, and the distributional summaries expanded to include the Pacific Northwest, here defined as comprising the states of Washington, Oregon, and Idaho, and the province of British Columbia (see map, page 4).

In the preparation of MAMMALS OF THE NORTHWEST, the literature was checked, specimens examined of almost all species included, thousands of photographs studied, and trips made to many parts of the Northwest area.

To the persons whose aid was acknowledged in WASHINGTON MAMMALS, the author reiterates his appreciation. His debt to the artist, Amy C. Fisher, who prepared the drawings, maps, half of the track diagrams, and the paintings for the covers is considerable. She spent many days in the bird and mammal museum at the University of Idaho preparing the drawings from actual specimens, photographs, and mounts. Mrs. Fisher, her husband Gregory, Stanlee Miller, and Gregory Pole provided advice and criticism, in addition to other services. Particularly appreciated was the kindness and hospitality afforded by Eugene Williams and his parents, Mr. and Mrs. Lawrence Williams, who invited the author to be their guest at their beautiful resort on Pickerel Lake, Minnesota, while the final assembly of the book was taking place.

Most helpful has been the cooperation and understanding of the SAS Publication Committee consisting of Pat Evans (chairperson), Anona Hales, Grace Patrick, and Hazel Wolf. Mrs. Wolf, SAS Secretary, has been, as always, most helpful in a hundred different ways. Of very great value have been the aid and advice of Kenneth Batchelder of the Portland Audubon Society and Donald Durham of Durham and Downey, the printers.

As stated in the previous book on mammals, it is the belief of many of us that true and enduring conservation will come only from an enlightened citizenry that appreciates the value of natural resources and is willing to do whatever is necessary to maintain them. May the interpretative value of this book provide some of that enlightenment!

Earl J. Larrison

Department of Biological Sciences
University of Idaho, Moscow
November 1, 1975

3

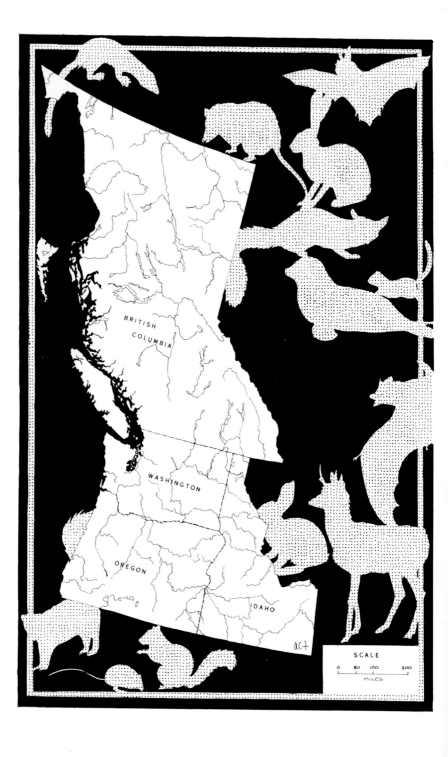

SCALE

0   50   100   200

MILES

INTRODUCTION

Mammal watching begins in the spring when the winter snows have melted and the first blades of new grass appear. Nowhere is this better demonstrated than in the area north of Pasco in Eastern Washington where the Washington Ground Squirrels may be said to come out of dormancy with the first green vegetation of spring and to re-enter suspended animation when the greenery dries out in early summer. Spring, then, is the time of appearance of hibernating mammals—the chipmunks, ground squirrels, marmots, bears, and jumping mice—to name just a few. The bleak, brown woods of spring, just after the snows have disappeared, are now populated with a noisy array of chipmunks and the open flats of the interior teem with ground squirrels. All are a part of the annual renewal of animal activity.

As spring merges into summer, mammal life is at its full. All of the hibernators are now out and mice are busy with feeding and breeding, young fawns are being born and carefully hidden by their mothers, and the squirrel tribe is adding to the woodland cacophony of sounds. As summer progresses up the mountainsides, the other mammals become apparent, the species of the high country, such as Elk, Mountain Goats, Hoary Marmots, and pikas. Some of these are reasons why hikers and mountain climbers take to the hills, not only "because the hills are there," but because there is a wealth of interesting plant and animal life among the cloud-spotted summits. We gain a special appreciation of the difficulties of alpine life and the niceties of environmental and behavioral adaptation necessary for its support when we study these high altitude species.

The author, in his many trips to the heights, especially on day climbs, has often had the feeling that those places were "forbidden," since he could visit them only for a few hours and then had to descend before night fell or a coming storm broke. How many times, before he began alpine camping expeditions, had he wished that he did not have to leave in mid-afternoon, but could remain overnight on equal standing with the local mammals and birds. Wonderful it was to be able to prepare the evening meal and to sit beside the campfire with the realization that at last he and the mountain animals belonged to each other!

Events occur as summer progresses. Those hidden fawns referred to earlier are now led forth and may occasionally be seen in early evening when they water by some lake margin. First appear the tiny tracks by the side of the mother's, then, if you are careful, you may see that little, spotted fellow itself—one of the most attractive of nature's sights.

About the first of August, a marked change takes place in the activities of many mammals. The shortened days and lengthening nights place a chill in the morning air and cloudy days become more frequent. Fruits, berries, and seeds are ripening, and all of these conditions trigger an often frenzied period of feeding and storage. Mammals that hibernate store their winter energy supplies in their bodies in the form of fat. To do this, they must eat continuously during their active hours. Other forms, which maintain some wakeful activity during cold months, must have well-stocked caches to use when blizzards and sub-zero chilling make outside foraging impossible. One of the most obvious of the latter is the Red Squirrel. Early in the summer, they are not too obvious, but in late July and August, the woods ring with their calls as they harvest cones and defend foraging territories. Little thuds are heard continuously through the woods as severed cones fall to the gound to be followed by scratchy-clawed squirrels gathering them up and stashing them away in hollow trees or holes in the ground. These are times of harvest and, like the days of our pioneer past, provision must be made for the approach of winter. How far our modern civilization has taken us from our earlier, closer relations with nature! Instead of putting vegetables away in the root cellar and smoked hams in the storeroom, we buy these articles any day in the local supermarket. Nevertheless, a special primordial delight is to be gained in some form of autumnal food gathering, even if it may be only the picking of a few mountain blueberries.

Certain species begin to disappear from the mammal scene as one by one the hibernators enter their winter inactivity. By October, most of the chipmunks have vanished from the mountain cabin feeding tray and woodpile. Bears are now busy in the timberline huckleberry patches, garnering the last of those fruits. Early fall storms reduce activity in the open and for a while, though small mice are still searching for food in protected places on the forest floor, little is to be seen of mammals. This is the time of late fall when the hunters enter the forests and mountains for the antlered game—deer, Elk, and Moose. The combination of fall foliage colors, brisk de-bugged days, and chilly nights, along with the primitive foraging urge mentioned earlier and the lure of the stalk, adds a zest to this outside activity that is unique. Undoubtedly, meat of equivalent quality could be purchased more cheaply in the local market, but the romantic aura of hunting and its associated woodcraft make these occasions very attractive to many people. We in the Pacific Northwest are most fortunate to have so much hunting area still available.

The first snows of early November reveal a whole new dimension in mammal watching. While previously the soft surface of the forest floor hid the activity of most mammals, the snow becomes a veritable tablet upon which, inadvertently, myriads of furry feet record the comings and goings of their owners. Few can pass by without leaving tell-tale records for those who can read such a script. We are impressed by the intricate designs of the Snowshoe Hare trails, the tiny filagree networks of the mice, the paired hop marks of the weasels, and the plodding foot marks and tail drags of the Porcupines. To the devotee of the winter scene, much can be learned, as will be indicated in a chapter in the appendix, of winter movements and behaviors, the stalking of prey, the foraging patterns, and much else. Many species, of course, carry on their work beneath the snow and seldom leave their records on the surface.

In the snow-bare lowlands, winter mammal activity is more normal, thus similar to that of summer. All seasons, however, have their interesting opportunities for mammal study and while these animals may not have the same mystique as birds, they do have their attractions as a part of the "wild kingdom."

How To Use The Guide

The bulk of this book contains a series of chapters, each devoted to a particular mammal group. These groups are informal clusters of similar species that differ noticeably from other such groups and may constitute an order, a family, or a genus, depending on the size of the cluster and its degree of difference from other clusters. See the list of groups in the discussion of mammal identification later in this introduction.

Each group begins with an illustration of one of its member species for characterizing the group. Then follows a general account of the group, containing a description of the cluster, notes on the habits, ecology, etc., of representative species, and other general information. This is followed by a series of species accounts which list the common name (the scientific name is to be found in the checklist of species in the appendix), dimensions (total length, tail length, length of hind foot, and ear height) in inches and millimeters, field characters of the species, the geographic range in the Pacific Northwest, and the habitat that the animal occupies.

For convenience in the range summaries, the words "mountains," "counties," "western," "eastern," "southern," "northern," "central," "Washington," "Oregon," and "British Columbia" have been shortened to "mts.," "cos.," "w.," "e.," "s.," "n.," "c.," "Wash.," "Ore.," and "B.C.," respectively.

To emphasize the complete common name in the body of the text, all such designations have been capitalized.

Principles of Mammal Identification

Identification is the first step in studying mammals, in addition to knowing where to find them. It is the dual purpose of this book in introducing its readers to the mammals of the Pacific Northwest to explain where they may be looked for and what their identifying characters are. However, this guide can be but an introduction. You must go to the mammals in their native haunts to know them which means searching in fields and forests, plains and mountains. Some species come only as the reward of much time spent in the field. To this group would belong the Fisher, Wolverine, and Bog Lemming. Others, like the Red Squirrels, deer, and chipmunks, are easily seen, often in the nearest city park or even in the backyard. Some species are encountered only by the field mammalogist in his trapping activities.

All species have unique characteristics and habits. All are the end products of millenia of trial and error genetic adaptation to their environments and ways of life.

An informal way of learning to recognize the mammals is to arrange similar species into groups (as has been done in this guide) and then to become acquainted with the characters of each of the groups. Once you can recognize a chipmunk or a mouse, the identification of which chipmunk or which mouse you have will be easy, since instead of comparing the species you wish to name with the almost 200 types in this book, you need compare it with only a few. Because similar species are usually closely related, these informal groups represent natural categories. Here is a list of these groups. Consult the index for their places in the guide.

opossums	chipmunks	kangaroo mice
shrews	marmots	kangaroo rats
moles	ground squirrels	beavers
bats	tree squirrels	cricetid mice
pikas	flying squirrels	wood rats
rabbits and hares	pocket gophers	voles
mountain beavers	pocket mice	muskrats

Old World rats and mice	dogs	seals
jumping mice	bears	deer
porcupines	procyonids	pronghorns
nutrias	mustelids	bovids
whales	cats	

After you have learned the characteristics of the above groups, read carefully the accounts and descriptions of the species making up each of them. In this way, you may become familiar with most Pacific Northwest mammals' forms and should be able to recognize immediately the name of the animal upon seeing it or find the name with a quick referral to this book.

Another valuable aid to identification is the consideration of the geographic and ecologic distribution of the various species. Excepting the bats, mammals do not have the powers of locomotion that birds possess and are much more fixed in their locations. The range and habitat summaries will tell you not only where the species occur but what types to expect in a particular area or environment. If you think that you have found a mammal in a considerably different location than that listed in the guide, you should re-check your identification. The illustrations should help you locate the group identity and probably will help a lot with the species. Treatment of subspecies has not been included in this manual, as they are difficult to separate and are mainly the concern of the professional specialist. Also, many are so poorly known in the Northwest that an adequate delineation of their variation and distribution would require a vast amount of new and well-planned field work. Not that such shouldn't be done, of course!

This book is heavily illustrated to aid the reader in his identification of mammal forms and understanding of the natural history of these animals. The line drawings are portraits of members of all the various groups and depict a large number of Northwest species. Numerous black and white photographs give an ecologic dimension to the presentation besides adding to the natural history portrayal. These features of the book are further enhanced by inclusion of a number of color photos. The author, the artist, and the photographers hope that these illustrations will flesh out the words of the text and present the mammals described herein in a more realistic manner.

SPECIES ACCOUNTS
OPOSSUMS

Figure 1.
American Opossum.

About the size of a domestic cat, the American Opossum has a grayish body with a white, pointed face, black ears and feet, and a long naked tail. The species is not native to the Pacific Northwest, having been introduced from the Eastern United States and possibly having spread northward along the Pacific Coast from California. As elsewhere, the Opossum will probably restrict itself to agricultural land with its variety of food and cover.

These animals are not often seen, being rather strongly nocturnal. They are omnivorous, feeding upon anything edible to them. The sense of smell is keen and a large part of the diet consists of car-killed mammals and birds which are sought in gutters and roadside ditches. The Opossum enjoys some reputation as a chicken thief, though such birds do not make up any sizable part of the diet, except under unusual local conditions. Often referred to as the "garbage man of the woods," the 'possum will kill rats and snakes, though it prefers the following, in decreasing order of usage: insects, fruits, invertebrates other than insects, mammals, reptiles, grain, birds, and birds' eggs.

Dens are located in hollow trees, rock piles, crannies under buildings, and abandoned burrows of other animals. They are lined with leaves and dry grass which the Opossum is reported to carry with its prehensile tail (or is this merely an animal tale?). At any rate, the Opossum's tail is really unique among tails of Northwest mammals, being capable of wrapping around branches as a fifth hand and also literally suspending the animal.

9

The breeding season is long, from late winter to late fall. Lacking a true placenta, a fact characteristic of the marsupials, the Opossum has a short gestation period of 13 days, the shortest term of any North American mammal! The young when born are extremely tiny, averaging about 14 mm—just a little over one-half inch in length. The entire litter, which may number as many as 25 young, may easily fit into the bowl of a teaspoon. The "larval" young find their way up through the saliva-moistened hairs of the female's abdomen to the marsupial pouch where those that successfully complete this hazardous journey and are in time to attach themselves to the 13 nipples will remain alive, the others perishing. Nursing takes almost two months. At the end of the third month, they are weaned. About seven young complete development.

Opossums are unsociable with their own kind and do not hibernate. They are not the most attractive of animals, being somewhat stupid in their actions, bad-smelling, and coarse-haired, and sometimes dripping at both ends. However, they are of value as carrion feeders and scavengers and their flesh is used as food, particularly in the southern states. The fur is of some value for coats. Scientists find them useful for experimentation in studies of sex development, hormone and drug action, nervous system development, and behavioral responses.

Essentially nocturnal in habit, the Opossum commonly remains close to its hollow tree or rocky cave home during the day, venturing out in darkness to secure food. Opossums are tremendously adaptable and their northern range seems limited only by the severity of the winters they can withstand. When frightened, the Opossum frequently bares its numerous teeth. Often, however, it may imitate death by falling on its side, closing its eyes, and extruding its tongue. While thought to be in shock, the "dead" individual seems to recover as soon as one's back is turned. These animals are good climbers, being most often found in deciduous growth along streams. The big toe of the hind foot is opposable. The prehensile tail also aids in getting around in the branches. Nevertheless, the Opossum is famous for falling out of trees and skeletons of many specimens show evidence of healed fractures of bones.

*　　*　　*

AMERICAN OPOSSUM 30-12-2⅕-1 (750-300-55-25) Fig. 1. Size, grayish fur, long scaly tail, and black ears and feet are distinctive. RANGE. Introduced into the coastal region of w. Wash. and w. Ore. from which it has spread throughout much of the lowlands, along the Columbia and Snake Rivers to s.e. Wash. and adjacent Idaho, and northward into extreme s.w. B.C. Populations have been recorded from e. Chelan Co., Wash. and the Umatilla area of Ore. HABITAT. Prefers stream bottoms in lowlands, especially in deciduous woods; forages also in agricultural fields, chicken farms, etc.

SHREWS

Figure 2.
Vagrant Shrew.

Shrews are the smallest of mammals. They are furred with thick, soft coats, except for their tails which are nearly hairless. Their snouts are sharply pointed, their eyes small, and their legs, though short, can carry them about rapidly. Shrews have a row of sharp teeth extending on each side of the jaw from the incisors continuously to the molars with no intervening space of a diastema, such as is found in rodents. Being so small, shrews have a very high metabolic rate, burning up "fuel" rapidly. Accordingly, they must be almost constantly in search of food. Shrews are mostly insectivorous, but consume almost any animal life they can subdue, even small mice. Tiny and secretive, shrews are seldom seen, though they are widespread and at least one species may occur in almost every natural or quasi-natural habitat in the Pacific Northwest. The collector of small mammals frequently traps them in sets baited with peanut butter, bacon, or rolled oats.

The author once caught alive a Dusky Shrew that had been attracted to a pile of skinned mouse carcasses just off the end of a table where specimens were being prepared by workshop students in the Selway-Bitterroot Wilderness of Idaho. We placed the little fellow, not without receiving a bitten finger, in a plastic drinking cup and observed him for some minutes. Its high metabolic rate was evidenced by the rapid breathing and heart beat. The nervous temperament was very obvious. The snap of a camera shutter would cause the animal to jump or twitch violently. Grasshoppers were killed and voraciously consumed when placed in the glass.

Twelve kinds of shrew occur in the Pacific Northwest, each species occupying a particular habitat and geographic range so that almost every ecologic type in the region covered by this guide contains a shrew. These animals are usually to be found in relatively dense vegetation where cover and shelter for such small mammals are readily available. Their preference for insects and various small invertebrates seems to require a fair amount of moisture, as well. Accordingly, the greatest density of shrews occurs in the moist, dark forests of the coastal regions while they are seldom encountered in the sparse grass or sagebrush in the arid interior.

The Cinereous Shrew is a forest species, usually preferring relatively dry, dark spots in the woods. The dark-grayish Trowbridge's Shrew is often a common denizen of the rain forest in the western part of the Northwest. Preble's and Pygmy Shrews are very rare in our region, the former being found mostly in dry pine areas in the Blue Mountains and in brushy areas southward while the Pygmy has been found only in yellow pine in the northeast corner of Washington, but widely in the more northern parts of British Columbia. The Dusky Shrew lives in a variety of mountain habitats. Water Shrews are often common along rushing streams of small to moderate size in mountainous terrain, while the Marsh Shrew prefers lowland sphagnum bogs and the vicinity of warm-water streams in the lowest parts of the mountains, occurring at higher elevations in the Olympic Mountains. The widely-occurring Vagrant Shrew is a frequenter of marshes, wet meadows, weed patches, grassy prairies, and even sagebrush, mostly in the lowlands. The little-known Merriam's Shrew lives in sagebrush and dry grassland. The Pacific Shrew is found in dark, marshy, brushy spots in the forest in parts of coastal Oregon, while in the Northwest the Ornate Shrew is found only in the Ashland area.

Some years ago, the author made a detailed study of the mammals of Mount Pilchuck, in Snohomish County, Washington. In analyzing the zonal distribution of mammals in that area, it was found that Vagrant and Marsh Shrews were the most abundant on the lowest levels of the mountain, while the Trowbridge's Shrew was common in the lower, coniferous forests. The Cinereous Shrew was an uncommon resident in the drier parts of the forest, while the Water Shrew was common along most of the streams at the intermediate elevations. Only a few Dusky Shrews were found in the Canadian Zone, but as one worked up through the Hudsonian Zone, shrews of this species became more and more numerous till on the summit ridges among the wet, moss-covered, spalling granite and along the little rills through the felsenmeers, this shrew became the only small mammal taken, having left even the usually abundant deer mice far below. This habitat and zonal distribution is reflected also in the more northern geographic range of the species. We have here, apparently in the Dusky Shrew, a species of the boreal areas seeking the alpine and mixed tundra ecosystems of our more southerly mountains.

Figure 3.
Ditch-side habitat of the Vagrant Shrew. All photos by the author, except where otherwise indicated.

13

Figure 4.
Stream-side habitat of the Water Shrew.

PACIFIC NORTHWEST SPECIES

CINEREOUS SHREW 4⅛-1¾-½-⅛ (105-44-12-4). A light, grayish-brown shrew with a relatively long tail. Usually light brownish tan to grayish tan on under parts with somewhat darker tannish or ashy brown on upper parts. Best separated from Vagrant and Dusky Shrews by the fact that the 4th unicuspid tooth on the side of the jaw is smaller than the 3rd unicuspid tooth. Has brighter colors than other NW brown shrews. RANGE. Throughout the NW, except for Ore. and the arid desert regions. HABITAT. Moist, forested areas, mostly in mts. and foothills, though also occurring in alpine tundra.

PREBLE'S SHREW 3½-1⁵⁄₁₆-⅜-⅛ (90-34-11-3). A small shrew with light brownish upper parts and whitish under parts. Tail bicolored in same pattern as remainder of the body. Total length less than 100 mm. RANGE. Extreme e. Ore. and s.e. Wash. and adjacent Idaho. HABITAT. Brush and willow growth around springs, bogs, marshes, and along streams; often in open, coniferous timber.

VAGRANT SHREW 4⅛-1⅝-½-³⁄₁₆ (104-42-12-4) Figs. 2 and 3. A medium-sized shrew, brownish above and brownish or buffy gray below. In winter, the upper parts become dusky (often flecked with white). The tail is slightly less than 2 inches long and very weakly bicolored; shorter than in the Dusky Shrew. RANGE. Wash., Ore., Idaho, and extreme s. B.C. HABITAT. Though widely distributed, prefers damp areas, such as marshes, wet meadows, ditch bottoms and sides, fern jungles, and saltwater beaches, mostly in lowlands and intermediate elevations. Rare in the upper parts of mts.; more of a lowland species. Occasionally found in semi-desert areas.

DUSKY SHREW 4⅜-1⅞-½-³⁄₁₆ (110-47-13-4). This species is similar to the Vagrant Shrew, but is dark tobacco brown above and silvery to brownish gray below. Tail mostly unicolored. Best recognized by its dark-brown color, darker under parts, and larger size. RANGE. Most of the Pacific NW, except s.e. Wash. and e. Ore. HABITAT. Wet places along streams and in marshy, boggy areas in mts.; also in rockslides and outcroppings, heather fields, and muskegs. More of a montane and alpine form than the Vagrant Shrew.

PACIFIC SHREW 6-2⅜-⅝-³⁄₁₆ (155-60-17-5). Upper parts very dark brown, becoming slightly paler below. Feet and tail (not bicolored) brownish. Large size and brown color distinctive. RANGE. W. Ore., mostly in coastal parts. HABITAT. Damp, marshy, brushy areas.

ORNATE SHREW 3⅞-1⅜-¾-⅛ (100-35-13-4). A small, short-tailed shrew with grayish-brown upper parts and pale grayish under parts. Tail very slightly bicolored. RANGE. Ashland area of Ore. HABITAT. Streamsides and damp vegetation.

WATER SHREW 6⅛-3-¾-³⁄₁₆ (156-76-20-5) Figs. 4 and 5. An easily recognized shrew, with its large mouse-like size, blackish or dark grayish upper parts, whitish under parts, and sharply bicolored tail (black above, white below). Toes fringed with long hairs. RANGE. Montane and intermediate elevations throughout the NW, excepting the Columbia Basin of Wash. and the lowlands of w. Wash. and w. Ore. Rare in the Olympics. HABITAT. Occurs in and along mt. and foothill streams and beaver ponds, particularly the rushing, white-water creeks of the montane forests. Also along alpine lakes and tarns.

Figure 5.
Water Shrew.

MARSH SHREW 6-3-⅘-³⁄₁₆ (150-75-20-5). A large shrew, similar in size to the Water Shrew, but blackish above and dark grayish black or brownish below. The race in the Olympic Mts. of Wash. is brownish above and brownish gray or buffy below. Tail unicolored or weakly bicolored. Toes of hind feet weakly fringed with stiff hairs. Tiny fleshy projections along outer edge of each nostril. RANGE. S.w. B.C., w. Wash., and w. Ore. HABITAT. Marshes and bogs (especially sphagnum and cedar bogs) and along warm-water streams in lowlands and lower mt. slopes. More of a mud shrew than a water shrew.

ARCTIC SHREW 4½-1⅝-⁹⁄₁₆-⅛ (115-42-14-4). Tricolored pattern distinctive: back dark brownish to blackish, sides light brownish, and under parts grayish to grayish brown. Heavy body, short tail (slightly bicolored), and color make for relatively easy identification. RANGE. In the Pacific NW, only in n.e. B.C. HABITAT. Edges of alder, willow, or aspen growth near water or marshy, boggy areas.

TROWBRIDGE'S SHREW 5-2⅓-½-⅛ (125-58-13-4) Fig. 6. A medium-sized shrew, blackish or dark sooty gray above; very slightly paler below. Tail is strongly bicolored, black above and white below, making for the best field character, along with size and forest niche. RANGE. S.w. B.C., w. Wash., and w. Ore. HABITAT. Dense coniferous forests, mostly in lowlands and intermediate elevations in mts. Often commonly and widely distributed in preferred habitat. Found on Destruction Island off the coast of Wash.

15

MERRIAM'S SHREW 3⅔-1⅖-½-⅛ (90-36-11-3). A small shrew, light grayish brown to gunmetal gray above and whitish below (including feet and under surface of tail). In summer, pale grizzled brown above, buffy white below; in winter, pale brownish gray above, white below. Tail strongly bicolored, brown above, white below. RANGE. Arid, open plains areas of e. Wash., e. Ore., and s. Idaho. HABITAT. Sagebrush and grasslands, particularly sage-grass and undisturbed bunchgrass types.

PYGMY SHREW 3⅖-1⅛-⅜-⅛ (85-28-9-3). A tiny shrew, the smallest mammal in North America. Upper parts reddish brown, sides tannish, and under parts whitish (being somewhat darker on the throat). Tail noticeably bicolored and proportionately quite short when compared with the head and body length. Only 3 unicuspid teeth are visible on the side of the upper jaw when the upper lip is pushed back, due to the minute size of the 3rd and 5th unicuspids. RANGE. E. B.C. and n.e. Wash.; n. Idaho. HABITAT. Dense to (mostly) open, coniferous woods, especially of the drier type. Dry pine forests and particularly the dry, grassy glades in the forests, as well as the edges of wet meadows and marshes.

Figure 6.
Trowbridge's Shrew.

16

C. Hart Merriam, the father of modern American mammalogy, was born December 5, 1855, at Locust Grove, New York, and died on March 19, 1942, at Berkeley, California. His contributions to the science of mammalogy were immense and came at the time of transition from the era of the cabinet naturalist to that of the modern worker. As Wilfred H. Osgood, himself a great student of mammals, wrote in the *Journal of Mammalogy* for November, 1943:

"His genius was of the kind that has the capacity for taking infinite pains. In his early work he was quick to see that his subject was shot with false conclusions due primarily to insufficient or faulty material. It became his passion, therefore, to put it on a sound basis, to correct the errors of his predecessors, and to lay a foundation for all time. He did this and much more. Perhaps his greatest contribution to his time lay in his perfecting of methods, in the use of large series of specimens, in the persistent emphasis upon exactness of geographic data, in the demonstration of a previously unsuspected importance of cranial characters in the finer divisions of mammalian classification, and in his steadfast belief in the combination of field and laboratory studies. His own concrete production was very large and space does not permit its enumeration. His published writings include well over 600 titles. New mammals discovered and described by him number approximately 660. The types of 651 of these are in the U. S. National Museum; 8 are in other American museums, and one in the British Museum. The collection of mammals which he started in his first years of government service was reported in 1940 to contain 136,613 specimens, vastly more than any other collection and all with full data and in prime condition. Contemporary opinion usually thought of him as most engrossed with studies of life-zones, laws of temperature control, and the general subject of geographic distribution, but his own secret pride was in his *Monographic Revision of the Pocket Gophers'*, a most exhaustive study which revealed him as a perfectionist. At the time it was published (1895) there is no doubt his intense desire was to go on with similar studies of other groups."

Merriam's boyhood was devoted to the study and enjoyment of the woods and fields with their birds and mammals. When a boy of 13, he had met and become inspired by the great Professor Baird. When 17, he served as an ornithologist on the 1872 Hayden Survey. He subsequently studied medicine, receiving his M.D. degree in 1879. Practicing medicine and continuing research on birds and mammals, he published his first book, MAMMALS OF THE ADIRONDACK REGION, in 1885. Merriam's growing interest in mammalogy, spurred on by the invention of the cyclone trap and acquaintanceship with a young collector by the name of Vernon Bailey, determined his research career—mammals. Largely through Baird's influence, Merriam was appointed the first chief of the Division of Economic Ornithology in the Federal government, later renamed the Biological Survey and still later the Fish and Wildlife Service, and served in this capacity till 1910. Too little space is available here to recite his multitude of interests and accomplishments, not the least of which

(continued on page 54)

MOLES

Figure 7.
Coast Mole.

Moles are recognizable by their specialized features which adapt them to subterranean life. They are chunky animals with pointed snouts, short legs, and naked to sparsely-haired tails. The broad front feet usually have the palms facing outward and are equipped with strong claws for digging. The pinhead-sized eyes are almost or quite invisible and external ears are not present. Colors range from velvety black to silvery with sometimes a coppery sheen.

Four species of moles occur in the Pacific Northwest: the large blackish Townsend's Mole of the coastal regions; the smaller, but very similar, Coast Mole of the western and central parts of the Northwest; the grayish Broad-footed Mole of southern Oregon; and the small, mouse-sized Shrew-mole of the region west of the Cascade crest.

The Townsend's is the largest of North American moles. It is often common in moist, grassy pastures in the Puget Sound lowlands where its large hills, often a foot in diameter, may readily be seen from adjacent highways. Dairy cattle pastures in river valley bottoms are particularly well populated by this species. The hills are approximately three feet apart and literally dot the meadows. The diet of this species is typically mole-like, consisting of grubs, earthworms, and small invertebrates. Little, if any, vegetable matter is utilized. The breeding season for this species begins in February and litters of two to four young are produced, with an average of three. Very little is known of the courtship of these animals, as they are mainly nocturnal and almost completely subterranean. Mammals so adapted for burrowing have very small posterior portions, such that the pelvis is too narrow to allow passage for the young at birth. Accordingly, the lower urogenital and alimentary tracts are on the ventral side, outside of the pubic bones, to allow birth to take place. The breeding season is in the early spring.

18

The Coast Mole appears to prefer a somewhat drier habitat than does the Townsend's Mole, accounting, no doubt, for its occurrence in parts of the Northwest interior. In the Puget Sound area, this species is most numerous in brushy and deciduous wooded regions, as well as the drier upland meadows. Some physical adaptations for the mole-like existences include the heavily-muscled neck and shoulders, long-snouted head, shovel-like feet, and velvety fur that may be rubbed forward and backward with equal ease. A number of skeletal features reflect the mole's peculiar life. Some of these are the enormous enlargement of the pectoral girdle and anterior limbs, strongly keeled sternum for muscle attachment, short and thick clavicle to withstand considerable strain in burrowing, elongated scapula for muscle attachment, short thick humerus to allow greater leverage for the associated muscles, right-angle arrangement of the forefeet for more effective digging, slender flexible ribs, short transverse processes of the vertebrae, reduced pelvic girdle, and small hind limbs. The eyes are minute, but the hearing is considered excellent.

The mole forages underground by using its snout to find suitable places to dig. The forefeet reach forward to acquire soil which is pushed sideways and backwards. The hind feet serve to kick the soil still farther back. The tunnel is made by the animal's pushing its head and shoulders alternately against the sides and roof of the burrow. Every so often, the mole must completely turn around in its tunnel and push the excavated soil to the ground surface or into an unused gallery with its front feet.

The Shrew-mole is not nearly as mole-like as its other three cousins in the Northwest. It is less adapted for sub-surface life in that its front feet are more normally constructed and less shovel-like. As its name implies, the Shrew-mole has habits resembling those of the shrew group. It hunts in shallow trenches that it makes under the forest leaf mat. There, it eats small arthropods, annelids, some vegetable matter, isopods, insect larvae, and other animal material. The Shrew-mole is so keenly sensitive to vibrations that it can feel the noise made by a burrowing earthworm and dig rapidly to its source. It spends a certain amount of its foraging time on the surface, occasionally tunneling in the upper part of the leaf mat, and less commonly digging down into the soil. Activity is not restricted to certain hours, for the animals forage day and night, usually resting only after a heavy meal. It is often common in its preferred habitat in moist, shady forest areas.

Figure 8.
The large hills put out by the Townsend's Mole.

PACIFIC NORTHWEST SPECIES

SHREW-MOLE 4⅗-1¾-⅔ (115-44-16) Fig. 8. This tiny mole is the size of a large shrew or a small mouse. Sooty or blackish gray in color above and below. The short, hairy tail is unicolored. Snout is long, pointed, and mole-like, while the forefeet have long claws for digging. RANGE. S.w. B.C., w. and w.c. Wash., and w. Ore. HABITAT. Moist forests with dense undergrowth from sea level to the Cascade crest; occasionally found on east slopes of that range. Occurs near water and occasionally in wet rockslides.

TOWNSEND'S MOLE 8⅘-1⅔-1 (210-41-26). A large mole with black, velvety fur on both upper and lower parts. Fur often with brownish or purplish luster. Tail naked; snout long and relatively devoid of hair. Forefeet are large and broad with long, flattened nails and rotated so the palms face outward. Separated from Coast Mole by size. RANGE. S.w. B.C., w. Wash., and w. Ore. HABITAT. Moist meadows and fields, especially in river bottoms, as well as grassy lawns and open, glacial prairies, mostly in lowlands, but also in subalpine areas of the n. Olympic Mts.

COAST MOLE 6½-1⅘-⁹⁄₁₀ (165-35-23) Fig. 7. Similar to the Townsend's Mole, but smaller. Colors somewhat variable according to subspecies. RANGE. S.w. B.C.; w., c., and s.e. Wash.; w. and n. Ore., and extreme w.c. Idaho (Cambridge area). HABITAT. Prefers drier, brushier, and more timbered habitats than those occupied by the Townsend's Mole. May penetrate mts. to the subalpine areas.

BROAD-FOOTED MOLE 7-1⅜-⅞ (180-36-22). Color grayish to light brownish. Forefeet broader than those of Coast Mole; feet and tail more hairy. Fur soft and silky. RANGE. S.c. Ore. HABITAT. Open, semi-dry areas and yellow pine woods.

William Healey Dall (1845-1927) was one of the pioneer modern naturalists in the Pacific Northwest and Alaska. As a boy, his interests in natural history, especially mollusks, brought him to the attention of Louis Agassiz who gave him great encouragement. From 1865-68, he was associated with the Russian-American Telegraph Expedition in Alaska, continuing the work of Robert Kennicott. Following the collapse of the expedition with the success of the Atlantic cable, Dall continued collecting in Alaska for Professor Baird at the Smithsonian and later worked on his materials at Washington, D.C. From 1871 to 1884, he explored the Aleutian Islands for the Coast Guard and amassed a great collection of specimens. From 1884 to 1911, he served as a paleontologist with the U.S. Geological Survey, writing numerous reports—he published over 1,600 scientific papers and several books during his lifetime. Though retiring from government service when he reached the age of 80, he continued working on his collections till his death. This devoted scientist had islands, mountains, and lakes in Alaska and the Yukon named after him, but we remember him by the Dall's Porpoise and the Dall's Sheep.

Figure 9.
Shrew-mole.

21

BATS

Figure 10.
Long-eared Brown Bat.

    The bats are unique in that they are the only truly flying mammals. The toes of the fore limbs have become greatly lengthened to form attachments for a nearly naked membrane which extends to the hind legs and then between the latter to inclose the tail. This allows these mammals, unlike other "flying" mammals such as the Flying Squirrels (which actually glide) to have powers of true, sustained flight. Bats' aerial navigation, which allows them to make exceedingly intricate maneuvers both in the laboratory and outside in order to avoid obstacles and to capture food, is accomplished by means similar to sonar. The animals utter short bursts of sound with frequencies between 25,000 and 75,000 cycles per second and receive echoes as the sounds rebound from objects in their path. Since the human ear can detect sounds of only 20,000 cycles per second at the most, we are unable to hear these ultra-high pitched utterances. Definite squeaks well within the range of human hearing, however, are also given off by bats both while they are in flight and at rest. Some of these animals are known to make annual migrations similar to those of birds and banding studies have shown them to return to the same cave or tree in the spring. Other species prefer to become torpid and pass the months of food scarcity in suspended animation.

    The Little Brown Bat is one of the most abundant species of bats on the North American continent and has a wide distribution in the Pacific Northwest. Like all brown bats, it feeds exclusively on insects, catching them on the wing. Due to its crepuscular habits, echolocation is used to secure the prey, some bats catching an average of 500 insects an hour. Commonly, Little Brown Bats will use foraging patterns from which they will not deviate from night to night. This species does not have a distinctive voice. Other than a few audible sqeaks, its calls vary from 7,500 to 48,000 cycles per second. There is a variance in the frequency in which these sounds are emitted, from 10 per second as the bat is preparing to fly, 30 per second as it is flying, and 50 per second as it approaches an object. Flight in this species averages about 11.2 mph.

The Little Brown Bat is highly colonial. It is often seen in large roosting colonies. During the summer, large groups of nursing females may be found. At this time, the males are usually roosting elsewhere, commonly in small numbers. Joint roosting of both sexes is practiced only during winter hibernation. At this time, the males will cluster in cooler parts of the cave while females prefer the warmer areas. Dormancy seems to be due to the ambient conditions, mainly temperature. Occasionally during warm periods of the winter, a few bats will come out of their torpor and show some activity. Mating is generally done in the fall, but can occur throughout the winter into the early spring. There is apparently a mechanism for delayed fertilization. Gestation is usually 50-60 days, parturition coming in mid-June to mid-July. With very few exceptions, only one young is produced per year.

Bat ticks are common ectoparasites in many species, though they have not been known to carry any disease. Rabid bats have occasionally been reported in the Pacific Northwest in recent years, although the extent to which this very serious and usually fatal disease is present in the bat population is unknown. Popular legends to the contrary, bats almost never attack humans. If a person should be bitten or otherwise attacked by a bat, every effort should be made to capture the bat so that it may be examined for possible rabies, and the incident reported to the health authorities immediately. Anyone who plans on studying or handling bats in research or field collecting should be immunized against rabies.

For the most part, bats are harmless and interesting denizens of the twilight hours, as far as many of us are concerned. They may, however, become a nuisance in attics of homes, particularly the less tightly-built summer cabins. Prevention of bat entry is most important with care taken to stop up all possible places where they might get into the building. In many summer homes (and some in the cities) it has been common practice by the builders to leave an opening above the projecting roof joist where it comes out through the wall. These are excellent places for bats (and other animals—the author once saw a snake) to enter the attic. Good results have been gained in keeping bats out by sprinkling several pounds of naphthalene flakes or mothballs (the flakes do the job quicker) on the floor of the attic or space under the roof. This chemical tends to discourage the residence of flying squirrels, pack rats, and tree squirrels, as well.

Various of the 18 species of Northwest bats have different habits. For example, the Western Pipistrel, smallest of our region's bats, seeks crevices and cliffs for shelter, giving it another common name of "canyon bat." It often occupies the same habitat as the Cliff Swallow, but because of its differing times of feeding and manner of foraging, it probably does not compete with the bird for food. Nevertheless, the pipistrels do emerge earlier in the evening than most bats and may be seen abroad before sunset. Some studies have

23

indicated that females appear more at night than do the males. The suggestion has been made that this habit may be due to the small amount of available water in the desert areas, combined with evaporation from high temperatures and water loss due to lactation, all endangering the water balance of the female. Roosting and breeding are done in crevices and small caves on the sides of cliffs in the driest parts of the desert areas. They swarm off the cliffs in the late afternoon or early evening and head for the nearest water. More than in other species of local bats, water seems to be a problem. The location of pipistrels in river canyons supplies both shelter and water. We have found that the best way to observe these midgets is to station oneself near water below a cliff in the bottom of a canyon just before sunset. Breeding is done in colonies and the two young are born in May, June, or early July.

Figure 11.
Little Brown Bat.

24

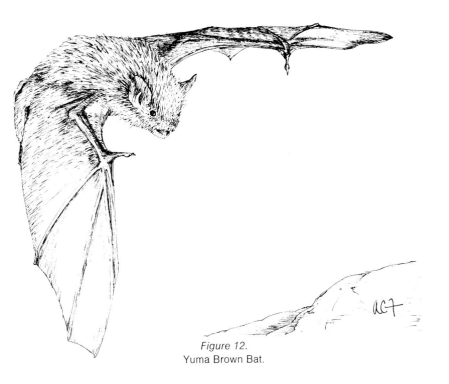

Figure 12.
Yuma Brown Bat.

PACIFIC NORTHWEST SPECIES

LITTLE BROWN BAT 3⅖-1⅜-⅜-⁹/₁₆ (85-36-11-13) Fig. 11. A small bat with yellowish-brown upper parts (the tips of the hairs being burnished with deep buff) and paler (light buff) under parts. Wings, interfemoral membranes (membranes between hind legs and including the tail), ears, and feet are blackish brown. Ears, when laid forward, do not extend past the nose and usually only just to the nostrils. RANGE. Occurs throughout the Pacific NW. HABITAT. found in a variety of places, though most commonly seen near water. May hibernate and roost in caves.

YUMA BROWN BAT 3⅜-1⅜-⅜-½ (85-35-9-13) Fig. 12. A small bat with buffy or light brownish back and whitish belly. Fore and aft parts of wing membranes are whitish, remainder of membranes dark brownish; interfemoral membrane sparsely haired and practically transparent. Fur of the back is dull colored. RANGE. Coastal and s. B.C. and throughout remainder of NW. HABITAT. Open areas in forests in lowlands and mts. Migrates, but also hibernates in lower part of NW.

KEEN'S BROWN BAT 3½-1⅘-⅓-⁷/₁₃ (88-35-8-14). A small bat with olive-brown to dark-brownish, glossy fur and dark-brown or blackish ears and wing membranes. Ears, when laid forward, extend about a quarter of an inch beyond tip of nose. RANGE. W. Wash. and w. B.C. HABITAT. Forests, particularly clearings and river banks.

LONG-EARED BROWN BAT 3½-1⅝-⅜-⅞ (88-41-10-22) Fig. 10. A small bat with light to medium brown-colored fur (slightly paler below) and black ears and wing and tail membranes. Ears are noticeably large and extend a quarter of an inch beyond the tip of the nose when laid forward. Free edge of interfemoral membrane with very sparse fringe of hairs. RANGE. Wash., Ore., and Idaho, as well as s. B.C. HABITAT. Mostly forested and wooded areas in lowlands and mts.

FRINGED BROWN BAT 3¼-1½-⁵⁄₁₆-⅝ (85-37-8-17). Similar to the Long-eared Brown Bat, but averages the same size or slightly larger and has shorter ears which extend less than three-sixteenths of an inch beyond the nose when laid forward. Color is yellow brown to dark olive, with little difference in shade between the upper and lower parts. The conspicuous fringe of short, stiff hairs at the free edge of the tail (interfemoral) membrane is distinctive. Pelage is rather full, with hairs dark at base, except on sides, and with light buffy tips on back and whitish tips on belly. RANGE. Ore., s. and c. Idaho, e. Wash., and s.c. B.C. HABITAT. Pine woods and broken country in the more arid parts of the NW.

LONG-LEGGED BROWN BAT 3½-1½-⅜-⅜ (90-38-10-11). A small bat, cinnamon to brownish above and buffy to light brown below. Membranes and ears dark brown to blackish. Pelage long and soft. Fur extends halfway down femur. Extension of fur on under side of wing membrane to elbow. Ears short, barely reaching tip of snout when laid forward. RANGE. S. and w. B.C., Wash., Ore., and Idaho. HABITAT. Forested and wooded areas and in broken country. Some hibernate in caves in winter.

CALIFORNIA BROWN BAT 3¼-1½-¼-⁷⁄₁₆ (82-38-6-11). A small bat with yellowish chestnut or brownish fur above and paler fur below. Ears dark brown, extending noticeably beyond the tip of the nose when laid forward. Membranes dark brown. Foot small, usually one quarter of an inch or less in length. RANGE. W. and s. B.C., and most of remainder of the NW. HABITAT. Variety of wooded or forested areas, usually near water.

SMALL-FOOTED BROWN BAT 3³⁄₁₆-1⅛-⁵⁄₁₆-½ (81-40-8-12). A small bat very similar to the California Brown Bat, but with slightly larger ears, blackish nose and face, and tip of tail free of tail membrane. General color yellowish to golden brown. RANGE. E. Wash., e. Ore., s. Idaho, and Okanagan Valley of s. B.C. HABITAT. Open, arid, desert-type areas; roosts in rocky crevices, caves, mines and old buildings. Forages commonly over water, ranging from desert sloughs to large cattle tanks.

SILVER-HAIRED BAT 4-1⅝-⅜-½ (100-40-9-13). A medium-sized bat with dark-brown to sooty-brown hairs tipped with white, giving a frosted appearance to the pelage. Most of the frosting is on the posterior half of the back. Hair on face, crown, and throat not frosted. Basal half of tail membrane furred dorsally. Ears short and broad. RANGE. C. and s. B.C., Ore., Wash., and Idaho. HABITAT. Forested areas at all elevations, preferring clearings, open waterways and lakes. Mainly a migrant in the NW.

WESTERN PIPISTREL 3-1³⁄₁₆-¼-⁷⁄₁₆ (75-30-7-11) Fig. 13. A very small bat with smoke-gray to buffy pelage and blackish feet, membranes, ears, and face. Size and color distinctive. RANGE. S.e. and c. Wash., e. Ore., and s.w. and s.c. Idaho. HABITAT. River canyons in the desert areas.

Figure 13.
Western Pipistrel.

Figure 14.
Pallid Bat.

27

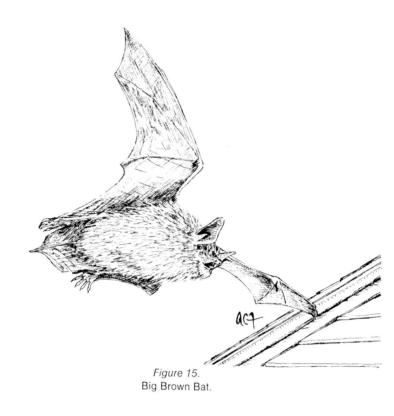

Figure 15.
Big Brown Bat.

BIG BROWN BAT 4½-1⅞-½-⅝ (116-48-12-17) Fig. 15. A large brownish or reddish-brown bat with blackish membranes, wings, and ears. The latter are short, barely reaching to the tip of the nose when laid forward. Under parts slightly paler than upper parts. RANGE. S. B.C., Wash., Ore., and Idaho. HABITAT. Forested areas near water, farmsteads, and metropolitan and urban areas in cities and town.

RED BAT 4⅖-2-⅓-½ (110-50-8-12). A medium-sized bat with reddish fur; occasionally with white-tipped hairs; ears broad and round. Dorsal surface of tail membrane is hairy. RANGE. One record for Skagit, B.C. Stragglers may occur rarely in w. Ore. and w. Wash. HABITAT. Forest openings, as well as urban areas, being attracted to the insects around street lights.

HOARY BAT 5½-2¼-½-⅝ (140-58-13-16) Fig. 16. A large bat with yellow-ish-gray or light-brown fur tipped with whitish to give a "hoary" appearance to the pelage. Under parts lighter and less hoary than upper parts. Dorsal surface of tail membrane well covered with white-tipped fur. Wings sooty brown with white or gray spots at wrists and elbows above. Ears round, partially furred, and rimmed with black. RANGE. S. B.C., Wash., Ore., and Idaho. Openings in forests, as well as wooded residential areas in cities and towns. Often begins flying in late afternoon.

28

SPOTTED BAT $4\frac{3}{8}$-2-$\frac{7}{16}$-$1\frac{3}{4}$ (110-50-11-46). Upper parts black, or nearly so, with three sharply contrasting white spots, one on each shoulder and one at the base of the tail. The only bat so marked. Under parts are whitish. The ears are extremely long, measuring about 40 to 50 mm. from notch to tip. RANGE. One record for s.w. Idaho. May occur as very rare straggler in s. Idaho and e. Ore. HABITAT. Apparently prefers the drier, more open regions.

TOWNSEND'S BIG-EARED BAT $3\frac{7}{8}$-$1\frac{3}{4}$-$\frac{3}{8}$-$1\frac{3}{8}$ (98-46-9-35) Fig. 17. A medium-sized bat with grayish-brown fur, sooty wings, limbs, and tail membrane, and very large (inch or more in length) ears. Large, glandular lumps between nostrils and eyes. RANGE. S. B.C., Wash., Ore., and Idaho. HABITAT. Occurs in a variety of places, particularly those provided with caves, abandoned mine shafts, old buildings, and crevices in cliffs.

PALLID BAT $4\frac{3}{4}$-$1\frac{7}{8}$-$\frac{1}{2}$-$1\frac{1}{4}$ (120-48-13-32) Fig. 14. A large bat, similar to the Townsend's Big-eared Bat, but lacks the glandular lumps on the face. Upper parts yellowish to light brownish; under parts buffy to buffy white. Ears long, but wider than those of the Big-eared Bat. Ears and membranes brownish. RANGE. E. Wash., drier parts of e. and w. Ore., extreme w. Idaho, and the Okanagan Valley of B.C. HABITAT. River canyons in semi-arid and desert regions. Roosts in caves, old buildings, and cliff crevices.

BRAZILIAN FREE-TAILED BAT $3\frac{1}{2}$-$1\frac{1}{8}$-$\frac{3}{8}$-$\frac{5}{8}$ (90-39-10-16). Body brownish, but slightly paler below. Ears and membranes dark brown to blackish. Hairs of body dark to base. Most of tail free, projecting beyond interfemoral membrane. RANGE. S.w. Ore. HABITAT. Open, semi-arid to arid areas, particularly favoring dwellings and old buildings for roosting.

BIG FREE-TAILED BAT $5\frac{3}{16}$-2-$\frac{3}{8}$-1 (133-51-9-25). Body brownish; slightly paler below. Ears and membranes blackish. Hairs of body whitish at base. Size larger. Most of tail free, projecting beyond interfemoral membrane. RANGE. One record for New Westminster area, s.w. B.C. Possibly rare straggler elsewhere in NW. Obviously our knowledge of the distribution of all bats, especially the less common ones, leaves much to be desired. HABITAT. Usually in desert areas.

There is a biological tenet known as the "principle of competitive exclusion" which may sound far from the scope of this volume but actually may be of interest and value to many of its readers in locating and identifying mammals. Briefly, this "law" holds that closely related (and thus closely similar) species cannot live in exactly the same ecologic niche, as in so doing they would be in competition with each other. If there is one thing that evolution seems to have provided against, it is untoward competition of two or more species for the same set of environmental resources. The process of natural selection removes the less fit in the competitive struggle for existence and, according to evolutionary dogma, only the best fit survives.

The end result of this process is that we usually find only one species, say of a genus, occupying a particular niche or habitat in a particular location. Even what would seem to be a case of complete overlapping (sympatry) is usually found not to exist, as the supposedly competing species differ in some ecological or behavioral way.

Let us take the chipmunks as an example. Six species of these little squirrels occur in the Pacific Northwest, all very similar in gross habits to each other, yet no two are to be found in exactly the same locality of habitat. Most of the populations of the Least Chipmunk occur in sagebrush or other northern desert shrub. Even their color pattern, or "uniform," matches the grayish desert surroundings and effectively camouflages the little fellows. Those races of the species which are to be found in timber occur in areas not occupied by other chipmunk species.

The medium-sized, brightly-colored Yellow Pine Chipmunk is an inhabitant of semi-open to open forests where bright sunshine enhances colors. It is widely distributed in the Western U.S. and well represented in our territory. No other species of the genus competes with it in its niche.

Occupying the dense fir, cedar, and spruce forests of the coastal regions is the large, somber Townsend's Chipmunk, a relatively silent and unobtrusive form. Dark like its background, it coexists with no other chipmunk in its particular fief. Like most other chipmunks, the species contains various races. Darkest in the lowland and rain forests, slightly lighter in the montane woods where the underbrush may be a little thinner, it reaches a rich reddish brown in the redwoods.

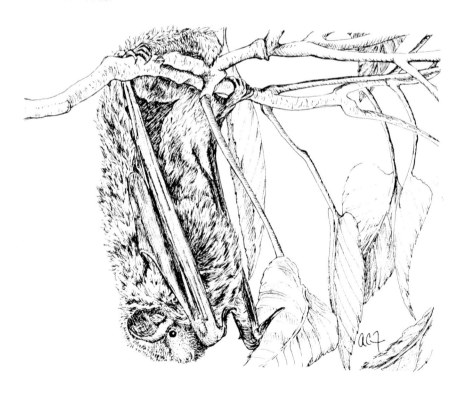

Figure 16.
Hoary Bat.

Figure 17.
Townsend's Big-eared Bat.

The Red-tailed Chipmunk occurs in the dense montane forests of the Idaho Bitterroots, contrasting strongly with the neighboring, light-colored Yellow Pine species. No other chipmunk exists in the rocky juniper and pinyon pine terrain of the bleached Cliff Chipmunk, nor in the Wasatch subalpine range of the Uinta Chipmunk.

By paying close attention to locale and habitat, the user of this book will find the environmental status of a species to be a very useful aid in its identification, to say nothing of its location in the first place.

PIKAS

Figure 18.
Common Pika.

Campers and hikers in the subalpine and alpine regions of the high mountains of the Pacific Northwest are likely to become acquainted with this small mammal during the cooler parts of the day by its peculiar short squeal or cry. Further evidence of the animal's presence is the occurrence of haystacks or forage piles in the cracks and crevices of the rockslides. If the weather is warm and sunny, these piles of harvested vegetation will sometimes be placed out in the open for drying, but are usually best cured in the shade of some over-hanging rock.

The boulder piles at the feet of cliffs provide the necessary openings in which these animals live and store their food. Pikas are diurnal and active throughout the year. They seldom travel more than several hundred feet from the shelter of their rocky homes. In these excursions, they generally remain on the rockslide. However, when they are gathering food for storage, they will venture away from the silde into the neighboring meadows and woods. These trips are made in the form of quick little runs, as though in fear of being too long away from the protection of the rocks. This caution is necessary because they are very vulnerable to attacks from predators. The pikas' coloring and freezing behavior provide excellent means of defense. They run through the galleries in the rocks aided by the fur padding on their feet which enables them to leap from rock to rock without losing their footing or suffering undue abrasion from the rough surfaces. Each animal has its own territory within the colony. It will have three to five pathways leading to the central nest and other pathways to the haystacks. Family units will share the central nest in some instances. During the short summer of the high country, the pika spends most of its time in gathering food for the long winter months. The animal holds the food crosswise in the mouth while carrying it from the supply source to the haystacks. These piles are located in crevices in the talus and are so situated that they will be protected from rain and snow during the winter. The stacks are interconnected by well-beaten paths which may even extend to neighboring slides. These caches have been found to contain as many as 34 different varieties of plants. Among these are grasses, thistles, and legumes. Thistles are commonly found in stacks and seem to be a favorite food.

Some divergence from natural habitat does occur, as pikas have been found living in log piles, abandoned stacks of slabwood, and even beneath the floor of a cabin. The animals use the central territory or nest as the breeding ground. Young are born during the early summer with two possible litters in a season. The gestation period is usually 30 to 33 days, and the litter generally numbers three to four. The young, although only half-grown at the time, are foraging for food before the end of summer. When they begin feeding for themselves, parental care ceases and they are forced to seek their own territories and homes elsewhere. Because most of these rabbits are confined to high mountain rocky areas, they are of very little economic value other than as a very interesting wildlife species. The common name, which is pronounced *pee-ka*, comes from the onomatopoetic term for the species used by the Tungus natives of northeastern Siberia.

While mostly to be found in the subalpine areas, pikas will occur scatteringly in rocky places in the forests or even in the desert areas. Additional habitats are occasionally provided by road cuts through massive rock along highways. Even though surrounded by forests, these newly-made habitats may be colonized by individuals dispersing from subalpine colonies. Rocks in slides and piles must be at least a foot in diameter, in order to provide the proper-sized crannies between boulders large enough for the animals to enter. Due to their restriction in habitat, the range of the pikas of the Northwest is broken up into a discontinuous pattern of endemic areas, many of which contain a separate, distinct subspecies. At least 15 of these races are to be found in our area, ranging from the light yellowish animals of the southern part of the Salmon River Mountains in Idaho to the blackish form inhabiting the Snake River lava beds of the same state. This pattern of divergent evolution in isolated populations is also to be observed in the pocket gophers where a great number of geographic races may occur within a single species.

Figure 19.
Rockslide habitat of the pikas.

PACIFIC NORTHWEST SPECIES

COLLARED PIKA 7½-⅝-1³/₁₆-¹⁵/₁₆ (190-15-30-24). Upper parts grizzled grayish brown to grayish above and lower parts whitish. Pale gray band on each side of neck behind the ears, on nape, and shoulders. Inner edges of ears black. Pads at bases of toes small and surrounded by stiff hairs. RANGE. Extreme n.w. B.C. HABITAT. Rockslides and felsenmeers (broken rock fields) in the high mts.

COMMON PIKA 8⅛-⅝-1-⅞ (203-15-25-23) Figs. 18 and 19; Color Plate 1. A small rabbit-like animal about the size of a guinea pig. In color, it is usually light to dark brownish. Some races have blackish wash over the upper parts. The rounded ears are scantily haired, white edged, and nearly rat-like in appearance. The hind legs are about the same length as the forelegs. The tail is very short and invisible except by close examination. The soles of the feet are densely furred. RANGE. Occurs in suitable habitat in mt. areas of the Pacific NW, excepting Vancouver Island, the Olympics and Coast Ranges, and the mts. of s. Idaho s. of the Snake River Plains except for the s.e. corner. May occur in desert lava areas as in e. Ore. and the region around the Craters of the Moon National Monument in s. Idaho. HABITAT. Talus slopes and rocky outcrops in the mts. and certain lava bed areas.

RABBITS AND HARES

Figure 20.
Black-tailed Jackrabbit.

Members of this family may be divided into two general types, hares and rabbits. "Hare" is the name applied to those lagomorphs whose young are born fully haired, with the eyes open, and able to run within a few minutes after birth. They are usually born in the open with very little preparation being made by way of a nest. All species of the genus *Lepus* are hares. Young of the genus *Sylvilagus,* the "rabbits," are born naked, blind, and helpless in a nest especially built for them and lined with fur. Relating to the degree of development of the young at birth, the gestation period is longer for the hares (36-47 days) and shorter for the rabbits (26-30 days). Vernacular names are misleading in the Family Leporidae. The names "jackrabbit" and "snowshoe rabbit" are applied to hares, while the "Belgian hare" is applied to a rabbit that is commonly bred in captivity. Rabbits and hares are active during early morning and late evening and do not store food as do their diurnal relatives, the pikas. They do have an unusual method of processing food. Two types of fecal pellets are produced, hard dark brownish pellets and soft greenish pellets which are re-ingested.

Eight species of this family occur in the Pacific Northwest: the Black-tailed and White-tailed Jackrabbits and the Snowshoe Hare, constituting the hares; the Pygmy and Brush Rabbits, the Eastern and Nuttall's Cottontails, and the European Rabbit, constituting the rabbits.

The Pygmy Rabbit occurs most frequently in areas where greasewood is abundant or where dense stands of sagebrush grow in the deep soil of hollows and gullies. Because this is the only species making and using extensive burrow systems, deep rather loosely packed soil is a definite habitat requirement. Other kinds of rabbits commonly use abandoned animal burrows. The burrow systems of Pygmies usually consist of from two to seven openings with the entrances being concealed in the thick sagebrush. Like most rabbits, the slate-colored Pygmy Rabbits are seen at most any time of the year except in mid-winter when the temperature is extremely cold or when the ground is covered with deep snow. They are most active in late spring and early summer and can be observed easily at this time. The home range is usually within 30 yards of the central burrow area. It is primarily a nocturnal animal with the major part of its activity being during the very early morning and late evening. Usually the Pygmy Rabbit can be approached quite closely, particularly if it is near a burrow entrance. Working with a red-colored spotlight at night, one mammalogist has been able to come within 15 feet of Pygmies feeding on sagebrush.

Eastern Cottontails usually inhabit heavy brush areas, strips of forest with open areas nearby, edges of swamps, and weed patches. In the Northwest, the small farming tracts provide excellent habitat. Cottontails are generally found where cover is abundant, the soil rich, and the land given to mixed usage. Various studies have shown that the Eastern Cottontail populations often exhibit a marked gregariousness. Both males and females periodically appear to shift their areas of concentration. These shifts seem to correlate with peaks of reproductive activity every seven days. Also, favored grazing areas tend to attract entire populations which feed and move as a loose band. Generally speaking, females appear to be more conservative in their movements than the males. Dominant individuals of both sexes seem to be more far-ranging than are the subordinates.

The habitat of the Nuttall's Cottontail varies with its distribution, but in general, it is essentially a species of the borderlands between forest and plain, being often found in brushy thickets. In the arid interior, the primary factors determining density are rock outcroppings and areas of thick sagebrush. Shrubby places close to cultivated lands are also preferred. The home range of the Nuttall's Cottontail is usually thought to be smaller than that of the Eastern Cottontail. Unless driven off by dogs or other animals, the native rabbits may spend their entire lives within the limits of a single acre. They also seem to have a foraging routine that is maintained for several days at a time, in which they follow the same paths. Besides these foraging routes, other trails are used for non-feeding travel. Like other rabbits, Nuttall's Cottontails are active during the early morning and late evening hours. Most of their daylight time is spent lying in forms and dusting. These dusting stations are located a few feet from their hiding areas to which they run when alarmed. Frequently, they sit motionless for long periods of time at the mouths of their hiding forms. Individual behavior patterns of this species are in general very similar to those of the Eastern Cottontail.

Nuttall's Cottontails seem to be able to adapt easily to a co-existence with man. While doing research in Eastern Oregon, Del Blackburn found a population of about 12-20 cottontails in a dense sagebrush area. During that summer, the sagebrush was completely destroyed and the land put to cultivation. Within

Figure 21.
Pygmy Rabbit.

two days, cottontails were observed in a junk pile half a mile away and were still maintaining their density two years later, nesting in old car bodies, abandoned refrigerators, etc.

A native of the timbered areas throughout the Northwest, the big brown Snowshoe Hare with the white tail can hardly be distinguished from the shadows into which it often seems to melt. If you return to the same spot in the dead of winter, the same animal might be there, but still almost invisible, this time wearing a coat as white as the snow on which it sits. Only the dark eyes and black-tipped ears betray its presence. Because of its varying color with the seasons, this species is often called the "varying hare." The only exception to this pattern is on the Pacific Coast where some subspecies maintain a constant dark coat color. This ability to change pelage color is the result of three types of hair and the seasonal molts. The shift is irregular and often occurs in a patchwork fashion. The change generally requires about two months and is completed about the time the ground is covered with a lasting snow.

Snowshoe Hares are typically found in the brushy thickets of the forested regions. They shun the bright daylight and are active chiefly during the early morning and late evening. These hares seem to be more sociable than other members of the genus *Lepus*. Three individuals were once found occupying the same hollow log in Northern Idaho. They typically maintain runways in the thick brush areas where they live. These well-kept paths are perhaps of greater importance to the welfare of the animals than is the protective winter coloring. By use of such runways, a hare can dash through the thicket brush, winter or summer, at great speed and so escape its fleetest enemies. Thus we can understand the necessity for the intricate network of runs made and maintained during the entire year by the Snowshoes living in a particular vicinity. They seldom take refuge in holes when pursued by predators. Not digging holes themselves, about the only time they will use them is to seek shelter from weather conditions and for concealment during the winter when no snow is on the ground. They do make and use forms for normal resting and hiding.

Two distinct vocal utterances have been reported from these hares. Adults and young utter a sort of grunt or growl indicating anger or fear. They scream in a piercing manner when wounded or being handled. They are also said to make a clicking sound, the significance of which is not known. Another sound is the drumming or thumping noise which they make by forcefully hitting the ground with the hind feet while hopping. This behavior seems to alert other hares in the vicinity and is also used during courtship behavior. The home range of the Snowshoe Hare has been determined to amount to 10-15 acres, depending upon the density of cover, availability of food, and population numbers. Movements of greater than one-fourth of a mile are usually observed only in young dispersing hares.

Figure 22.
Nuttall's Cottontail.

The sexual development of the male hare usually becomes noticeable by the middle of March and mating takes place two or three weeks later. Premating activities are quite pronounced, involving drumming and chasing one another in a fantastic series of circles. The somersaulting behavior wherein several individuals circle around, jumping over each other, is an amazing sight. Called the "ghost dance" by Ernest Thompson Seton, this routine was once observed for about five minutes by Larrison and his father at a distance of a few feet, on the shore of a lake in Northeastern Washington.

The White-tailed Jackrabbit was once common in the sagebrush-bunchgrass habitat of Central and Eastern Washington, but at the present time it is restricted and scarce in that state except in the Okanogan Valley. It occurs in reduced numbers in Eastern Oregon and in Idaho. Because of this drastic lessening in distribution and populations, the White-tailed Jackrabbit is coming to the attention of conservationists in the Pacific Northwest. In Washington, "white-tails" favor the hilly bunchgrass territory of the arid sub-division of the Transition and Upper Sonoran Life Zones. In winter, they will descend to the lower sagebrush valleys. Not too long ago, this species was the only jackrabbit in Eastern Washington, keeping mainly to the higher slopes in the bunchgrass and coming to lower elevations during the winter. This "clawhold" of the native form held the region west of the Columbia, in Eastern Washington, as late as 1920, but the Black-tailed Jackrabbits by that time were swarming over lands east of the river and native competitors were gradually backing off the map. This has been the pattern of history in the invasions of the Black-tails in the years preceding their sweep into Eastern Oregon and Washington after invading the plains and prairies as far east as Kansas. With the invasion and spread of the Black-tailed Jackrabbit and the reduction of the native bunchgrass through over-grazing by livestock and conversion to cropland, the splendid large White-tailed Jackrabbit may well disappear from Washington, and even large parts of the remainder of the Northwest. Another possible reason for the disappearance of the White-tailed, which turns white in winter, is that it is selected against by predator pressure in the predominantly gray background of sagebrush. Del Blackburn once observed a large hare of this species to escape through thick sagebrush onto an open snow-covered burned-off hillside. It was quite easily sighted while in the sage, but the instant this individual broke into the white background, it was nearly impossible to see. Mortality in this species must be very high during mild relatively snow-free winters. At the present time, the most serious threat to the White-tail seems to be alteration of the habitat by over-use and conversion to other forms of agriculture.

PACIFIC NORTHWEST SPECIES

PYGMY RABBIT 10⁵/₁₆-1-2⅝-1⅝ (270-25-68-42) Fig. 21. The smallest rabbit in the NW, next to the pikas. It is dark grizzled gray above and pale buffy white below, but by mid-winter, the upper parts may wear down to a silvery gray. The feet are buffy and the short ears are tinged on the inside with rich buff. The tail is short and does not show a large white undersurface as in the cottontails. RANGE. S.c. Wash., e. Ore., and s. and c. Idaho. HABITAT. Tall, dense sagebrush or greasewood. Also in sand dune areas, as in the Juniper Forest preserve in e. Wash.

BRUSH RABBIT 13⅜-1⅛-2⅞-2⁵/₁₆ (340-30-75-60). A small rabbit, dark brownish above and lighter brown to brownish or buffy gray below. Slightly lighter in summer. No "cottontail." Legs relatively short. RANGE. W. Ore. HABITAT. Brushy areas in valleys and river bottoms.

EASTERN COTTONTAIL 15-1½-3½-2¼ (382-38-90-58). Recognizable as a cottontail by the white "powder-puff" tail. Upper parts mostly brownish with tan-colored lower back and rump. Ears are darker than the back. Under parts are white, though the pale cinnamon color of the sides may extend partly or entirely over the belly. The inside of the ears is whitish. RANGE. Introduced into extreme s.w. B.C. and variously into w. and e. Wash. and w. Ore. HABITAT. Prefers brush, edges of swamps, weed patches, railroad rights-of-way, and other similar areas with varied vegetation.

Figure 23.
Snowshoe Hare.

Figure 24.
White-tailed Jackrabbit in summer pelage.

Figure 25.
White-tailed Jackrabbit in winter pelage.

41

NUTTALL'S COTTONTAIL 13³/₁₆-1¾-3⅝-2½ (340-45-93-58) Fig. 22. This species is grizzled grayish with a yellowish overwash above; whitish below. The tail is nearly black above and white below and is usually carried so that the white area is conspicuous. The edges of the ears are tinged with white or buffy on the inside and with black on the outside. Somewhat smaller and paler than the Eastern Cottontail, though the main differences are in the skulls. RANGE. E. Wash., e. Ore., w. and s. Idaho, and the Okanagan Valley of B.C. HABITAT. Sagebrush, dry gullies, canyons, weed and tall grass patches, brushy thickets, orchards, wrecked car dumps, etc., mostly at low elevations.

SNOWSHOE HARE 17-1½-5⁵/₁₆-2¹⁵/₁₆ (430-38-135-75) Fig. 23. This species is a medium-sized hare presenting in summer a reddish-brown or brownish dorsal coloration with whitish or buffy under parts. The large feet (whence the name) are brownish or white, depending on the race. The ears are short for a hare and are brownish like the back with dark tips. In winter, the pelage usually changes to white, except for the ear tips which remain dark. Hares in the lowlands w. of the Cascades become only slightly paler in winter. RANGE. Occurs throughout the NW, except the arid areas of e. Wash., e. Ore., and s. Idaho. HABITAT. Coniferous forests and woodland swamps and brush patches.

WHITE-TAILED JACKRABBIT 23-3⅛-6-4⅛ (585-80-153-105) Figs. 24 and 25. A large hare, appearing to have twice the bulk of the Black-tailed Jackrabbit. In summer, upper parts grayish and under parts white, with an almost entirely white tail. In winter, white or nearly white above and below, except for dark ear tips. RANGE. E. Wash., e. Ore., Idaho (excepting the tip of the Panhandle), and the Okanagan Valley of s. B.C. HABITAT. Grasslands and higher grassy sagebrush of the foothills and lower mts.

BLACK-TAILED JACKRABBIT 21-3¼-4⅞-4¹¹/₁₆ (535-82-124-120) Fig. 20; Color Plate 4. Somewhat smaller than the White-tailed Jackrabbit, this species is grayish brown above, grizzled with black, and buffy white below. The large ears are tipped with black and the tail has a conspicuous black streak on its dorsal surface with buffy gray on the ventral surface. RANGE. E. Wash., e. and s.w. Ore., extreme w. part of lower Idaho Panhandle (may be extirpated from that area), and s. Idaho, as regards its NW range. HABITAT. Sagebrush, lower foothill grasslands, and (in late summer) adjacent hay fields. Elimination of much of the sagebrush has strongly reduced the populations of this species.

EUROPEAN RABBIT 16¼-3⅛-3¾-2¾ (445-80-95-70). Coloration of this species variable, though usually reddish brown to dark grayish, with varying admixtures of blackish hairs. May be brown on belly or whitish. Ears relatively short, not reaching beyond the muzzle when laid forward. RANGE. Introduced and now abundant on San Juan Island and also on some other islands of the San Juan Archipelago of Wash.

MOUNTAIN BEAVERS

Figure 26.
Mountain Beaver.

The first adventurous fur traders who penetrated the Pacific Northwest found the Chinook Indians provided with robes made of the skins of the Mountain Beaver. From that time until recently, little accurate information has been available concerning the habits of this curious mammal. Locally, it is known by several other names, including "sewellel," "mountain boomer," and "chehalis." Incidentally, it should be pointed out that the animal is definitely not a true beaver and does not always occur in the mountains.

This mammal belongs to the genus *Aplodontia* which contains only a single living species with several poorly marked races, all having a close resemblance to a thick-bodied, tailless Muskrat, except for the coarse, harsh fur. Mountain Beavers are the oldest known living rodents, the existence of these "living fossils" going back to the late Paleocene. They have a remote relationship to the squirrel family.

The musky odor of the Mountain Beaver is immediately and extremely noticeable to the human nose. It is much like that of the Muskrat and is not repulsive to most people. Ordinarily silent, this creature will whine when annoyed or in pain. A fight between two Mountain Beavers is punctuated by loud squeals of rage.

Much of the animal's range was originally covered by dense forests of great spruces, firs, or redwoods. Since the country was settled, a vast acreage of this woodland has been cleared away. Some of it has been cultivated, but the rougher slopes and unfertile areas have grown up to a jungle of shrubs, vines, and ferns. The Mountain Beaver has found this growth much better suited to its needs than the original forests. There is an abundance of food in great variety throughout the year. The dense tangle of vegetation is good insurance against birds of prey. The Mountain Beaver has very poor eyesight and is at a disadvantage on cleared ground which it seldom enters. The species is a burrowing mammal, honey-combing the areas it inhabits with a maze of tunnels and chambers. These occasionally have access or escape openings which are not sealed. A No. One steel trap placed on the floor of the tunnel at such a place seldom fails to capture a specimen, should control be necessary. A strict vegetarian, the Mountain Beaver feeds on a variety of plants, herbaceous in summer and somewhat more woody in winter. Food is temporarily stored in warehouse chambers in autumn and winter. Two or three young constitute the litter. The males are antagonistic during the rutting season and the author was once attacked by a vicious male which he killed with a club. They are difficult to maintain in captivity but recent studies into the nature of their ecologic needs have produced success in keeping them in an artificial environment.

In most cases, the Mountain Beaver, living as it does in wild or scrubby country, does not interfere with man's activities. In some parts of its range, man and beaver come into close proximity and there the gardens and truck areas may suffer. There is some evidence that these animals may inhibit reforestation on tree farms. They are easily caught, however, and a few steel traps will usually solve the problem quickly, if only temporarily.

*   *   *

MOUNTAIN BEAVER   14-1½-2⅓-1 (350-38-58-25) Fig. 26.   The Mountain Beaver is a small woodchuck- or rabbit-sized mammal with blackish-brown fur over upper and lower parts (where slightly paler). White spot behind the ear. Claws on forefeet relatively long and straight. Head round and short and rests solidly on the shoulders with little obvious neck. Some individuals have varying amounts of white in spots or patches on the under parts. RANGE. Occurs in w. Wash. and Ore. and s.w. B.C., including the Cascade and Olympic Mts. and Coast Ranges, from sea level to subalpine country. Found in the n.e. Cascades as far east as Loomis. HABITAT. Prefers the moist open parts of coniferous forests, being widely distributed and occasionally numerous on hill slopes and in damp ravines, alder bottoms, and bracken fern jungles. Commonest in the lowland regions and less abundant, though sometimes present, at higher elevations. Much of the lowland habitat is now being usurped by suburban and country home development and the species is gradually being restricted to the foothills and mountains.

CHIPMUNKS

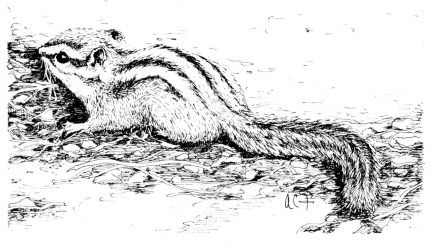

Figure 27.
Least Chipmunk (light-colored sagebrush form).

Chipmunks, the smallest Pacific Northwest squirrels, are bright, active, vociferous, diurnal rodents with a series of alternating light and dark stripes over the back and upper sides running from the shoulders to the rump. The sides of the head are similarly striped and the lower sides are plain colored and of the same hue as the central portion of the undersurface of the tail. The bellies are white or buffy. Their size is about halfway between that of a mouse and a rat. Chipmunks are restricted to coniferous forests or brush, hibernate during the winter months, and are active during daylight hours, mostly on sunny days. Unlike many of their squirrel relatives, chipmunks spend most of their time on the ground or in low bushes and seldom climb trees. They are not often found in the open habitats preferred by the ground squirrels.

Six species of chipmunks occur in the Northwest, each strongly characteristic of a certain environmental type. The large, dark-colored, sluggish Townsend's Chipmunk prefers the dense Douglas fir and hemlock forests of the west-side lowlands, the Olympics and Coast Ranges, as well as the hemlock and pine-larch-fir montane forests of the Cascade Mountains. The bright-colored Yellow Pine Chipmunk is a denizen of the semi-open to open subalpine forests of the higher mountains, as well as the yellow pine woods of the more arid east-side mountains and foothills. The smaller Least Chipmunk is restricted to the sagebrush areas of eastern Washington and Oregon, as well as open forests of parts of Idaho and northern British Columbia. In parts of the eastern reaches of the Northwest occurs the dark-colored Red-tailed Chipmunk, preferring the dense fir, cedar, and white pine forests. The pale, almost stripeless Cliff Chipmunk barely enters extreme southern Idaho, while the dull-colored Uinta Chipmunk occupies subalpine and other parts of southeastern Idaho.

Figure 28.
Sagebrush habitat of the Least Chipmunk.

46

Figure 29.
Open woods habitat of the Yellow Pine Chipmunk.

These little fellows are the author's favorites among mammals and he has studied all of the Northwest species in detail and finds them just as attractive today as when he began those studies some 40 years ago. Though many persons think that all chipmunks look and act alike, close familiarity with them, such as the author has had, reveals a number of striking differences in appearance, distribution, and behavior. Some species are tame and easily seen, while others are shy and hard to find.

While most chipmunks prefer forests or heavy brush areas, the Least Chipmunk has several subspecies which are restricted to sagebrush, the remaining races of the species in the Northwest occurring in open coniferous woodlands. To see the grayish sagebrush forms, which have even been suggested to belong to a separate species, one must go to their habitat and search carefully for them. The author has seen these sagebrush chipmunks in the barren sage hills between Vantage and Ellensburg in Washington and in the sagebrush-covered plains and foothills of southern Idaho. In walking through the brush, one occasionally observes the flash of a little grayish animal as it scurries from the protection of one bush to that of another. They are not vocal and sight reveals most of them. Strangely enough, they are also fond of the low-growing shadscale of the northern Great Basin area of southern Idaho. In specimen collecting, the biologist gets the majority of his animals with mousetraps baited with dry rolled oats. Larger, darker races of the species are to be found in the open timber of the Owyhee Highlands and Targhee areas of Idaho and the northern parts of British Columbia.

Campers and hikers in the subalpine parks and pine slopes of the Northwest soon make acquaintance with the small, agile, brightly-colored Yellow Pine Chipmunk. Curious, vociferous, and not adverse to stealing food scraps about the camp, this little sprite is abundant in the open coniferous forests of the upper parts of the mountains and in the yellow pine woods of the intermediate elevations in the eastern sections of the Northwest. It may be identified by its habitat, small size, and bright colors. No other chipmunk occurs within its ecologic and geographic ranges.

This species is something more of a tree climber than are the other chipmunks, although its arboreal excursions are limited mostly to the smaller pines and firs and it seldom ascends much above 10 or 15 feet. One exception to this general rule is the subspecies *Eutamias amoenus affinis* of the east slopes of the Cascade Mountains of Washington and British Columbia. This race, interestingly enough, readily takes to trees for escape and the author has seen individuals well over 100 feet up in tall pines. Seeds, other vegetational material, and some insects make up most of the diet of this species. In captivity, it will accept peanuts, rolled oats, sunflower seeds, dried bread crusts, cantaloupe rinds, and meat scraps. The nest is usually placed at the end of a short burrow a few feet in length or in a small cave or crevice in rocks. A favorite spot is in the cracks or narrow clefts in spalling granite if vegetation is nearby. The food caches are placed in the nest burrow or chamber and in shallow holes in the ground. Mating is done in April with the young born some 30-40 days later in May or June. Five to seven young chipmunks constitute a litter of which only one is had a year. The young are naked, blind, and helpless. Though without fur, the dorsal stripe pattern is revealed by dark streaks of pigment in the skin of the back of these infants. They are weaned some six weeks later and appear outside as two-thirds to three-fourths grown animals

Figure 30.
Yellow Pine Chipmunk.

with a thinner fur and duller color pattern than those of the adults. They will retain this pattern until the spring molt of the second year. By the end of the first summer, they are almost as large as their parents.

Chipmunks occur mostly in non-agricultural areas—almost entirely in forested regions—so seldom come in conflict with man's economy. It is true that they may garner a few seeds from barn, forest, or garden, but their attractiveness as a part of the wild fauna, their confiding ways, and their contribution to the food base of carnivores make them a valuable part of the natural scene without which the life of the outdoor enthusiast would be a little drab.

As one walks down a trail in some dense fir forest in western Washington or western Oregon, he may be greeted by a sharp *kwiss* from a nearby brush patch in a small clearing or burn. If our observer remains motionless and does a little lip squeaking, he will soon see a dark-brownish chipmunk climb slowly out on some half-exposed branch to look the situation over. Phlegmatic in behavior and preferring to keep well within vegetational cover, the Townsend's Chipmunk is the only member of the genus in the thickly forested regions. This fact, plus the relatively large size and dark coloration (one lowland race having no dorsal light stripes, being, rather, the same color as the sides; montane races only slightly lighter) make the identification of this species easy. It is not nearly as common in its range as the other species are in theirs and is more often heard than seen.

Chipmunks feed on a variety of plant food, with the inclusion of a few insects. Vegetational material consists of seeds, leaves, stems, fruits, corms, and some fungi. Seeds probably form the bulk of the diet. In spring and summer, they consume the soft immature seeds of ripening flowers. Later mature seeds are eaten or stored for winter. Fruits are probably the next most important food when available. A few specific foods are pine and sedge seeds, huckleberries, raspberries, thimbleberries, and yarrow, knotweed, and thistle seeds. Chipmunks do not typically depend on a deposit of fat to supply energy during the winter. In late September and early October, they begin storing food in the den, usually covering over the cache with a layer of grass. At times during the winter, they dig down through the grass and consume some of their stores.

The Red-tailed Chipmunk occupies somewhat the same ecologic niche in northeastern Washington, northern Idaho, and southeastern British Columbia that is filled by the Townsend's Chipmunk of the coastal areas. While the Yellow Pine Chipmunk, in one race or another, occurs in the open forests along the eastern borders of the region, the Red-tailed Chipmunk prefers denser stands of conifers where its short warning bark is a part of the auditory scene. The two species come together at the margins of dense and open woods. One such place is at "Kingbird Lake" where the author had the opportunity to study these animals for a number of years. In a dense grove of lodgepole pine, called "The Piney Woods," only Red-tails were originally present. The lower limbs of half of the grove were removed, opening up the timber and increasing the density of pine grass on the forest floor. In two years, the Yellow Pine Chipmunk had invaded and taken over the open part, the Red-tails remaining in the dense portion. Then, the second half was limbed, to be subsequently taken over by the Yellow Pines. Where direct competition is in-

Figure 31.
Townsend's Chipmunk.

49

Figure 32.
Rocky habitat of the Cliff Chipmunk.

volved, as at a feeding tray visited by both species, the Red-tail definitely dominates the Yellow Pine, members of the former species not tolerating close proximity of the latter. Thus, we see that both habitat preference and differ-ential behavior act to keep the distribution of two such closely similar species separate.

One good place, if there is such a thing, to meet the Cliff Chipmunk is in the Silent City of Rocks in extreme southern Cassia County in the southern-most part of Idaho. Here in this mysterious place of great stone outcroppings and brooding history of Indian massacres, one may, if lucky, spot a gray-colored chipmunk with practically no dorsal striping scurrying over some rock or climbing through dense bitterbrush or pinyon pine. Seldom will the chip-munk call and it will not show any of the usual chipmunk curiosity about a campsite. In this area, the Cliff Chipmunk lives out its life in the scattered rocks and conifer groves of the Albion Range and Black Pine Mountain, and seen only by the diligently-searching naturalist and an occasional passing cowboy.

Equally sequestered in the Northwest area covered by this guide is the dull-colored Uinta Chipmunk. The best place to see it is in the Bear River Range of extreme southeast Idaho. We suggest that you go to the Bloomington Lakes region where you will find *umbrinus,* which means "clouded," along the edges of the timber running over fallen logs and scattered rocks. The species can also be found in the Raft River Mountains and Big Hole Mountains of Idaho. You will have to search for this species to find it!

Figure 33.
Cliff Chipmunk.

Figure 34.
Uinta Chipmunk.

51

Let us enter the world of the chipmunk! What activities compose the daily life of this little mammal? What are its problems, its enemies, its accomplishments?

Its problems are probably very similar to our own—getting enough food to remain strong and healthy, finding mates to satisfy the reproductive urge, locating shelter from the elements and enemies, securing enough sleep to rebuild the tired body, and providing against a both certain and uncertain future.

The life of the chipmunk includes a variety of behavior types. Perhaps the most important is food getting, the searching, storing, eating, and digesting of seeds, berries, nuts, insects, buds, and all that fuels these animals. Searching for food is a part of their investigative behavior which also involves locating dens and nest sites as well as proper habitat to live in. Reproductive behavior includes searching for and selecting mates, courtship, and mating. The young seek care (care-soliciting behavior) which is provided by the mother (care-giving behavior). The young are furnished with certain hereditary behaviors, but learn by imitating habits observed in their parents (mimicking behavior). The rituals involved in eliminating body wastes constitute eliminative behavior.

An easily-observed activity in chipmunks is the setting up and maintenance of territories, areas which include the dens and resources to support and protect the adults and offspring. These often must be defended (agonistic behavior) again other chipmunks. The scraps and chases that we occasionally see between a couple of chipmunks are probably territorial disputes. However, these little animals do seem to be somewhat social, as individuals will often feed together on a feeding tray, especially if they are all of the same species.

It is an interesting learning experience to spend an afternoon with a chipmunk and to record all of the things done and places visited during that time. Try it sometime!

Figure 35.
Brush pile, a favorite haunt of the Yellow Pine Chipmunk.

Figure 36.
Red-tailed Chipmunk.

PACIFIC NORTHWEST SPECIES

LEAST CHIPMUNK 7½-3⅜-1⅛-1¹/₁₆ (190-85-29-17) Figs. 27 and 28. Mostly a small, shy chipmunk of the dry sagebrush areas and characterized by a general grayish color, black mid-dorsal dark stripe, brownish lateral dark dorsal stripes, and buffy or grayish sides. Hind foot averages less than 31 mm. and the tail is relatively short. However, some subspecies in Idaho and British Columbia may be larger and darker than the sagebrush varieties, but basically the Least Chipmunk is smaller and grayer, with yellowish rather than ochraceous or cinnamon colors in its bright areas. RANGE. N., n.e., and s.e. B.C., the arid areas of c. Wash. and e. Ore., and s. and s.c. Idaho. HABITAT. Occurs irregularly in sagebrush areas and lodgepole pine and open fir forests in s. part of range and in alpine tundra and coniferous forests in the northern section of the NW.

YELLOW PINE CHIPMUNK 8¾-3¹⁵/₁₆-1⁵/₁₆-¾ (223-101-34-19) Figs. 29, 30, and 35. A brightly-colored chipmunk with sharply contrasting light and dark stripes on its back and upper sides. The dark stripes are dark brownish with blackish centers while the light stripes are whitish or at most light grayish. The facial stripes are strongly marked. The ears are dark sooty gray or black with conspicuous white post-auricular patches. The sides are bright yellow or orange. The rump is grayish and the belly white or buffy. The undersurface of the tail is the same color as the sides. RANGE. S. and c. B.C., mts. of Wash. (including the Olympics), c. and e. Ore., and most of Idaho (excepting the s.w. portion). HABITAT. Open to semi-open coniferous forests (as in yellow pine and subalpine fir groves), clearings, large brushy areas, and rocky places, from lowlands to high mts.

TOWNSEND'S CHIPMUNK   10⅓-4⅗-1½-⅔ (258-115-38-17) Fig. 31.   A large, dark-colored chipmunk. The dorsal dark stripes are blackish with the dorsal light stripes brown or grayish. Tail reddish on under surface. Sides of body brownish. Individuals in the redwoods area of s.w. Ore. are reddish brown. The coastal race farther n. has black stripes on a brown back. RANGE. S.w. B.C., w. Wash., and w. Ore., including the Olympics, Coast Range, and Cascades. HABITAT. Clearings, slash, and other semi-open, brushy places in dense coniferous forests. Heavy cover of thick underbrush with dense over-head canopy preferred.

CLIFF CHIPMUNK   8¼-3⅝-1³/₁₆-¹¹/₁₆ (210-91-31-18) Figs. 32 and 33.   A large, shy, easily-overlooked chipmunk. The general coloration is grayish with indistinct dorsal stripes. Under surface of tail is bright reddish. Only the mid-dorsal dark stripe may be evident. RANGE. Extreme s. Idaho, in Goose Creek and Cassia areas. HABITAT. Rocky juniper and pinyon pine growths.

RED-TAILED CHIPMUNK   9¼-4⅜-1½-¾ (235-110-33-18) Fig. 36.   A large, dark-colored chipmunk with reddish shoulders and sides, black and white (mixed with reddish) dorsal stripes, red under surface of tail, and white belly. Separable from Yellow Pine Chipmunk which it occasionally overlaps by larger size, darker colors, preference for denser cover, and tendency to dominate former in direct confrontation. RANGE. N.e. B.C., n.e. Wash., and n. Idaho. HABITAT. Dense, montane, coniferous forests, as well as more open subalpine groves at timberline.

UINTA CHIPMUNK   9-4-1⁵/₁₆-¹¹/₁₆ (230-100-33-18) Fig. 34.   This species is a large, rather drab-colored chipmunk with brownish-gray sides, grayish head and rump; broad, blackish, dark dorsal stripes; and a white belly. RANGE. Limited areas of s. (Raft River Mts.), s.e. (Bear River Mts.), and e. (Targhee Plateau) Idaho. HABITAT. Semi-open timber and fallen logs and brush at edges of forests.

(continued from page 17)

was the life zone system. His eccentricities, his difficulties with congressional committees, and his adventures on the Western frontier are legendary. A recent book, LAST OF THE NATURALISTS: THE CAREER OF C. HART MER-RIAM, by Keir B. Sterling (Arno Press, 1974), is a detailed study of this remarkable man.

To quote Osgood again, "In the history of American mammalogy his place is a very large one, in fact it can scarcely be judged as less than preeminent. What he did is scarcely less important than what he influenced others to do. He was a power in the land with a reach into posterity that will long be felt. His contemporaries familiar with his whole career are now few in number and need no reminder that his was a remarkably complicated personality. For others, his record stands, but it cannot reveal the nuances of his unique character nor the warmth of his personal relations."

MARMOTS

Figure 37.
Hoary Marmot.

The marmots, also locally called groundhogs, rockchucks, woodchucks, chucks, and whistle-pigs, are the largest of the Pacific Northwest squirrels. Five species are represented in the region covered by the guide, the Olympic and Vancouver Island populations, as explained later, being considered to represent separate species. These large, phlegmatic squirrels are mainly terrestrial, seldom climbing bushes or small trees. They are often seen in rocky habitats where ready cover may be found among the larger boulders. The food is mainly plant material. One litter of two to nine young has been reported.

In the Northwest, the Yellow-bellied Marmot occurs in suitable habitats in Washington, Oregon, and Idaho, as well as southern British Columbia. Only the coastal areas are unoccupied by this species. The Hoary Marmot is to be found scatteringly in the subalpine country of northern Idaho, Washington, and much of British Columbia. The Eastern Woodchuck has a wide distribution across North America, but in the Pacific Northwest is to be found mostly in British Columbia with restricted ranges in northeastern Washington and northern Idaho.

The Eastern Woodchuck feeds mainly on grasses and herbs which it sometimes stores for the winter in its burrow, lining the walls, though apparently not eating this food. The Woodchuck usually does not forage very far from any of the openings of its den. Mating begins in March or April when the animals come out of hibernation. Four or five infant "chucks" are born about 35 days later. They are naked and blind at first, but by another month they open their eyes, are covered with soft hair and able to walk about. The young increase their weight to about three pounds by August, leaving the parents at this time to locate a place for their own den and to begin the serious job of putting on weight for the winter fast. Foxes, Coyotes, and Badgers are among the principal enemies of the Woodchuck, though even they have little success unless they can surprise it outside its burrow. Once inside, the chuck can produce a wall of earth faster than the predator can dig.

Preferring rocky places, the Yellow-bellied Marmot is replaced in many parts of the mountains by the Hoary Marmot, but where the latter is absent, the former species may penetrate well up into the subalpine. The Yellowbelly whistles or chirps in alarm when danger is sighted and is thus one of the prominent guardians of rocky places. The animal is herbivorous and generally gorges itself before winter sleep. Unlike the Woodchuck, this species forages far from its rocky haven. The den is fairly deep in the rocks and lined with dry grass. Here, the marmot has almost complete safety from predators. Breeding is done upon leaving hibernation and the young, varying from six to eight in a litter, are born in May. By late May and early June, they are frequently to be seen scurrying along road shoulders and rock piles. Though sometimes abundant where they occur, colonies are widely scattered and much "good" marmot country is unoccupied. In wild areas, the marmot causes no trouble to man, makes an interesting animal to watch, and contributes to the health and welfare of certain carnivores. In agricultural localities, however, it may invade hay fields, pastures, and vegetable gardens where local control measures must be taken. Shooting or trapping are effective methods and success has been obtained with poison bait or gas. If one has severe problems with these squirrels, the county agricultural agent should be consulted.

Experiences with mammals often remain with us for many years. Witness this scene in the Monte Cristo Range of Washington. After a few hours' hiking, we had just entered the beautiful cirque at the foot of the final slope to the summit of Vesper Peak. We had not proceeded far when the air was shattered by the shrill whistle of a Hoary Marmot. A little searching revealed the author of this blast watching us from a slab of granite halfway up a rockslide, the self-appointed but very effective watchman of the cirque. Our party remarked at the time that if we were to select a totem of the high places, we could do no better than choose this species.

The Hoary Marmot is the largest of North American marmots. It is similar in proportion but twice the size of the Eastern Woodchuck. Grayish in color to match the granites that it frequents, it is easily identifiable. In its high mountain habitat, the Hoary Marmot is active for only a few months of the year, the remaining time spent in deep torpor. In such a condition, the heart beats only four or five times a minute. One full breath is taken about every minute. Body temperature is only a few degrees above freezing. Recovery from dormancy may take only some two hours. After a short period of high metabolic activity, the normal basal rate is resumed. Green grass and succulent herbs make up most of the diet of this mammal, to be gathered during daylight hours. Eagles, Cougars, Bobcats, Coyotes, and bears are its enemies. The average litter runs three to five in number, though as many as eight have been reported. The young are born from late March to mid-May, depending on location. Development is slow and mating is seldom done before the young are two years old. Although the fur of the Hoary Marmot had considerable value at one time in the past, the worth of this species at present is strictly esthetic. For nature lovers who like to get up in the mountains where this mammal lives, it is of great importance.

Basically, then, the marmots are large, slow-moving, bulky squirrels which characteristically inhabit—in fact are strongly restricted to—rocky places where they find shelter in the crevices between large boulders. Such a niche is to be found mostly, in our region, in the basaltic areas of the interior where outcroppings and the talus slides of canyons and coulees are available and in the felsenmeers and rockslides among the cliffs and cirques of the high country above or near timberline in the mountains.

Figure 38.
Woodchuck.

Figure 39.
Yellow-bellied Marmot in typical rocky habitat.

Figure 40.
Talus slope habitat of the Hoary Marmot.

Figure 41.
Yellow-bellied Marmot.

PACIFIC NORTHWEST SPECIES

EASTERN WOODCHUCK 21⅓-5-3⅛-¹³⁄₁₆ (541-127-78-20) Fig. 38. This species is a small, dark marmot. Its upper parts are cinnamon brown, densely frosted with white-tipped hairs, while the under parts are reddish brown. The tail is dark brownish. Unlike other marmots, the head is mostly unmarked with no dark bar over the nose. The feet are black or blackish brown. RANGE. N.e. Wash., n. Idaho, and e., c., and n. B.C. HABITAT. Open forests, edges of fields and meadows, and subalpine meadows and rockslides.

YELLOW-BELLIED MARMOT 23¼-6¾-3¼-1 (590-170-82-25) Figs. 39 and 41. A large marmot with grizzled, dark-grayish upper parts, strongly marked black and white face, yellow under parts, and yellowish-brown feet. Sides of neck have conspicuous buffy patches. RANGE. E. and c. Ore., Idaho, e. Wash., and s.c. B.C., down the Fraser R. to Hope, B.C., and to the n. Puget Sound area (Bellingham, one record). HABITAT. Talus slides, outcroppings, rimrock, rock fills along highways, and other rocky places. Also in old log piles, under old buildings, and in burrows in cut banks.

HOARY MARMOT 30-8⅝-4-1 (750-220-100-25) Figs. 37, 40, 169, and 178; Color Plate 1. This is a large subalpine or alpine marmot with grayish upper parts, slightly darker sides, black feet, and dark brownish tail. The face is strongly marked. The under parts are whitish. RANGE. Cascades and w. Okanogans of Wash., mts. of n. and c. Idaho, and the mts. of much of the mainland B.C. HABITAT. Talus slopes and broken, rocky areas in subalpine and alpine regions. Irregularly distributed. Seems to favor granite or gray rock.

VANCOUVER MARMOT 26½-8⅝-3⅞-¾ (675-221-98-20). Body is dark, glossy, chocolate brown in color with a grayish-white patch on the muzzle, scattered white hairs on the back, blackish gloss over the rump, and a few white spots on the belly. RANGE. Mts. of Vancouver Island, B.C. HABITAT. Subalpine and alpine meadows; less commonly in montane parks and forests.

OLYMPIC MARMOT 28-8-3⅞-1³⁄₁₆ (714-204-100-31). Body drab brownish mixed with white, with a broad white patch in front of the eyes and white sides of nose, lips, and chin. RANGE. Olympic Mts. of Wash. HABITAT. Open, rocky areas and subalpine and alpine meadows near timberline.

———————————

The Vancouver and Olympic Marmots are occasionally included with the Hoary Marmot as a single species. When all of the facts are in covering the North American origins and Eurasian relationships of New World marmots, it may be that the Olympic and Vancouver Island populations represent relatively unaltered, isolated branches of the Old World *Marmota marmota* which became isolated in their present ranges during the withdrawal of the last continental glaciers, some 10,000 to 12,000 years ago. Similarly, the marmots of Mount Pilchuck in the western Cascades resemble closely these dark brown species farther to the west. The latter mountain evidently was a nunatak during the last ice age and its marmot population may be a relict group of an earlier, widespread species now mostly gone from the mainland. The grayish-backed Hoary Marmots may be more divergent descendants of the original Eurasian marmot. On the other hand, the Olympic and Vancouver Island marmots may be isolated off-shoots of an original North American alpine form of which the grayish Hoary Marmot, so commonly occurring in granitic batholith areas, is also descended. The Eastern Woodchuck is, perhaps, the most primitive (and antecedent?) of New World marmots, while the Yellow-bellied Marmot is a lowland, dry country type which has become secondarily alpine (mostly in desert ranges) where the Hoary Marmot is lacking. Just another example of the intriguing mysteries surrounding the origins of many of our Pacific Northwest mammals. For further interesting speculations of this nature on a number of Washington state mammals, the reader is referred to discussion in Walter W. Dalquest's MAMMALS OF WASHINGTON published in 1948 by the University of Kansas Museum of Natural History. Long out of print, copies may be found in a few libraries.

GROUND SQUIRRELS

Figure 42.
White-tailed Antelope Squirrel.

These mammals are small to medium-sized, diurnal, rock or ground in-habiting squirrels. They usually have plain or dappled backs without dorsal stripes, but if stripes are present, such markings then occur only along the sides of the back. Ground squirrels may be referred to locally as sage rats, gophers, or gray diggers. One species, the Mantled Ground Squirrel, is often confused with the chipmunks.

Ground squirrels are active dispersers and readily invade newly available habitats, as is shown by the northward movement of the California Ground Squirrel. The author has removed the Golden-mantled Ground Squirrel from clearings in the west Cascades' forests, only to have them re-populated within a year or two by individuals dispersing from places of origin farther up the mountain slopes.

The author had stopped his car after topping the Umptanum Ridge after the long pull up from Ellensburg on the way to the Audubon Society's campout at Wenas Creek. Down the road ahead sat a couple of small grayish ground squirrels cautiously eyeing the idling automobile. The dry barren ridge was well populated with these little mammals and numbers seemed to have busi-ness along the edges of the gravel road. This is a scene that may be repeated in many places in eastern Oregon and southern Idaho as well. In early spring, highway shoulders and borrow pits seem literally to swarm with Townsend's Ground Squirrels which usually appear with the first green grass and disappear into estivation when the last of the grass has dried up. In some areas, as much as seven or eight months may be spent in dormancy. The total period of active life that such a mammal may experience may come to less than 12 months, which at that is more than the life span of a mayfly, come to think of it!

This same Townsend's Ground Squirrel may enter nearby alfalfa and grain fields to cause a certain amount of trouble. It is a voracious eater, consuming almost anything, including dead members of its own species. No doubt, run-over ground squirrels attract more individuals to live along roadsides. Green vegetation, however, is the preferred food. In low hot places, there may be little or no water for drinking and the only water the animals get is obtained from the metabolic breakdown of their food. The burrow system may be rather extensive, some tunnels having been measured at more than 50 feet, with numerous openings, and reaching an occasional depth of several feet. One litter per year of some four to 10 young is produced. Enemies of the Townsend, as well as of most ground squirrels, are numerous, including snakes, hawks (particularly the Red-tailed Hawk), weasels, Badgers, and Coyotes. Ground squirrels often occur in colonies where they may be very common. If any of our readers are plagued with too many of these animals, the local county agent or Fish and Wildlife rodent control man will be glad to help.

The east-west course of the Columbia River where it separates Washington and Oregon has provided an important barrier to the northward range expansion of many mammals. One of these was the California Ground Squirrel,

Figure 43.
Townsend's Ground Squirrel.

Figure 44.
Uinta Ground Squirrel.

a large sciurid very common in the California valley area. Some squirrels got across the river in 1912 and established a colony at Bingen on the north bank and were at White Salmon by 1915. First, the Klickitat area was populated. Later, the crest of the Simcoe Mountains was passed and the invasion continued northward along the lower east slopes of the Cascades. Here, the squirrels have come to occupy a zone between the yellow pine haunts of the Golden-mantled Ground Squirrel and the arid domain of the Townsend's Squirrel. Northward extension has been reported as far as the Naches area and lower Wenas Creek and Umptanum localities. It will be interesting to see how far this rapid range extension will go, especially if it should swing around the northern fringe of the Columbia Basin and bring the California and Columbian Ground Squirrels together. What an interesting competition that might be!

A peculiar ground squirrel of the arid west is the little White-tailed Antelope Squirrel which in the Pacific Northwest occurs only in parts of southeastern Oregon and southern Idaho. This mammal, on which considerable physiological research has been made, is most likely to be found in the hottest, driest parts of the Great Basin desert. Often abroad during the heat of the day, it may occasionally be found active during the winter months as well. Sparsely vegetated ground surfaces, even alkali flats, are attractive to it in the author's experience.

Figure 45.
Townsend's Ground Squirrels often occur in grassy clearings in the lower yellow pine country.

Figure 46.
Arctic Ground Squirrel in typical stiff, upright posture of the ground squirrels.

Figure 47.
Columbian Ground Squirrel.

PACIFIC NORTHWEST SPECIES

WHITE-TAILED ANTELOPE SQUIRREL 8¼-2³/₁₆-1½-⅜ (210-56-38-11) Fig. 42. A small, coarse-haired ground squirrel with dark-grayish upper parts marked on each side with a single white stripe. The legs are pinkish and the under parts are white. The tail is grizzled black above, white below, and usually carried up over the rump so that the white under surface shows conspicuously, as the name indicates. RANGE. S.e. Ore. and s.w. and Raft River Valley areas of Idaho. HABITAT. Roadside ditches, alkali flats, and open places in the sagebrush areas. Seems to prefer the hottest, driest regions of the desert.

TOWNSEND'S GROUND SQUIRREL 8⅞-2-1¼-⁵/₁₆ (225-50-32-8) Figs. 43 and 45. This species is a small buffy-gray ground squirrel with pale dots on the upper parts. The face and legs are reddish buff with pale buff on under parts. Under surface of the tail is dark cinnamon. Some races paler than others. At any distance, the back appears to be unmarked. RANGE. E. Ore., s. Idaho, and s.e. Wash. (west of the Columbia R.). HABITAT. Mixed sage-grass areas, especially where small patches of grass occur in the sagebrush. Also found in extensive short grass plains and in cultivated fields. Colonies often located on hillsides. Prefers the hotter, drier parts of the open desert country.

WASHINGTON GROUND SQUIRREL 9⅛-2-1½ (229-50-35). Similar to the Townsend's Ground Squirrel but has darker (brownish gray) upper parts

65

Figure 48.
California Ground Squirrel.

which are distinctly marked with large grayish spots. Under parts are dark buff. Face, hind legs, and tail are dull reddish. A more strongly marked species than the closely related Townsend's Squirrel. RANGE. S.e. Wash. (east of the Columbia R.) and n.e. Ore. HABITAT. Prefers grasslands, either extensive or scattered as small prairies in the sagebrush, as well as roadside ditches and edges of grain fields.

IDAHO GROUND SQUIRREL 8½-1⅞-1⅜-⅝₆ (215-48-34-8). A small, un-striped ground squirrel less than 250 mm. in length and with the hind foot less than 38 mm. The upper parts are dappled grayish brown; the nose, outer parts of hind legs, and under surface of tail, rusty brown; the belly, grayish fulvous; and the chin, white. RANGE. Washington and Adams Cos. of Idaho. HABITAT. Open, dry, rocky ridges and grassy flats.

RICHARDSON'S GROUND SQUIRREL 12⅛-3⁵⁄₁₆-1¹³⁄₁₆-1³⁄₁₆ (308-85-46-20). A medium-sized, plain-backed, unstriped ground squirrel with a buffy wash over the grayish back and sides, buffy white under parts, and a tail blackish above and buffy below. The shoulders are not noticeably more grayish than the rest of the upper parts. RANGE. N.e. and s.e. "lower" Idaho, as well as s.w. part of that state, and extreme s.e. Ore. HABITAT. Grassy prairies on higher plateaus and openings in the timbered areas; occasionally in grain fields.

UINTA GROUND SQUIRREL 11¾-3-1¾-$1\frac{1}{16}$ (300-76-45-17) Fig. 44. A medium-sized unstriped ground squirrel with grayish-brown back and sides but with head and shoulders distinctly grayer than the remainder of the upper parts. The central part of the under surface of the tail is grayish. RANGE. E. Idaho, mostly in the mts. and mt. valleys; uncommonly to the lowlands. HABITAT. Dry meadows, pasture lands, cultivated fields, and montane meadows, usually near water.

BELDING'S GROUND SQUIRREL 11-2$\frac{9}{16}$-$1\frac{1}{16}$-⅝ (282-66-44-17). This species is a medium-sized, unstriped ground squirrel with grayish upper parts faintly washed with pinkish down the center of the back, grayish sides, and buffy under parts. Central part of the under surface of the tail is chestnut brown, margined by black and white bands. The reddish band down the center of the back is distinctive. RANGE. E. Ore. and s.w. Idaho. HABITAT. Meadows, open juniper slopes, sparse timber, and brush from intermediate elevations to timberline. Favored place is where there is a grassy meadow with a stream on one side and a sagebrush slope on the other.

COLUMBIAN GROUND SQUIRREL 14-3⅞-2⅛-⅝ (368-98-53-15) Fig. 47. A large ground squirrel—dark grayish buff above, marked with small white or

Figure 49.
Golden-mantled Ground Squirrel.

67

buffy dots; forehead brownish; back part of head and nape, dark grayish; face and hind legs, cinnamon color; under parts deep buff, becoming grayish buff on belly. Tail relatively long and bushy, dark above and below (undersurface with gray-tipped hairs). RANGE. N.e. and e. Wash., n.e. Ore., n. and c. Idaho, and s.e. and s.c. B.C. HABITAT. Grasslands, meadows, grain fields, and mt. parks from lowlands to subalpine areas. Also in open yellow pine forests.

ARCTIC GROUND SQUIRREL   15⅞-4½-2½-⁹⁄₁₆ (400-115-64-14) Fig. 46. Largest of our northern ground squirrels. Head and shoulders cinnamon. Nape and back grayish to buffy brown, distinctly marked with whitish spots. The sides, under parts, and legs are tawny. Under surface of the tail is tawny with a black terminal brush. Pelage is thicker and more woolly than that of the more southern ground squirrels. RANGE. N.w. B.C. HABITAT. Open meadows, forest clearings, and brushy subalpine areas.

CALIFORNIA GROUND SQUIRREL   18⅓-8-2⅖-1¹⁄₁₂ (458-200-60-22) Fig. 48. A large ground squirrel with general brownish or grayish-brown color, conspicuously marked with gray on nape of neck. A dark band runs back from the head to mid-back, narrow at first and becoming wider posteriorly. Grayish sides of nape narrowing on proceeding back to center of dorsum as stripes. Under parts buff. Tail long, covered with buff-tipped hairs. Dark areas of back and sides with small, buffy dots. RANGE. W. Ore. and in Wash., along the Columbia R. in Skamania and Klickitat Counties, north over the Simcoe Mts. and along the e. base of the Cascades to the Naches and Wenas areas. HABITAT. Grasslands, oak groves, rocky outcrops, and talus slopes.

GOLDEN-MANTLED GROUND SQUIRREL   9⅝-3½-1⅝-⅝ (245-90-40-15) Fig. 49; Color Plates 1 and 4. This is a chipmunk-like ground squirrel with conspicuous light and dark stripes on the sides. Back is brownish gray with a white stripe, bordered by two black stripes, on each side of back, and with buffy sides. Head and shoulders brownish to yellowish (constituting the "mantle") with a narrow white line above and below the eye. Tail of medium length, grizzled above and light brownish below. Very much like a chipmunk in habits, behavior, and ecology. RANGE. C. and e. Cascades, Blue Mts., and n.e. corner of Wash.; most of Ore., except the n.w. coastal area; most of Idaho; Rockies and lower Cascades of B.C. HABITAT. Open coniferous forests, clearings, and rocky outcroppings and slides, from intermediate elevations to the alpine areas. Particularly abundant and familiar in campgrounds and picnic spots in national parks.

There is very little to fear from wild mammals. No Northwest species makes a practice of stalking humans, though some may occasionally follow you—unseen—out of curiosity. The large mammals, such as bears, Moose, Elk, Buffalo, etc., must not be approached too closely, especially if they have young, or they may take defensive measures. Any mammal, large or small, will put up a fight if attacked or if it considers itself in danger. Give mother bears with cubs a wide berth, and all park bears should be treated with extreme caution. Mooching chipmunks, skulking deer mice, and raiding pack rats are a nuisance, but not a danger. Diseases are rarely contracted from wild animals, but it is probably best not to handle rodents or jackrabbits, especially if they are found dead.

TREE SQUIRRELS

Figure 50.
Western Gray Squirrel.

Three native and two introduced species constitute this group of medium to large-sized squirrels in the Pacific Northwest. Although spending considerable periods of time on the ground, these forms are more at home in trees where they leap from branch to branch and climb along the trunk with graceful ease. The Eastern Gray Squirrel and the Fox Squirrel have been introduced into several localities in the region, while the native Western Gray Squirrel is found in western Oregon and parts of western and south-central Washington. The Douglas' Squirrel, or chickaree, inhabits southwestern British Columbia, western Washington and the Cascades of that state, and western and central Oregon, while the related Red Squirrel occurs in the forests of Idaho, northeastern Oregon, eastern and northeastern Washington, Vancouver Island and much of British Columbia.

Eastern Gray Squirrels are active most of the year, holing up only during exceptionally cold weather. Fierce fighting may occur among the males during the beginning of the mating season. Nests are placed in holes during the

69

Figure 51.
Fox Squirrel.

winter, but may be built out in the open during the summer. Such nests are masses of twigs and leaves in a fork on a high limb, looking much like a hawk or crow nest. The gestation period of this squirrel averages 44 days. The young number three to five in a litter and sometimes there may be two litters in a summer. The value of this species is mainly esthetic. The small amount of neighborhood pilfering it does should be considered only a just award for its presence.

Western Gray Squirrels are rather shy and do not mix well with civilization. Only in a few places have they entered settled areas. While the Douglas' Squirrel is easy to observe, the Western Gray Squirrel keeps hidden from the watcher. Nests may be placed in cavities in trees or in large masses of material on branches. The young are born early in the spring, in late March or April. The number of young in a litter averages four and there may be two litters in a season. Acorns and pine seeds, especially those of the yellow pine, are preferred, though a variety of other foods may be taken depending on availability.

The Fox Squirrel is the largest of all North American squirrels. A full-grown adult may weigh two to three pounds and the average life span may reach 10 years. The Fox Squirrel gets its name from its fox-like face and tail and reddish color. In its native range, it prefers oak, hickory, and beech woodlots in the Northeast and broken pine forests in the southern states. The species is strictly diurnal and does not hibernate, though severe weather may force it to remain inside its nest. Hunger sometimes will bring it out, however. The Fox Squirrel feeds on a variety of foods such as nuts, acorns, seeds, fungi, insects, buds, birds' eggs, and soft bark. Nuts stored for winter use are usually buried throughout the territory of the individual and many are not retrieved. These squirrels have also been known to feed on soft unripe ears of corn.

The Red Squirrel occurs strictly in coniferous forests. These animals spend much time on the ground, as their tracks in the winter snows will attest. Individuals remain close to their nests and it has been estimated that the home range may average about two and a half acres, though this depends somewhat on the quality of the habitat. Nests may be placed in hollow trees or on branches, or, rarely, in the ground. Breeding occurs during March and July with litters born in April and in early fall. The average litter contains four to five young. The author was once camped by a large hollow snag in the Seven Devils Mountains of Idaho that contained a family of Red Squirrels. In the mid-afternoon on almost every day, the mother would escort the five young out of the nest hole and let them scramble along several nearby branches. After an hour or so of play, they would be shooed back into the nest. Martens, goshawks, and horned owls constitute the principal enemies of these squirrels. Not particularly good to eat, they have no value to humans but numbers are shot each year by plinkers. The Red Squirrel is one of our most abundant diurnal mammals and should be strictly protected.

The Douglas' Squirrel is similar to the Red Squirrel, but differs in details of coloration and behavior. Both occupy approximately the same coniferous forest habitat in their respective ranges. The Douglas' Squirrel makes its home in tree cavities or in nests constructed of twigs, needles, and bark. The nests are placed in the upper parts of trees and are round in shape and a foot or more in diameter. The inner chamber is often lined with cedar bark. Five or six young are born in late spring or early summer.

Figure 52.
Cone caches and shucking station of the Red Squirrel.

PACIFIC NORTHWEST SPECIES

EASTERN GRAY SQUIRREL 18⅘-9-3-1³/₁₆ (480-230-68-30). This is a large, bushy-tailed tree squirrel usually seen on the ground, when observed. Upper parts and sides grayish with a strong overwash of reddish in summer (more grayish in winter); under parts whitish. The tail is long and bushy with long, white-tipped hairs. Some melanistic individuals are completely black. The hairs on the tail may be grayish with white tips. RANGE. Introduced into several states in the NW, such as at Seattle and Spokane, Wash.; also at Vancouver, B.C. Has not spread beyond urban areas.

WESTERN GRAY SQUIRREL 22⅓-10⅘-3¼-1⅛ (570-270-82-28) Fig. 50. A large, native, bushy-tailed tree squirrel usually not seen in urban areas. Upper parts and sides dark, grizzled grayish with pure white under parts. The tail is dark blackish gray, edged with white. RANGE. W. Ore. and w. and w.c. Wash. HABITAT. Prefers oak, maple, or yellow pine woods. Occurs in oak woodlands and open coniferous forests in the lowlands s. of Puget Sound and e. along the Columbia R. to Klickitat Co. and then n. through the oaks and pines to the walnut groves s. of Lake Chelan, preferring above all the groves of *Quercus garryana* for winter food, and yellow pine for summer sustenance.

FOX SQUIRREL 20⅞-9-2¾-1⅛ (530-230-70-28) Fig. 51. This non-native squirrel is a large, reddish-gray, bushy-tailed member of the genus *Sciurus*, the tree squirrels. Though variable (from silver gray to blackish), upper parts usually are dark grayish with reddish-brown cast. Ears, feet, and edges and under surface of the tail are rusty red; under parts of body are orange to deep buff. May easily be distinguished by the presence of reddish or blackish colors and not so strongly gray colored as in the gray squirrels. A white nose may be present. Somewhat slower moving than the gray squirrels. RANGE. Introduced into Asotin, Seattle, and Okanogan areas in Wash.; the Boise, Rupert, Aberdeen, Bruneau, Nampa, Weiser, and Caldwell areas in Idaho; and possibly some other places in the Pacific NW. HABITAT. Urban areas, for the most part, but has spread into some surrounding agricultural land, particularly in the Boise River Valley of Idaho.

RED SQUIRREL 12½-5-2-⅞ (320-128-52-22) Rigs. 52, 53, and 55. A medium-sized tree squirrel with dark reddish or brownish upper parts, the brown of the upper sides separated from the white of the lower sides by a black lateral line. Rest of under parts are grayish white. The tail is blackish; feet, dark buff to light brownish. RANGE. N.e. and e. Wash. (including the n.e. Cascades), n.e. Ore., most of Idaho (excepting the s.w. corner), and all of B.C., except the s. humid coastal belt, but present on Vancouver Island. HABITAT. Coniferous forests, especially yellow pine and semi-open fir woods.

DOUGLAS' SQUIRREL; CHICKAREE 11⅞-4¹¹/₁₆-2⅞-¾ (304-120-48-20) Fig. 54. This coastal species is slightly smaller than the Red Squirrel. Upper parts are dark, dusky brown or olive and the under parts are orange or yellow, separated from the upper sides by a black line. The tail is blackish brown, edged with white or yellow. The *pee-oo, pee-oo, pee-oo* call is distinctive. RANGE. S.w. B.C., w. Wash. (including the Olympics and most of the Cascades), and Ore., excepting the n.e. and s.e. parts. HABITAT. Coniferous forests.

Figure 53.
Red Squirrel.

Figure 54.
Douglas' Squirrel

73

Figure 55.
Red Squirrel (Klaus Sonnenberg).

The author was once standing on the muddy margin of a small pond near the head of Wenas Creek when his attention was directed to some activity associated with his right foot. On looking down, he found a Douglas' Squirrel excavating a cavity under the forward portion of the boot. It seemed wise on the part of the owner of the shoe to remain motionless and find out, if possible, what was going on. After sufficient mud had been removed and the cavity large enough to suit the squirrel, it inserted a Douglas fir cone which it had brought with it under the sole and proceeded to close in the sides of the hole with mud which it carefully patted against the leather. When the author told this story to Professor William T. Shaw, that expert on squirrels reminded him of a study he had made in the Palouse Range near Moscow, Idaho, of the storing of green pine cones in mud by squirrels of this genus.

FLYING SQUIRRELS

Figure 56.
Northern Flying Squirrel.

The rays of the full moon filtered down through the great cedars like light falling between the pillars of some Gothic cathedral. Except for the water rippling over the pebbles in the creek bottom, all was silent. The distant hoot of a Horned Owl sounded irregularly. But there were other sounds, however; occasional chirps coming from the trees and the soft slap as a furry body glided down through the air and landed against a trunk, to be followed by a scratching of clawed feet. Here and there through the streaks of moonlight floated small bodies like the shades of Homer's heroes gliding down the dark tunnel to Hades after death. The field biology class lay in their sleeping bags watching this scene, not caring that it was already after midnight along the banks of Granite Creek in the far northeastern corner of Washington.

Unlike other North American members of the squirrel family, the Flying Squirrel is completely nocturnal, and for that reason is very poorly known to most people as they almost never see it. Studies have shown, nevertheless, that it is often common; in some places as numerous as the day-time chipmunk. Flying Squirrels are mostly seen during the daylight hours only when frightened from their nests, as when the tree or snag in which they are hidden is cut down, necessitating a sudden change of residence. The food consists of the

75

usual squirrel provender of seeds, nuts, and fungi, but also a wide variety of berries, fruits, blossoms, and even bark. The species is more carnivorous than most squirrels and consumes many insects, as well as small birds and birds' eggs. Dens are placed in holes in trees, usually lined with shredded bark. Caches are made of food materials, as these animals do not hibernate.

The most obvious feature of this squirrel is its ability to glide through the air by means of the furry membranes stretching between the fore and hind feet. This is gliding or soaring, not true flying, which in mammals is accomplished only in the bats. The gliding of the Flying Squirrel is always downward, the animal depending on its weight to force its gliding membranes against the air. Considerable maneuverability is possible through the application of different tensions to the gliding membranes and positions of the tail. Thus, the squirrel may make sudden twists and turns in mid-air to change direction or to avoid obstacles.

The two to five young are born in late spring after a gestation period of 40 days. In two months, they are able to make short glides. Besides the usual array of enemies, not the least of which is the Marten, Flying Squirrels suffer from man's activities in cleaning up the forests and woods of den trees. These, which are usually old snags, are carefully removed by the forester in an honest, though ill-informed, concept of forest housekeeping, much to the detriment of the Flying Squirrels. Bluebirds suffer from the same activity, and it may be necessary, if we are to preserve these interesting squirrels in certain overly-managed woodlots, to install nest boxes for denning. The recent interest in leaving snags in the forests augers well for these nocturnal squirrels.

*   *   *

NORTHERN FLYING SQUIRREL 11¾-5⅛-1⅝-1⅛ (300-130-42-28) Fig. 56. Fur over body very soft and silky; prominent fur-covered membranes on sides of body between fore and hind limbs. Upper parts brownish or dark grayish; under parts ashy gray to light grayish buff. Tail colored as body. Ears very small. RANGE. Occurs, often abundantly, in coniferous forests throughout the Pacific Northwest with the exception of Vancouver Island, s.e. Ore., and s.w. Idaho. Strictly nocturnal and seldom seen. HABITAT. Prefers coniferous forests, frequenting most commonly and abundantly the denser portions where a thick canopy lessens the penetration of light, plenty of brush and a small stream make for a copious insect supply, and fallen logs provide convenient highways for surface travel. Here, on a fallen tree, a live trap, preferably of the Havahart type, baited with an apple or prune or some rolled oats will probably capture a Flying Squirrel and this interesting little rodent can be observed for a day or two before being released to its sylvan habitat.

POCKET GOPHERS

Figure 57.
Northern Pocket Gopher.

Pocket Gophers are medium-sized rodents distinguished by their externally opening fur-lined cheek pouches used for carrying food, large yellow incisors, and long-clawed front feet suitably adapted for digging. Their fur is short, their eyes are small but clearly evident, and their scantily-haired tails are relatively short. They may be separated from the moles with which they are often confused by several means. Moles' eyes are not apparent, their front feet are more spade-like, their tails are shorter, and their muzzles are less rodent-like. Pocket gophers are excellent diggers and, unlike the moles which often merely push the soil out of their way, dig true tunnels, the soil from which is removed from the burrows to the surface to form mounds or hills. Only in the Townsend's Mole do we find expertise in tunneling comparable to that of the gopher. The group of mammals treated here are active in winter and continue their burrowing, either in the soil or in the snow.

Six species of pocket gophers occur variously in the Pacific Northwest. The Southern Pocket Gopher has two small ranges in s.w. Oregon. The large Townsend's Pocket Gopher likewise occupies areas of small extent in s.e. Oregon and s. Idaho unlike the widely-occurring Northern Pocket Gopher which extends throughout the Pacific Northwest except for timbered lowland areas in s. B.C. and w. Washington and Oregon. Gopher areas in the coastal parts of Washington and Oregon contain the closely similar Mazama Pocket Gopher. The large, dark Camas Pocket Gopher exists entirely in the Willamette Valley of Oregon, while the small Idaho Pocket Gopher is found in eastern Idaho.

As is indicated above, much of the Northwest is populated by pocket gophers. Their presence is revealed by the numerous hills of excavated earth in summer and the earth cores or cables lying on the ground uncovered by melting snow in early spring. In some alpine areas, the meadows may be literally laced with these mysterious cores. They are the work of the pocket gophers which, having tunneled in the ground after burrowing in the snow during the winter, place the soil tailings in old snow tunnels. As the snow slumps and melts, these cores are slowly lowered to the earth's surface and finally liberated from their snow molds as the white stuff disappears. After a few weeks of drying out, the cores fall apart and their rope-like shape is destroyed. Pocket gophers are active throughout the winter. The author and a companion, while traveling over a snowy meadow in a snowmobile, surprised a Coyote in the act of digging a gopher out of its snow burrow. The Coyote fled the scene with the gopher, but left one of the rodent's legs in the dug-out burrow.

In spite of their biological interest, pocket gophers may constitute a serious menace to man's economy in gardens and agricultural fields by consuming food and piling up hills of dirt over young plants. If a few individuals are the culprits in a small garden, a few gopher traps will suffice. In large areas, however, the use of strychnine-poisoned grain or diced cubes of potatoes or carrots must be employed.

Gophers forage by underground tunneling, seeking roots, tubers, and bulbs of various plants. Most activity of the animals is spent below the surface with only brief visits above ground, mainly for pushing out excavated soil. In its underworld domain, the gopher patiently tunnels along, seeking food, extending its burrow system, well away from whatever weather may be prevailing "outside." Gophers are consistently solitary and each burrow system possesses only a single occupant which is not at all agreeable to the approach of other gophers. This antagonism is relaxed during the breeding season in meetings of opposite sexes. After a gestation period of shortly less than three weeks, the five or six young are born. The pocket gopher does not hibernate, but burrows through the snow, if present, in its search for food.

No treatment of Pacific Northwest gophers would be complete without mention of the Mima Mounds on Mima Prairie south of Olympia. Literally immense gopher hills, these are an amazing sight and should be watched for by anyone driving through the area. The subject of long and continuous controversy, Victor B. Scheffer and Walter W. Dalquest originally suggested the origin of the mounds by pocket gophers. Great were the expostulations of the geologists that followed. One of the latter group's hypotheses has it that these mounds are the result of permafrost activity. The last glacial period ended some 10,000 years ago and it is difficult to imagine how permafrost boils could remain uneroded that long, unless, of course, permafrost heaving still exists in the area!

Figure 58.
Townsend's Pocket Gopher (light phase).

Figure 59.
Townsend's Ground Squirrel (dark phase).

Figure 60.
Fresh pocket gopher hills.

80

Figure 61.
Earth cables or cores of the pocket gopher.

PACIFIC NORTHWEST SPECIES

SOUTHERN POCKET GOPHER 9⅜-3-1¼-¼ (240-78-32-7). Upper parts rusty or reddish brown; under parts light buffy ochraceous, contrasting with upper parts. Feet, cheeks, and chin are whitish. In some individuals, the incisors are white-tipped. RANGE. Pistol River, Chetco, Cottage Grove, Klamath Valley, and Umpqua areas in s.w. Ore. HABITAT. Reported as frequenting hard clay and volcanic soils in open non-forested places.

TOWNSEND'S POCKET GOPHER 11-7⅛-1⅜ (280-80-35) Figs. 58 and 59; Color Plate 16. A large pocket gopher with colors ranging from buff through brown to brownish with a black wash. A completely black, melanistic phase also occurs. Best identified by size and distribution. RANGE. Restricted areas in s.e. Ore. (Alvord Lake, Narrows, Owyhee, and Vale localities) and the lower Snake and Boise River Valleys and American Falls-Fort Hall localities in s. Idaho. HABITAT. Moist river valleys and irrigated regions. Frequents sides of ditches and irrigation canals.

NORTHERN POCKET GOPHER 7⅞-2⅜-1-⅓ (200-60-25-8) Figs. 57, 60, and 61. The color of this species varies considerably, depending on the particular geographic race being examined. It is usually uniform, though somewhat paler below and generally of a yellowish-brown or grayish-brown hue. There are prominent dark patches behind the ears. The nose is often dark colored and there may be a white spot or patch on the chin. Probably best identified by size and distribution. RANGE. E. Wash. (including the Cascades), e. and c. Ore., most of Idaho, and s.c. and s.e. B.C. HABITAT. Open to semi-open places, such as meadows, grasslands, pastures, sand dunes, mountain parks, and grassy streambanks where soft soil for burrowing is present.

IDAHO POCKET GOPHER 6⅝-1⅞-1-⁷⁄₁₆ (170-48-25-6). This recently-described species is a very small gopher with the head and body usually less than 150 mm. in length and the hind foot less than 26 mm. The color of the body is yellowish or buffy, rather than reddish; the feet are whitish; and dark ear patches are not present. RANGE. N.e. (Dubois, Idaho Falls, Lost Rivers sinks areas) and extreme s.e. (Bear River Mts.) portions of Idaho. HABITAT. Open sagebrush, grassland, mountain parks, and subalpine meadows and hillsides.

MAZAMA POCKET GOPHER 8⅓-2⅔-1⅛-⅓ (208-66-28-8). This species is practically indistinguishable externally from the Northern Pocket Gopher and for the general purposes of this guide one may separate the two species on the basis of regional occurrence. Gophers of this size of the western parts of Oregon and Washington and the Olympic Mts. are probably this species and those of the Cascades and the regions to the east are most likely the Northern Pocket Gopher. Technically, the baculum, or penis bone, of the Mazama Pocket Gopher varies from 22-31 mm. in length, while that of the Northern Pocket Gopher ranges from 12-17 mm. Coat colors of *T. mazama* are usually reddish brown with larger post-auricular (ear) dark patches than in *T. talpoides*. The incisors of the former are weakly grooved. RANGE. N.w., s.w., and Cascades areas of Ore. in both valley and higher mt. regions; scattered prairie localities and higher Olympics in w. Wash. HABITAT. Open prairies and subalpine meadows.

CAMAS POCKET GOPHER 11¾-3½-1⅝ (300-90-42). Largest of the pocket gophers. Color dark brown to sooty black, darkest on the underside. Pelage long and furry in winter, but short and harsh in summer. RANGE. Willamette Valley area of Ore. HABITAT. Open places, such as cultivated fields, pastures, meadows, orchards, and lawns.

Certain mammals, which are apparently closely associated with the soil as in burrowing or foraging, may show very close preferences as to the type of ground they live on or in. An excellent example of this is in the case of the Idaho Pocket Gopher described above. In carrying on biological studies in the Bear River Mts. of southeast Idaho some years ago, the author noted that a small, pale pocket gopher, then thought to be a race of the Northern Pocket Gopher, lived only a few feet from a much larger, darker gopher; the former in hard, dry, limestone soil and the latter in soft, meadow loam. Jerry Ferrara and the author found a large, grayish gopher in the lower parts of sand dunes in the Juniper Forest preserve in south-central Washington, living just a few feet from a smaller, darker gopher in the loessal silt surrounding the dunes. These are more examples of this principle of competitive exclusionism referred to earlier in the book, where closely-related species or even subspecies may differ in distribution on the basis of very fine ecological or behavioral differences.

POCKET MICE

Figure 62.
Great Basin Pocket Mouse.

The small nocturnal pocket mice are restricted largely to the more arid regions of the Pacific Northwest. About the size of the deer mouse, or smaller, pocket mice range in color from nearly white through buff and yellow to grayish on the back and sides to whitish on the belly. A definite line running backwards from the nose separates the colors of the back from the lighter shades of the under surface. The tails of these animals are typically as long as, or longer than, the combined head and body length. Fur-lined cheek pouches opening externally are characteristic of the family to which these mice belong and are used to transport food, usually in the form of seeds, to the underground burrows in which they spend the daylight hours, for these are strictly nocturnal mice. These pouches, however, are detectable only through careful scrutiny. Like their relatives, the kangaroo rats, pocket mice can live on a diet free from water, since moisture in sufficient quantity can be manufactured metabolically from their natural forage. Two species of pocket mice are included in the Northwest mammal fauna, the Little Pocket Mouse and the Great Basin Pocket Mouse.

These mice are almost entirely denizens of the sagebrush lands and it is to such places you must go if you wish to become acquainted with these silky-haired little fellows. Many people, perhaps with the dirty-brownish House Mouse in mind, consider all mice nasty and horrible, but this is not so. Mice are beautiful and attractive little mammals with distinctive color patterns, habits, and distributions.

The more wide ranging of the two species, the Great Basin Pocket Mouse, is basically a seed eater, but also may take green vegetation and insects when available. Food, while gathered above ground, is usually eaten below the surface. It may also be stored in special chambers in the burrow complex. In gathering food, the animal usually sits on its hindquarters, using the hand-like paws to secure the bits of food and then stuffs them into the cheek pouches. Food is removed from the pouches by a back-to-front sweeping movement of the forefeet which presses out the materials within. Territories of the pocket mice are small, often less than an acre in size. The food of these mice is abundant in desert areas and long treks to seek it are unnecessary. The average-sized litter numbers four and one or two groups of young may be produced in a year.

The Little Pocket Mouse, tiniest of Northwest rodents, occurs in southeast Oregon and extreme southern Idaho. The author of this book was the first worker to find individuals of this species in Idaho and duly reported the fact to the authorities at the university for which he works, they in turn sending the information out in a press release. Larrison, who was spending the summer in the field in southern Idaho, was greatly surprised to see a headline in a Salt Lake City paper reading "Two Hundred Pound Scientist Finds Tenth Ounce Mouse." Some people have a greatly perverted sense of humor!

Although positive evidence of hibernation is lacking, pocket mice are at least inactive above ground during the winter months. Seeds comprise the staple of the Little Pocket Mouse's diet, although stomach analyses reveal that insects and caterpillars may be consumed in varying quantities. It is doubtful whether any economic loss caused by these rodents through seed consumption is significant. Their ingestion of insects may relegate them to a neutral or even positive economic status. With their host of natural enemies, such as predatory birds, Badgers, Coyotes, skunks, snakes, and even grass-hopper and deer mice, the Little Pocket Mice serve as a food source in the natural scheme and apparently have little direct effect on man. In fact, with the continued and relentless destruction of the sagebrush and desert shrub biome, the Little Pocket Mouse, with its restricted occurrence in the Pacific Northwest, could well become an endangered species, at least in our region.

Pocket mice, in one species or another, may contain what are often called "soil color races" by the mammalogist, subspecies which closely resemble in their body appearance the surface color of the ground they live on (and in). Almost pure white individuals are found on the gypsum sands of the Tularosa Basin in the Southwest while blackish pocket mice occur on nearby black basalt areas. The same situation occurs in the Craters of the Moon National Monument in Idaho where a pale race typical of the Snake River Plain sur-rounds a blackish form in the lava and cinder cone areas.

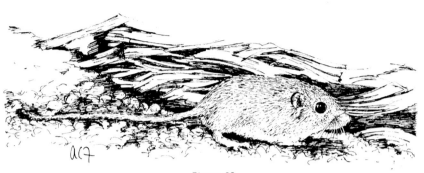

Figure 63.
Little Pocket Mouse.

PACIFIC NORTHWEST SPECIES

LITTLE POCKET MOUSE 5⅛-2¾-1¹/₁₆-³/₁₆ (130-71-18-6) Fig. 63. This smallest of the Pacific NW rodents is buff to buffy gray on the back with an overlay of blackish hairs and lighter buff or white on the under parts. There is a white patch on the chest. The fur is soft and silky. Tiny size and distribution are distinctive, as are the typical pocket mouse's large hind legs and very small forelegs. RANGE. S.e. Ore. and extreme s. Idaho in the Raft River Valley area. HABITAT. Shadscale, sagebrush, or greasewood areas, particularly on the lower slopes of alluvial fans.

GREAT BASIN POCKET MOUSE 7⅛-3½-⅞-⁵/₁₆ (180-90-23-8) Fig. 62; Color Plate 2. A medium-sized mouse with soft, silky fur, long tail, large hind legs, very small forelegs, and externally opening cheek pouches. Upper parts olive gray to grayish, thickly mixed with brownish or blackish hairs; sides buffy; under parts buffy white. Tail weakly bicolored. Pocket mice in the Craters of the Moon National Monument and surrounding lava bed areas in south-central Idaho are almost black. RANGE. Suitabie habitats in e. Wash., e. Ore., s. and w.c. Idaho, and s.c. B.C. (Anarchist Mt. and Okanagan, Thompson and Similkameen River Valleys). HABITAT. Sagebrush, bitterbrush, and rabbitbrush areas, as well as grassy places and nearby grainfields.

KANGAROO MICE

Figure 64.
Dark Kangaroo Mouse.

The author must confess that he has had no personal field experience with this group of rodents, his knowledge of them being limited to preserved museum skins. The species in the Northwest, the Dark Kangaroo Mouse, is apparently limited to southeastern Oregon. One could hardly improve on the account of this mouse in Vernon Bailey's *The Mammals and Life Zones of Oregon* published in 1936 and now long out of print. The following remarks are quoted from that source.

"Like their relatives, the kangaroo rats and pocket mice, these quaint little gnomes are desert dwellers, lovers of sandy or mellow soil among the sagebrush, and able to live where there is little rain and long periods of drought. They are nocturnal burrowers, sleeping underground during the day and rarely seen except when taken in traps at night. The little paired tracks of the two hind feet, too large for pocket mice and too small for kangaroo rats, are easily recognized in the dusty trails, but the closed burrows, well hidden under the sagebrush, are not easily found. . . .

"They run in little short hops on the two hind feet, rarely leaving a print of the little hands, which are generally folded on the breast and used mainly for feeding, digging, and all the general purposes of hands rather than feet. Their speed is so great that when frightened they disappear like a flash of light over the sandy soil of their own color. In captivity, if quietly handled, they are gentle and unafraid. They are closely like the kangaroo rats in disposition and habits. . . .

"Near the Narrows, where Preble found them in 1896, the writer camped overnight on July 13, 1927, to collect more specimens. In a sandy sagebrush spot near a point of lava rocks about 2 miles southwest of Narrows tracks of the gnome mouse were found and a line of 66 mousetraps set in the most promising localities. The next morning the traps contained the usual numbers of pocket mice, kangaroo rats, white-footed and grasshopper mice, but only one gnome. Their tracks were around many of the traps, and they had taken the bait from several without being caught, but they seemed not to care much for rolled oats. Their tracks in the early morning before the wind and ants had obliterated most of them were easily followed and generally led from the burrows out into patches of the abundant little desert weed, *Mentzelia albicaulis,* then well laden with flowers and green and ripe seed capsules on which they were feeding. . . .

"It would be difficult to accord any commercial or economic value to these dainty little denizens of the desert nor can any serious sins of omission or commission be laid to them. Still they have a value sufficient to warrant many in making a long journey into the desert to gain a few specimens of a unique type and to learn a little of the causes that have guided its development along lines different from all other forms of life. As the writer looks back more than 45 years to the capture of the type of this genus and the first thrill of realizing its remarkable characters, so different from even its nearest relatives and opening up a whole new field of possibilities for the multiform kinds of desert life, it is no wonder that the hardships of bitter winter and scorching summer camps should have vanished before the fascination of this first-hand study of desert life. With all our intelligence and versatility of adaptation we are still far behind such animals in the perfection of physical mechanism for our needs, and we can surely learn humility if not wisdom from many of our inferior mammalian brothers."

*　　*　　*

DARK KANGAROO MOUSE 6¼-3⁹⁄₁₆-1-⅜ (160-92-25-10) Fig. 64. A small, mouse-sized, kangaroo rat-like mammal with fur-lined cheek pouches and a tail that is thickest in the middle and tapering to a point at the end. Upper parts buffy gray with white ear patches; lower parts white to cream-colored; sides of nose, edges of ears, and lateral line buffy; feet grayish; tail bicolored, dark buffy above, light buffy below, with black tip. Size, nature of tail, and color distinctive. RANGE. S.e. Ore. HABITAT. Soft, sandy soil in hot, dry sagebrush.

KANGAROO RATS

Figure 65.
Ord's Kangaroo Rat.

Kangaroo rats are distinguished by their large, strong, hind legs and small, weak forelegs; smooth, silky fur; and long, bicolored tails which because of long hairs on the tip appear "bannered." Large, fur-lined cheek pouches opening to the outside are used to carry food to subterranean caches. Colors range from pale buff through shades of tan, brown, and gray on the back, while the under parts are whitish. A white stripe extends across the haunch or thigh to the base of the tail. These rats are restricted to the drier parts of the Northwest, mostly east of the Cascade Range, where the soils may be of ash, sand, or fine gravel. The greatest part of the diet of these animals is composed of seeds, although arthropods and the stems or fleshy parts of plants may afford a supplementary diet. Large quantities of seeds may be stored underground and caches containing a bushel or more are not uncommon. Through a series of behavioral and physiological adaptations, kangaroo rats are able to manufacture and conserve metabolic water from a dry diet, thus negating their need for free water. Limiting their above-ground activity to the nocturnal hours, they spend the remainder of the day in underground burrows which may form vast subterranean networks. Some species characteristically build mounds above ground which are honeycombed with burrows and runways.

The common kangaroo rat of the Northwest is the Ord's "K" rat, occurring widely in the arid parts, often in sandy soils. The animal shuns sand dune areas where there is no vegetation but will be found abundantly where a scant cover of grass has invaded the dune areas. Here, their myriad tracks and tail marks literally cover the surface giving one the idea that they are more numerous than they actually might be.

The Chisel-toothed Kangaroo Rat is more restricted in its distribution in the region covered by this guide, occurring with us only in southeastern Oregon and southern Idaho south of the Snake River. While the ranges of it and the Ord's rat often overlap, there seems to be a marked ecologic separation between the two. The Chisel-tooth (its name coming from the chisel-shaped lower incisors which do not taper to points as in other kangaroo rats) prefers more or less pure stands of such chenopods as shadscale, winterfat, or salt sage, while the Ord's rat prefers a mixed vegetational cover of various species, particularly weeds. These habitat preferences are reflected in the diets of the two in which, when a variety of foods may be available to each, the Chisel-tooth will demonstrate a choice for chenopods alone while the Ord's will feed on a variety of seeds. It was recently shown that the chisel-tooth pattern of the lower incisors in the kangaroo rat of that name is used to scrape off the skin of the chenopod leaves, usually saltbush or salt sage of some kind, which contains the high salt content so that only the fleshy, inner parts of the foliage may be used. The other rats apparently do not have this habit, so do not need the chisel-shaped scrapers. This is a neat adaptation which the author is amused to confess that he had spent considerable time watching captive kangaroo rats of both these species feeding on seeds and foliage of chenopods and other desert types and never watched closely enough to observe the Chisel-tooth rat's method of feeding, thus allowing another worker to make an important discovery. Close observation and the relating of obscure facts are the name of the game in natural history! One is reminded of Thomas Henry Huxley's remark of "Why in the world didn't I think of that!", upon his finishing reading of Darwin's *Origin of Species*.

In non-range lands, the kangaroo rats probably play no significant economic role. They do have a status in range or crop lands. In their favor, lie the increased soil aeration and greater water seepage as a result of their burrowing. It is reported that the Banner-tailed Kangaroo Rat of another region adds plant nutrients to the soil in an amount equal to 30 cents per acre. Their depletion of range grasses or crop seeds is probably negligible. Studies conducted in southern Idaho some years ago by the author and a student of his revealed that the total weight of forage consumed by all rodents—kangaroo rats, as well as other species—in a salt desert range amounted to about 20 grams per day per acre, out of a total acreage reserve of some 300,000 grams, in which the daily renewal was more than the 20 grams the rodents used. In cultivated lands, most of the rats' destruction is caused in the marginal areas since the cultivation destroys their natural habitat and lessens the rats' population density.

The studies of the author alluded to above also revealed that over-utilization of a range land produces bare areas which come to be populated by weeds, thus a variety of plant species, which in turn attract a variety and increased number of rodents with differing food habits. A monoculture or climax vegetation supports a minimum variety of mammals in range lands. There must be a message in these facts!

Figure 66.
Burrows and tracks of the kangaroo rat.

PACIFIC NORTHWEST SPECIES

ORD'S KANGAROO RAT 9¾-5½-1⅝-8¾ (250-140-31-19) Fig. 65. Upper parts dark tan; under parts white. Tail is brownish gray with white lateral stripes and a dark ventral band tapering to a point near the tail tip. The soles of the feet and linings of the cheek pouches are whitish. The lower incisors taper to sharp points at their tips. RANGE. S.c. Wash., e. Ore., and s. Idaho. HABITAT. Open sandy or soft soil areas with sparse cover of vegetation, such as sagebrush, forbs, or grasses.

CHISEL-TOOTHED KANGAROO RAT 10⅝-6⅜-1⁹/₁₆-¾ (270-160-40-16) Color Plate 5. Similar to the Ord's "K" Rat, but slightly darker with sooty fur on the soles of feet and linings of cheek pouches. Best told by the broad, chisel-like shape of the lower incisors. RANGE. S.e. Ore. and s.w. and extreme s. Idaho (Owyhee Co., Raft R. Valley, and Salmon Falls Reservoir areas). HABITAT. Light, ashy soils and growths of chenopods such as shadscale, salt sage, or winterfat.

HEERMANN'S KANGAROO RAT 12¼-7³/₁₆-1¾-⅜ (312-184-46-15). Large, dark "K" rat. Upper parts dark, cinnamon buff overlaid with much black on head and back. Under parts white. Face marked with black. RANGE. S.w. Ore. in Klamath and Brownsboro areas. HABITAT. Soft or sandy soil in open, brushy places.

90

Figure 67.
Beaver.

As evening progressed, the shadows cast by Ceanothus Ridge slowly moved over the surface of "Kingbird Lake." The author's rowboat was situated in the center of the lake near the aerator outlet at a spot where the big cut-throats were particularly fond of Royal Coachman flies. The surface of the lake was mirror-smooth with only an occasional dimple where a "cut" rose to the surface for a low-flying insect. Soon all of the lake was in shadow. Suddenly, a dark-brown head appeared in the water near the east-shore beaver lodge. It surveyed the scene, dark eyes alert and ears upright, then it swam rapidly by the boat toward the west-shore lodge. Moving steadily, it left a V-shaped wake in the wave-less surface with a white cut-water in front of its muzzle. A sudden motion by one of the fishermen in the boat alarmed it, and it turned over forward in the water, striking the surface with its tail to produce a resounding crash and flying spray. The giant Beaver of "Kingbird Lake" had begun its nightly foraging.

The Beaver is one of the best known of all North American mammals. Largest of the continent's rodents, it has a wide distribution, there being few ponds, lakes or streams on which they do not occur, at least originally. They have been, and still are, extremely valuable to man. During the early part of the 19th

91

century, no well-dressed gentleman could appear in public without a Beaver hat. This fashion made possible the great Beaver trapping era of the Rockies and north country. The exploits of the mountain men and fur trappers, such as Jim Bridger, the Sublettes, and Peter Skene Ogden, are a part of the glorious history of western North America. After the collapse of the Beaver hat fashion, many of these men turned their knowledge of mountains and plains gathered in exploring for new Beaver waters to the guiding of the emigrants and military forces which were penetrating westward. The Beaver thus played a unique role in the discovery of the West.

A characteristic feature of the western mountains are the small to large, flat valleys scattered here and there. These are largely the products of silted-in Beaver ponds. Well-watered, level, and with a rich grass growth, these "holes" were most valuable to the early settlers and still offer much of the hay-growing meadows of the hill country. Even today, Beavers play an important part in water conservation. Their chains of dams and ponds on a stream distribute the runoff during the summer and keep the water tables high in pastures and hay meadows. Because of value and quantity, Beaver hides still rank high in the fur trade. In recent years, pelts have brought an average price of $16 per skin in the Northwest.

Beavers sometimes live in burrows dug into the banks of larger rivers. More commonly, however, they build the familiar lodges and dams in streams and lakes. Entrances to the lodges are below the level of winter ice formation, allowing access during the year-round activity of the animals. However, if the pond freezes over hard, the animals are "in" for the winter and must have sufficient food in the way of submerged branches to carry them over. The accumulation of soil and debris above their dams and the ultimate silting in of their ponds often force the occupants to seek new sites. Many kinds of aquatic and herbaceous plants serve as food for these animals, among them the bark and cambium from aspen, willow, cottonwood, birch, or alder trees, and cat-tails.

As mentioned above, Beaver impoundments are important in irrigation and reforestation, and in forming habitats for trout, aquatic birds, and other fur-bearing animals such as Mink and River Otter. Embankments deter water run-off, but Beavers can become nuisances by attacking crops when their pre-ferred foods are unavailable. Their dams may plug up irrigation ditches or flood tillable soil. Their low mortality often leads to conditions of over-popula-tion so that colonies on ponds and lakes need constant management to prevent untoward depletion of their food supplies. Trapping offers the best control for these animals and live traps are usually recommended so that Beavers can be removed to areas where their activity will benefit, rather than hinder, man. The gradual encroachment of humans and their alterations of the environment, however, are spelling out a problematical future for the Beaver in many parts of the Northwest. In discussing the decline in Beaver pelts in the 1965-66 fur harvest season, the fur report of the Idaho Game Department sounded the following warning: "Sixty-seven percent of the stream mileage in Idaho is now not suitable for Beaver management. It has been necessary to remove Beaver from extensive complaint areas. Curtailed production of Beaver in these areas is an important factor contributing to this decline."

Figure 68.
A Beaver pond in northeastern Washington.

93

Figure 69.
Materials used in a Beaver dam.

Figure 70.
Large tree felled by a Beaver.

BEAVER 39½-17¾-6⅞-1⅜ (1,000-450-175-35) Figs. 67, 68, 69, and 70; Color Plates 3 and 7. This is a large, dark-brown rodent weighing some 30 to 60 pounds with a broad, flat, scale-covered tail. RANGE. Occurs in suitable habitat throughout the Pacific Northwest. HABITAT. Semi-aquatic, restricting itself closely to streams and standing water such as ponds and small lakes. Forage is found in close proximity to the water in the form of trees and branches from which the bark is removed for food. Streams are frequently dammed to produce the Beaver ponds which isolate and protect the lodges and form the reservoirs of water where food may be stored beneath the surface for later consumption.

CRICETID MICE

Figure 71.
Common Deer Mouse.

Of the Pacific Northwest rodents, nine species are here considered members of the Family Cricetidae of which six are mouse-like and treated in this chapter. The remaining three are wood rats and follow in the next chapter. The vole-like rodents are included in the Family Microtidae and discussed later in this manual.

The cricetid mice are mostly characterized by darker upper parts contrasting with lighter under parts, large ears, and (in most species) long tails. The bodies of these rodents are slender and the fur is soft.

The Harvest Mouse looks enough like the common House Mouse to be easily mistaken for that grubby immigrant. Small, lean, brownish, and long-tailed, the Harvest Mouse may be distinguished in the hand by the tan-colored hairs inside the ears and the grooved upper incisors. Also, there is a habitat difference. The Harvest Mouse is very seldom found in buildings or human habitations, preferring instead the grassy areas in the dry parts of the interior of the Northwest. In fact, giant wild rye patches are a favorite haunt. A few House Mice may be found in such places, but not often. Though one of the smallest of our mice, the Harvest Mouse is a fighter and proficient in biting. Though sometimes abundant, the places of occurrence of these mice are scattered and it is not nearly as common as the deer mice.

The Harvest Mouse usually builds its nest above the ground level, often in bushes, vines, or holes in fences or small trees. The nest resembles a ball or

95

Figure 72.
Harvest Mouse.

clump of densely matted grasses, finely woven together with one or two tiny openings near the lower level. The nests are often lined with fine grasses or down from cattails, willows, or cottonwoods.

The attractive little Common Deer Mouse has the distinction of being one of the most abundant and widely-distributed mammals in the Northwest. It is found almost every place where there is cover of brush, trees, or rocks. Nocturnal for the most part, deer mice appear shyly in the late evening to scamper about the forest floor in the protection of the sides of some fallen log or large boulder. Often several will be seen together. Timidly moving about searching for food, they dash to the protection of a burrow or crevice at the slightest noise. Unlike most wild mice, deer mice do not hesitate to enter cabins, tents, or other human habitations. In such places, they can be a nuisance, leaving their numerous droppings scattered about and getting into unprotected food, particularly bread and cereals. They are easily controlled, however, by closing up all the means of entry and a few mousetraps will take care of those individuals already "in." The deer mice are prolific breeders, with the season ranging from February to November, depending on location and climate. After 21 days of gestation, the three or four young are born. There may be two to four litters a season. The young disperse some six weeks after birth and sexual maturity may be reached in females six to seven weeks after birth.

The large, long-tailed Mountain Deer Mouse is the most abundant mammal in the mountains of the Cascade and Olympic Ranges of western Washington and southwestern British Columbia. Studies have revealed that while this mouse occupies the dense coniferous forests of the mountain slopes and certain lower elevations, the Common Deer Mouse is to be found in the more open lowland forests. In mountainous terrain elsewhere in the Pacific Northwest, the Common Deer Mouse reigns supreme.

Predatory carnivores need not be coyote- or cougar-sized. Body dimensions vary in the animal kingdom and are not necessarily related to habit. All of which demonstrates that the Grasshopper Mouse, in spite of its size, is a full-fledged, efficient prey stalker and meat eater. If you would find this species, you must search in the dry sagebrush with your live traps and be patient, for the Grasshopper Mouse is never abundant. While feeding on grasshoppers and crickets to a considerable extent, the species also includes mice in its diet and stomach analysis commonly reveals animal flesh and bits of fur.

It has been said that the Grasshopper Mouse resembles a weasel in some of its feeding habits. While in captivity, one was observed to slash at captive deer mice and other mice in the same cage with its sharp incisors. This habit closely resembles that of some of the larger carnivores which possess canine teeth. These mice seldom dig their own burrows, but commonly occupy those of other mice, kangaroo rats, ground squirrels, and Badgers.

Figure 73.
Canyon Mouse.

PACIFIC NORTHWEST SPECIES

WESTERN HARVEST MOUSE 5½-2¹¹/₁₆-¹¹/₁₆-⅝ (141-69-18-16) Fig. 72. This is a small, delicately-built mouse with brownish upper parts (becoming sooty brown down the center of the back) and buffy-gray under parts. The long tail is strongly bicolored, sooty brown above and gray below. Similar to the House Mouse, but has tan-colored hairs inside the ears and longitudinally grooved upper incisors. RANGE. Prefers the arid interior of the NW (e. Wash. and Ore. and s. Idaho, including the dry parts of the Snake, Salmon, and Clearwater Rivers in n. Idaho), as well as s.w. Ore. and the Okanagan Valley of B.C. n. to Okanagan Landing. HABITAT. Dense grass in dry, open, semi-desert to desert areas; often common in wild rye patches along streams, dense patches of grass in sagebrush, and cattail marshes.

CANYON MOUSE 7¼-3¾-¾-¾ (185-96-20-21) Fig. 73. A small, medium-sized mouse with long, lax, buff or olivaceous-buff pelage above and whitish fur below. The bicolored tail is fur-covered and longer than the length of the head and body and is tufted at the tip. Usually a conspicuous oil gland in the middle of the back. RANGE. Narrowly restricted to its preferred habitat in e. Ore. and s. Idaho. Distribution is discontinuous, the species occurring in scattered, isolated colonies. HABITAT. Rocky slides and crevices in cliffs in hot, dry canyons in open, desert country. Often at bottom of talus slope near a small stream.

98

Figure 74.
Sagebrush habitat of the Grasshopper Mouse.

Figure 75.
Common Deer Mouse (upper); Pinyon Mouse (lower).

COMMON DEER MOUSE 7-2¹⁵⁄₁₆-⅞-¾ (180-74-22-20) Figs. 71 and 75. A medium-sized, long-eared, long-tailed mouse with brownish upper parts (darkest along center of back), white under parts and lower sides, and a strongly bicolored tail (dark brown above and white below). Chin and throat white. Total length usually under 200 mm. RANGE. Occurs abundantly and widely throughout the Pacific NW with the exception of the Cascades of Wash., the Coast Range of B.C., and the Olympic Peninsula where it is replaced by the Mountain Deer Mouse. HABITAT. Prefers a variety of habitats, though favoring the coniferous forests. Also to be found in considerable numbers in grain fields (especially stubble), weedy fence rows and ditches, and in sagebrush and slide rock in the arid interior.

MOUNTAIN DEER MOUSE 7⅞-4⁵⁄₁₆-⅞-¾ (202-110-23-19) Fig. 76. Very similar in color to the Common Deer Mouse, but much larger. Total length usually more than 200 mm. and tail more than 100 mm. Dusky brownish on upper parts with sooty streak down center of back. White below. RANGE. The Cascade Mts. and Olympic Peninsula of Wash. (including the s.w. part of the state) and the Coast Range of s.w. B.C. HABITAT. Prefers the dense, dark forests of the mts. and foothills.

SITKA DEER MOUSE 8⁹⁄₁₆-4¹⁄₁₆-1-⅝ (219-104-26-16). A large, dark-colored deer mouse with a long, bicolored tail. Upper parts brownish with a broad, dusky stripe down the middle of the back. Ears grayish, edged with white.

99

Legs brownish; feet grayish. Under parts whitish, sometimes streaked down the middle with reddish. Black-phased individuals occasionally to be found. RANGE. Occurs on the outer islands (Frederick, Hippa, Gordon, Anthony, Ramsay, and Hotspring) of the Queen Charlotte group off coastal B.C. HABITAT. Prefers the dense spruce-cedar forests, particularly the forest edges.

PINYON MOUSE 7¼-3⁹/₁₆-1-1 (185-91-25-25) Fig. 75. Upper parts grayish brown or brownish buff, grizzled with black. Under parts white. Tail about the same length as the head and body and distinctly bicolored. Easily recognized by the very long ears which are an inch or more in length, much longer than those of any other dry country deer mouse. The fur, in length and texture, is intermediate between that of the Canyon Mouse and the Common Deer Mouse. RANGE. The Deschutes, Klamath, and Rogue Rivers areas of Ore. and the Raft R. and Silent City of Rocks in s. Idaho. HABITAT. Open forest, particularly pinyon pine and juniper, brush, and rocky areas, as well as greasewood flats.

NORTHERN GRASSHOPPER MOUSE 5³/₁₆-1⁹/₁₆-¾-¾ (138-40-20-21) Figs. 74 and 77. This predatory little fellow is a stocky, medium-sized mouse with grayish upper parts, white under parts, and a short tail which is pale gray above and white below. Feet and face below eyes are white. The fur is short and woolly. A short, white tuft of hair lies in front of each ear. The claws are long and straight. RANGE. The arid areas of e. Wash. and Ore. and s. and extreme w. Idaho. HABITAT. Mostly restricted to sagebrush.

Figure 76.
Mountain Deer Mouse.

Vernon Orlando Bailey was born in Manchester, Michigan, June 21, 1864, and died in Washington, D.C., April 20, 1944. As a young boy in Elk River, Minnesota, he mastered the amazing skills of trapping and observing mammals that were to make him famous as a field mammalogist. Concurrently, he developed a skill in writing that was at once concise and interesting. He began field work for the Department of Agriculture in 1887 and continued his studies for 46 years until he retired as Chief Field Naturalist of the Biological Survey, though he remained active in biological research to the time of his death.

Bailey's chief interest lay in studying the life histories and distribution of mammals. He published numerous books and papers, including biological surveys of Texas, New Mexico, North Dakota, and Oregon, as well as revisions of the meadow mice, red-backed mice, and pocket gophers. Two studies on the animals of Glacier and Yellowstone National Parks were in print for many years. He was very much interested in nature education, being active in the Boy Scout movement and the Audubon Society.

Victor Scheffer has written that Bailey's "career as a field naturalist spanned the rich and exciting years when new faunas were being discovered in various parts of North America, and his career is thoroughly interwoven with the activities of this era. Bailey himself contributed more than ten thousand specimens of mammals to the National Museum, besides many birds and other animals" (*Murrelet,* May-August, 1942).

Figure 77.
Northern Grasshopper Mouse.

101

WOOD RATS

Figure 78.
Desert Wood Rat.

Perhaps no animals are more maligned, due to their distasteful imported Old World relatives, than the wood rats. Several characteristics serve to distinguish the wood rats from their less desirable kin, the Norway and Roof Rats. In gross appearance, there are many similarities. Wood rats, however, have larger ears that are usually covered with hair. Their under parts are whitish. The best field mark for the native rats is their fur-covered tails which in the Bushy-tailed Wood Rat may be just that—bushy-tailed. These rats are very deserving of the other common name of "pack rat." It is here that their habits may be qutie annoying, as they filch various and sundry items from the camps of man. Unlike many other animals which spend their time seeking food, these rats drag human artifacts, stones, and sticks to their houses in amounts up to 50 or more bushels for no apparent reason other than to incorporate them into their nest or stick pile. Wood rats commonly live among rocks, in caves or crevices, or on elevated rocky ledges. Look under the largest boulder on a mountain rockslide and you may find evidence of their presence. Houses of sticks and brush may be built in trees or shrubs or on the open ground and the nest buried well within. Their structures on the ground are commonly four or five feet in diameter and a foot or two high. Although common around old buildings or abandoned houses, wood rats usually prefer to live well away from the habitats of man. They are nocturnal in habit and are, therefore, seldom seen. Vegetable food, such as seeds, stems, berries, and bark is preferred, but insects are eaten and small amounts of carrion. More than their thieving habits, the most undesirable feature of these animals is that in some parts of the Northwest they may carry Rocky Mountain spotted fever ticks that serve as hosts for that disease as well as fleas carrying bubonic plague.

Similar to the more common Bushy-tailed Wood Rat in color, the Desert Wood Rat is smaller and has much shorter hairs on the tail, giving it a rounder appearance than the squirrel-like appendage of the other species. The upper parts are grayish or buffy gray while the under side, the feet, and the ventral part of the tail are light gray or pale buff. Relatively scarce and irregular in its range in the Pacific Northwest, these animals may be found in some numbers in the Owyhee Desert and the Raft River Valley in Idaho. Sagebrush-covered slopes, rocky outcroppings, and hop sage areas are favorite haunts. Small colonies of these rats may occur on foothill slopes where the openings to the animal's burrows may be seen. Also, nest piles of cactus and sage leaves, goosefoot, saltbush, seepweed, nettles, and dock may occasionally attain considerable size. The bleached white bones of jackrabbits are frequently incorporated into the nest, as well as the stem joints of prickly pear cactus placed around the entrances. Desert Wood Rats probably seldom come into competition with man. They serve as food for some predators, but their nocturnal habits undoubtedly save many from their natural enemies.

Figure 79.
Stick-pile of the Desert Wood Rat.

Figure 80.
Rockslide home of the Bushy-tailed Woodrat. The larger the boulders, the more likely are the rats to be present.

Students of animal behavior differ as to why pack rats "pack," but the existence of the habit is certainly not disputable. Many campers have had embarrassing experiences with these little thieves. Anything loose, especially if metallic or shiny, is likely to be pilfered. The author well remembers a rat at his camp at Soda Springs on the Ahtanum Creek southwest of Yakima which made off with the entire lima bean supply one night. Knives and forks, wristwatches, rings, etc., must not be left in the open if wood rats are around. In old cabins and buildings, the stick piles may be made out of trash, mattress linings, pieces of cloth, etc. Oregon grape leaves are commonly included, especially in nests in rock crevices which may be almost entirely of leaves and stems of this plant.

Wood rats commonly have three or four young in a litter and two litters a season are often the rule. The female is bred as soon as the first litter is born and weans them upon the appearance of the second. The earlier group often remains around the nest, but the young males soon challenge their father who drives them out. Most of the dispersing rats that the author has caught have been young animals.

PACIFIC NORTHWEST SPECIES

DESERT WOOD RAT 11-4⅝-1³⁄₁₆-1⁵⁄₁₆ (280-118-31-34) Figs. 78 and 79; Color Plate 7. Upper parts grayish to buffy gray; under parts, feet, and ventral side of tail, light gray or pale buff. Much shorter hairs on the tail, giving it a rounder appearance than the squirrel-like appendage of the Bushy-tailed Wood Rat. RANGE. S.e. Ore. and s.w. and s.c. Idaho. HABITAT. Prefers greasewood, sagebrush, and hopsage areas; less frequently rocky habitats. Uses old buildings less commonly than the Bushy-tailed Rat.

DUSKY-FOOTED WOOD RAT 18⅝-8⁷⁄₁₆-1⅝-1 (445-216-43-25). Upper parts dark cinnamon brown, overlaid with blackish; lower parts whitish, clouded with buffy or cinnamon. Feet dusky with whitish toes. Tail round, not bushy. RANGE. The Rogue, Umpqua, and Willamette River areas of Ore., n. to the Columbia R. HABITAT. Brush and open forests, preferring the drier regions of their range, where they build extensive nests and appear to shun old man-made structures.

BUSHY-TAILED WOOD RAT 15¾-6⅞-1¾-1½ (400-175-44-39) Figs. 80 and 81; Color Plates 1 and 6. A large, thickly-furred, bushy-tailed rat with grayish brown upper parts and whitish under parts. Tail gray above, white below. Feet are white. Sub-adults are bluish gray on upper parts. RANGE. Occurs throughout most of the NW from sea level to high mountain peaks. HABITAT. Prefers slide rock and cliff and canyon areas, caves, mines, and old, abandoned buildings; both in forested and open, desert regions.

Figure 81.
Bushy-tailed Woodrat.

105

VOLES

Figure 82.
Gapper's Red-backed Mouse.

These rodents, the meadow mice, lemmings, and their close relatives of the Family Microtidae form a group of economically important mammals. They are medium-sized rodents with blunt snouts and stout chunky bodies. Legs, fur-covered tails, and ears are short and the small black eyes are bead-like in appearance. The fur is generally soft and dull colored. "Vole" is a more correct name than "meadow mouse" or "field mouse" for some of these animals, since their habitats range from meadows to marshy areas, forests, dry plains, prairies, and even ocean beaches for certain species. However, members of the genus *Microtus* are referred to as meadow mice in this book for purposes of uniformity and the fact that they are more likely to be found in grassy or meadow habitats than any other.

Most voles are meadow or marsh dwellers but the Gapper's Red-backed Mouse is a denizen of the dense coniferous forests, often being most numerous in the thickest, driest parts of the timber. It is easily recognized by its short tail, reddish back, and close-set eyes. Red-backs are often common, sometimes rivalling the deer mice in abundance. They are gentle little creatures of the forest floor, easily tameable, and make interesting pets, not at all adverse to being handled. The red-backs of the low coastal areas are dull in color and considered to belong to the Western Red-backed Mouse species while true Gapper's Red-backed Mice are bright of color and in the upper forests in the Cascades and generally in coniferous timber to the eastward. Red-backed mice feed chiefly on green vegetational material, but seeds, nuts, bark, fungi, and a few insects are also included in the diet. They are active both day and night and climb well. The nests are lined with grass and usually placed under logs or tree roots. The young, as in the case of most mice, are born naked, blind, and helpless, the average litter numbering from four to six. As the gestation period is some 17 to 19 days, there would be room for two or more litters per year from a single female. The young are weaned in about three weeks after birth. Red-backed mice do not hibernate, moving about freely under the snow.

The Heather Mouse is one of the most interesting rodent species in the Northwest. Ranging widely through the forested mountainous region, it is, nevertheless, spotty in distribution and rare to uncommon in occurrence. The finding of an individual is always an event, giving notice that this mouse is in one's study area. The names "heather mouse" or "heather lemming" are commonly used, as many occur in the rocky, heather meadows at or above timberline. They have, however, been taken in rocky, grassy meadows, talus slopes, dry lodgepole pine woods, and even in woodsheds. The species feeds on the bark of various trees and shrubs, seeds, lichens, berries, and miscellaneous green vegetable material. Some storing is done. It is most active at twilight and at night. It builds a large nest of soft grasses, mosses, and lichens above ground in the snow in winter. In early spring, these cantaloupe-sized nests may easily be found on the surface of the ground, often beside a pile of droppings almost as large as the nest. In summer, the mouse lives below ground, under rocks or debris, or among the roots of trees.

Meadow mice are among the most strictly vegetarian of mammals. They feed to a considerable extent on green material. In captivity, they must have fresh green leaves and grass. One biologist, experimenting with keeping vari-

Figure 83.
Heather Mouse.

Figure 84.
Red Tree Mouse.

Figure 85.
Pennsylvania Meadow Mouse.

ous mice in confinement, found that he was successful with meadow mice when he supplied them daily with fresh grass clippings from the lawn mower. The presence of meadow mice is revealed by the typical runways in the turf which are usually in or below the dead grass mat. To find them, one must part not only the blades of living grass but the fallen intermeshed leaves and stems of the previous season's growth as well. There, next to the ground, will be found the myriad highways and byways of this Lilliputian world, here running to a sub-surface burrow opening, there literally tunneling in the grass mat itself. We often think of meadows as open habitats (at least they are from our coign of vantage) but we must consider a stand of grass from the mouse's point of view as an extremely dense jungle.

The differences in habitat that one often finds between related species was dramatically illustrated in field investigations conducted by the author one summer on a ranch owned by friends in British Columbia, in the west Kootenay district. Along a small creek were colonies of two voles. Above the ranch house, a number of Richardson's Water Voles had a dense colony where the stream flowed between steep grass banks. Below the house, where the ground was more level and the banks were very low, there existed a colony of Long-tailed Meadow Mice. Runways of the former species indicated a close dependence on water while the latter species spread out more from the creek site and apparently was attracted only to the stream margin by the denser growth of grass.

The palest of the voles in color is the Sagebrush Mouse. Color patterns of our mammals frequently reflect the habitats in which they live. Animals of the deserts or grasslands, where grays and light yellows abound, are usually light in color, apparently to make them less contrastive when seen against their native backgrounds. Conversely, species of the dark, thickly-vegetated rain forests of the coastal part of the Pacific Northwest are dull brownish in color. This condition is particularly striking when one compares east- and west-side races of a single species, the east-side one usually being noticeably paler. Such a situation, produced through adaptive evolution, has often accounted for many of our mammal (and bird) species that occur in the Northwest having pairs of subspecies, one eastern and the other western, the principal difference being the variation in coat color.

The brownish, long-haired lemmings of the Arctic barely get down into our area in northern and north-central British Columbia. They are among the most interesting of small mammals and are well worth looking for in their proper habitat, as indeed are all of the lesser mammals which may have habits and life histories just as fascinating as those of their larger cousins.

Figure 86.
Montane Meadow Mouse.

PACIFIC NORTHWEST SPECIES

NORTHERN RED-BACKED MOUSE 5¹¹/₁₆-1⁹/₁₆-¾-⅝ (146-41-20-15). This is a small, slender, brightly-colored vole with a bright red back, ochraceous sides, and a buffy belly. Tail bicolored. All-gray phase occasionally found. RANGE. N.w. B.C. HABITAT. Brush, open taiga forests (both coniferous and deciduous); tundra, and less commonly, rocky areas.

GAPPER'S RED-BACKED MOUSE 6-1¾-¾-½ (150-45-19-12) Fig. 82. General coloration grayish brown with distinct reddish overlay on back. Sides buffy gray; feet and under parts buffy white. Tail bicolored, dark brown above and grayish below. Red back may be absent in the uncommon gray phase. RANGE. Occurs widely in the coniferous forests of the NW, except for n.w. B.C., w. Wash. and Ore., and s.w. Idaho. HABITAT. Restricted mostly to the damper, darker, coniferous forests, where they may at times become abundant, even rivalling the deer mouse in numbers. At higher elevations, may occur in subalpine brush and rock slides.

WESTERN RED-BACKED MOUSE 5¹¹/₁₆-1¾-1¹/₁₆-⁷/₁₆ (146-45-18-11). Similar to the above species, but much darker and less reddish. Upper parts dark brown with faint reddish wash on back; sides slightly paler; under parts dark buffy; tail bicolored, sooty brown above, buffy white below. RANGE. Lowlands of w. Ore. and Wash, and extreme s.w. mainland of B.C., w. of the Cascades but including the Olympics. HABITAT. Dense, moist coniferous forests of the coastal lowlands and the Olympics.

110

HEATHER MOUSE 6-1⅜-¾-½ (152-34-18-12) Fig. 83. A medium-sized vole, ashy gray to brownish above and grayish white below. Tail sharply bi-colored, dark brownish above and whitish below. Fur thicker and more woolly than in meadow mice. Difficult to identify. Best technical character is the fact that the inner reentrant angles of the lower molars are much deeper than the outer ones. RANGE. Occurs widely in the forested and subalpine areas of mts. and foothills throughout the NW, except for s.e. Ore. and s.w. Idaho. HABITAT. Favors a variety of habitats ranging from heather and heather-rock areas in subalpine country and rocky, grassy places in hilly and montane terrain to moist brush along forest streams. Also taken by the author in woodsheds and under cabins in the mt. forests and wet, marshy areas. Seems to prefer open, seral, forest vegetation in drier sites, though near water.

WHITE-FOOTED TREE MOUSE 6¹¹⁄₁₆-2⁷⁄₁₆-¾-⅜ (171-63-20-10). Brown above; clear gray below. Tail sharply bicolored. Back sprinkled with black-tipped hairs. Feet white. RANGE. Humid, coniferous-forested regions from the Columbia R. s. to the California line in w. Ore.; in the Willamette Valley and along the coast. HABITAT. Dense, tangled vegetation adjacent to streams in thick coniferous forests, often along the water margin; also alder-filled canyon bottoms. Apparently more terrestrial than the Red Tree Mouse.

RED TREE MOUSE 7⅛-2⅞-1³⁄₁₆-⅞ (182-73-21-11) Fig. 84. Upper parts bright reddish brown; under parts whitish; tail dark brown to black. Claws sharp and strongly curved. RANGE. W. Ore. from the foothills of the Cascades

111

Figure 87.
A wet meadow, the favorite habitat of the Pennsylvania Meadow Mouse.

Figure 88.
Long-tailed Meadow Mouse.

w. to the coast and from the Columbia R. s. to the California line. HABITAT. Douglas fir forests (less commonly spruce and grand fir) where the animals spend most of their lives in the branches and crowns of the trees. *Note:* The slightly larger and darker (more brownish, less reddish) "Dusky Tree Mouse" (*A. silvicola*) is now considered a race of the Red Tree Mouse.

SINGING MEADOW MOUSE 5¹⁵⁄₁₆-1³⁄₁₆-¾-½ (152-30-19-13). A medium-sized vole with a very short tail. Light brownish above, slightly paler below. Buffy ear spot and bicolored tail, grizzled brown above, buffy below. RANGE. Probably occurs in the alpine areas of the mts. of the extreme n.w. tip of B.C. HABITAT. Dry, open, alpine tundra; also in brush along water.

PENNSYLVANIA MEADOW MOUSE 7-1¾-¾-½ (176-46-21-13) Figs. 85 and 87; Color Plate 10. A moderately-large vole with blackish-brown upper parts, dark brownish sides, dark grayish under parts, and a short, weakly bicolored tail. Fur is distinctly glossy in appearance and not grizzled. RANGE. Most of B.C. (excepting the coastal region), n.c. and n.e. Wash. (including an isolated population in the c. Columbia Basin), and n.e., c., and e. Idaho. HABITAT. Wet, grassy meadows; scattered bogs, cattail, and sedge habitats along lake shores, creeks, marshes, and springs. Often occurs in dense colonies in sedges standing in or near water.

MONTANE MEADOW MOUSE 6¼-1½-¾-⁹⁄₁₆ (160-39-19-15) Fig. 86. Upper parts dark brownish; under parts dark grayish. Tail short; feet grayish. Small size and range distinctive. RANGE. Occurs mostly in the drier, open parts of the NW, such as e. Ore., much of Idaho, e. Wash., and s.c. B.C., particularly the Okanagan Valley and Kamloops regions. HABITAT. Moist, weedy, or brushy areas near water at edge of grasslands. Tall vegetation, such as is found near water, is desired. Often common in grain fields. Prefers the grass-land zone.

GRAY-TAILED MEADOW MOUSE 6-1⅓-¾-½ (154-34-19-13). Upper parts yellow brown to yellowish gray; sides paler; under parts grayish white; tail short and bicolored, dark brown above and gray below; feet grayish. RANGE. N.e. Ore., s. of the Columbia R. from Hood R. w. to the Portland area and s. in the Willamette Valley. Also in the Vancouver, Wash., area. HABITAT. Grass-lands and open, grassy meadows and pastures.

CALIFORNIA MEADOW MOUSE 6¹¹⁄₁₆-1⅞-1³⁄₁₆-⁹⁄₁₆ (171-49-21-15). Upper parts brownish; lower parts grayish. Tail bicolored, brown above, grayish below. RANGE. S.w. Ore. in the Rogue R. and Umpqua Valleys n. as far as Cottage Grove. HABITAT. Dry upland meadows; less commonly marshes and wet grasslands.

113

Figure 89.
Sagebrush-grass habitat of the Sagebrush Vole.

TOWNSEND'S MEADOW MOUSE 9-2⅔-1-⅗ (225-66-25-15). A large vole with glossy, dark-brownish upper parts; sides more brownish and less black-ish; and dark, grayish under parts. Tail long, mostly unicolored. More reddish brown in summer. Fur mostly not grizzled. RANGE. W. Wash. and Ore. and extreme s.w. B.C.; also on Vancouver Island and certain nearby islands. HABI-TAT. Occurs mostly in lowlands, preferring wet swamps and marshes, espe-cially where dense tall grass or cattails exist. Also salt marshes. Usually not found in forests or mts., but does occur in subalpine meadows in the n. Olympics and on Vancouver Island.

TUNDRA MEADOW MOUSE 6¹³/₁₆-1¹⁵/₁₆-¾-½ (174-50-20-13). Colors griz-zled brown above and buffy gray below. Tail bicolored, dark brown above and grayish white below. Sides yellowish brown. Feet grayish. RANGE. Extreme n.w. tip of B.C. HABITAT. Moist tundra, sedge, and cottongrass areas, usually near water; also alpine tundra in higher parts of mts.

LONG-TAILED MEADOW MOUSE 7¼-2⁷/₁₆-¾-⅝ (183-63-20-16) Fig. 88; Color Plate 10. A medium-sized, long-tailed vole with grizzled brownish or grayish-brown upper parts, dark grayish sides, and bluish-gray under parts. Tail relatively long for a vole and bicolored, dark brown above and grayish below. RANGE. Occurs throughout most of the NW with the exception of n.e. B.C., Vancouver Island, and the lower Columbia R. and Willamette Valley areas. HABITAT. Often occurs in small colonies in more or less isolated, moist, grassy or herbaceous areas along streams or ditches; also in wet, boggy places along the ocean coast, alpine lakes, and sagebrush plains. Common in the original bunchgrass prairies.

CREEPING MEADOW MOUSE; OREGON MEADOW MOUSE 5¼-1⅗-⅔-⅖ (140-42-17-10) Fig. 90. A small, to medium-sized vole, almost completely dark brown on both upper and lower parts. Tail and ears short. Size, habitat,

Figure 90.
Creeping Meadow Mouse.

114

Figure 91.
Richardson's Water Vole.

115

Figure 92.
Streamside haunt of the water vole. Note the tandem arrangement of traps
necessary for securing these large rodents.

Figure 93.
Sagebrush Vole.

and overall dark coloration distinctive. RANGE. W. Wash. and w. Ore., including parts of the Cascade Range e. along the Wash.-B.C. border into the Okanogan Highlands, and in the lowlands of extreme s.w. B.C. HABITAT. Various, ranging from wet meadows and damp woods to subalpine meadows and dry, grass fields. Prefers banks along rivers, forest edges, and moist, sloping, semi-open ground. In scattered colonies. More in the woods than any other of our *Microtus.*

RICHARDSON'S WATER VOLE 8-2¾-1⅛-½ (220-70-28-12) Figs. 91 and 92. A very large vole, usually found close to water in mts. Upper parts dark brown, under parts grayish. Tail of relatively medium length and bicolored, dark brown above and grayish to light brownish below. Fur tends to be rather dull in appearance. Stiffened hairs on edges of hind feet. RANGE. Cascade Mts. of s. B.C., Wash., and Ore., and the Rocky Mts. and associated ranges of e. Wash., Ore., Idaho, and B.C. HABITAT. Largely restricted to stream banks, moist meadows, and lake shores in subalpine and forest areas in the mts. Often found along small brooks in the meadowy parts of glacial cirques. Must have grass or forb cover and the proper banks for burrowing and landing places at edge of water. Occasionally found in suitable habitat as low as 2,500 feet in s.e. B.C.

SAGEBRUSH VOLE 4⅛-¾-1¹¹⁄₁₆-⅜ (105-20-17-10) Fig. 93. A small, light-gray vole with a very short tail. Upper parts light, buffy gray; under parts whitish. Tail very weakly bicolored, dark buff above and pale buffy below; feet buffy white; soles of hind feet densely haired. Size, color, and short tail distinctive. RANGE. The dry, semi-desert to desert areas of e. Wash. and Ore. and s. Idaho. HABITAT. Grassy sagebrush and bunchgrass, often on the intermediate slopes and plateaus above the valley floors. Recorded in Ore. to hollow out cow chips, using them for shelter and food.

BROWN LEMMING 5⅞-1³/₁₆-1³/₁₆-⅜ (151-21-21-10) Fig. 94. A medium-sized, chunky, large-headed vole with very long, lax fur and a very short tail. Upper parts are chestnut brown, being somewhat lighter on the head. The under parts are buffy gray and the feet are grayish. Pelage grayer in the winter. RANGE. N. B.C. HABITAT. Moist, grass- and sedge-covered swales, as well as stream banks, wet meadows, and alpine tundra; rock slides in the mts.

NORTHERN BOG LEMMING 4¾-1-¾-½ (122-23-19-12) Fig. 95. A medium-sized vole with a very short tail and weak, longitudinal grooves near the outer sides of the anterior faces of the upper incisors located between the white and yellow tooth surfaces. Some specimens from n.e. Wash. are without such grooves. Upper parts grayish brown to brownish; under parts grayish to whitish. Tail slightly bicolored, dark brown above and grayish brown below. Stout, thick-set body, very short tail, and long, woolly fur are distinctive. RANGE. Occurs throughout B.C. (except Vancouver Island) south to extreme n. and n.e. Wash. and n. Idaho. HABITAT. Occurs locally along boggy, sphagnum-banked mt. streams, wet grassy meadows, and margins of Beaver ponds. A pale race is found on sagebrush slopes in the s. Okanagan Valley of B.C.

Figure 94.
Brown Lemming.

117

In spite of the current high cost of books, it is possible to economically build a good working library on mammals. Careful consideration of what to buy is the key. You are already off to a good start with this book. Next, to get a continental survey of the mammal kingdom, buy Burt and Grossenheiders' guide (see list on pages 252-253). A book on general mammal habits should come next; those by Cahalane, Morris, or Orr are suggested. The Ingles volume supplies much detail on Pacific Coast species. If you live in British Columbia or adjacent areas, you should purchase the excellent B. C. Provincial Museum handbook on mammals and Banfield's *Mammals of Canada*.

Now, you may wish to consider mammals on a world-wide basis. The two-volume set by Ernest Walker is recommended. Not only is it the best thing of its kind in English, but the hundreds of photos will give you an understanding of the entire mammal class.

Two journals, *The Murrelet* (Pacific Northwest Bird and Mammal Society) and *The Journal of Mammalogy* (American Society of Mammalogists) will be useful for updating your mammalogical knowledge.

If still more information on mammals is desired, the student is now ready to obtain the two volumes by Hall and Kelson. These books make an excellent introduction to the details of systematics and distribution of North American mammals. There is a variety of state books on mammals and these would likely come next in the building of a mammal library. New titles will appear from time to time—the building of a library never ends!

Figure 95.
Northern Bog Lemming.

MUSKRATS

Figure 96.
Muskrat.

Playing second fiddle to the more colorful Beaver as an aquatic mammal personality and denizen of the swamps and muddy lowland creeks, the Muskrat is a humble creature that, interestingly enough, is our most economically valuable furbearer. The price of a Muskrat pelt is often rather low, often less than a dollar, but the sheer numbers of skins taken each year and the relative ease of their capture makes for a nationwide sum of many millions of dollars. They are easily seen in their preferred habitat in early morning or evening and thus may become a familiar animal to the watchful field observer.

The Muskrat is widely distributed in the Northwest, occurring in most lowland fresh waters, often in small creeks and ponds that hardly would be attractive to any mammal and are little better than open sewers. It is a gentle creature, carrying on its activities in twilight or darkness. Muskrats swim rapidly with their narrow, flattened tails vibrating behind them.

These semi-aquatic rodents excavate deep burrows into the banks of deep streams or lakes. The tunnels extend back for some distance and then curve up to a chamber where the nest is constructed. Lodges are often built on stream or river bottoms and their domes may extend three, four, or even five feet above the water's surface, though usually only a two or three-foot height. The one or two entrances enter from below the waterline and extend into the single large room. One litter is produced in the spring and often another in the late summer from the same female or from those of the spring brood. Cattails and various aquatic plants, as well as freshwater mussels, snails, and young

119

Figure 97.
Typical habitat for the Muskrat on Lake Osoyoos.

frogs make up the diet. Turtles and crayfish are also taken, as in addition such items as alfalfa, water lilies, and cultivated corn and other grains if available.

Three to nine, with an average of six, make up the usual litter, of which there may be two or three a year. The gestation period is about one month.

Though the price per pelt fluctuates from year to year, the total value of the Muskrat harvest in the Pacific Northwest may reach a third of a million dollars or even more, representing a sizeable part of the total fur industry of the region. The flesh of the Muskrat, though lacking in much fat, is firm and tasty when properly prepared. The musk glands serve as the base for some perfumes and for trapping scents. Crops along waterways may suffer from these animals' feeding but it has been recorded that the pelt harvest on many farms more than compensates for the crop injury. More serious loss may be incurred from "rats" burrowing into ditches and canal banks, causing breaks and washouts.

MUSKRAT 22¾-10¾-3⅛-⅞ (580-279-80-23) Figs. 96, 97, and 98; Color Plates 3 and 11. This is a large vole-like rodent, about the size of a small house cat, with dense dark-brown fur, short ears, hair-fringed hind toes, and a naked, laterally compressed tail. Under parts are dark grayish to silvery gray. Nearly always seen in or near fresh water. RANGE. Occurs extensively and commonly in suitable habitat throughout the NW with the exception of the mts. of s.c. Ore. and s.w. B.C. Found on Vancouver Island. HABITAT. Marshes and swamps, and along streams, rivers, and lakes, mostly in the lowlands; less commonly entering the mts.

The mass of men lead lives of quiet desperation. What is called resignation is confirmed desperation. From the desperate city you go into the desperate country, and have to console yourself with the bravery of minks and musk-rats. . . .

The life in us is like water in the river. It may rise this year higher than man has ever known it, and flood the parched uplands; even this may be the eventful year, which will drown out all our muskrats. . . .

Thoreau

121

Figure 98.
Scent-marking station of the Muskrat.

OLD WORLD RATS AND MICE

Figure 99.
Norway Rat.

Though including some 450 species in world-wide distribution, the Family Muridae can boast of only three species in North America, none of them native. Our murids are rat- or mouse-sized and mostly brownish or blackish in color. The long, naked, scaly tails are distinctive. All three species in the Northwest are closely associated with the dwellings and buildings of man, practically living in commensal relation with him. As such, they cause much damage to food and fiber and constitute our most widely spread and injurious mammalian pests. The Norway (Brown) and Roof Rats are more denizens of storage facilities and garbage cans, but the little House Mouse is all too familiar to most of us.

Originally a native of Europe, the Norway Rat has now spread to most parts of the temperate and tropical regions of the world, usually as an inadvertent guest of man. Few mammals have had as striking an economic impact as this species. Tremendously prolific, it can produce as many as 12 young at a time and have a litter a month. It largely restricts itself to man-made habitats where its burrows are placed under buildings or in heaps of trash. It eats anything not downright poisonous and thus is able to scrounge a living under difficult circumstances, usually in unsanitary situations. The species is a particular problem in grain elevators, flouring mills, and food warehouses, but stringent inspection and strict laws have helped to keep its activities to a minimum in despoiling food and fabric.

As a transmitter of disease, the Norway Rat is also infamous. The following may be spread by this species: trichinosis, paratyphoid, glanders, mange, spotted fever, tularemia, epidemic jaundice, rat-bite fever, cholera, tuberculosis, dysentery, rabies, foot and mouth disease, Haverhill fever, and salmonella food poisoning, as well as other less spectacular germs and parasites. Strangely enough, even this mammal has its brighter side. The "white rat," so commonly used in medical and nutritional research, is merely an albino strain of the Norway Rat and is also commonly used as a children's pet.

It was the Roof Rat, brought from the Near East during the Crusades, that introduced plague- and typhus fever-carrying fleas into Europe and caused the scourge of the Black Death during the latter part of Medieval times. It is hard for us in these sanitary days to visualize the terrors of the plague. One of the more moving descriptions of it is to be found in the opening pages of the novel SIR NIGEL by Sir Arthur Conan Doyle. A third to a half, or even more, of Europe's population was destroyed. Fortunately, health and sanitation measures have removed this threat and only recently has man himself manufactured a worse menace, the nuclear bomb. Let us fervently hope that he may control it as effectively as the Black Death! Otherwise, mankind, like the plague-ridden army of Sennacherib before Jerusalem may suffer a similar fate when

"Like the leaves of the forest when Summer is green,
That host with their banners at sunset were seen;
Like the leaves of the forest when Autumn hath blown,
That host on the morrow lay withered and strown."

It is unfortunate that the mammal people come in contact with most frequently (other than themselves and domestic cats and dogs) is the House Mouse, for this species is hardly a decent representative of the mammalian tribe. "Mousey" in color, dirty, odoriferous, sneaky, and destructive, this common pest is a sanitation and health problem of urban life. Non-native to North America, it arrived with the early colonists, strictly as a stowaway, and has since spread throughout the settled parts of the country. Unintenionally or negligently provided cover and wasteful spillage of food have enabled it to live in practically a symbiotic co-existence with man. In this condition, however, lies the solution to its control. If hiding and breeding places and food sources can be eliminated, it, like the House Sparrow and Starling, can be brought under a fair degree of control.

One must, nevertheless, admire the House Mouse's adaptability to its mode of existence. Able to be transported under what, to a native mouse, would be almost impossible circumstances and to eke out an existence in conditions of uncertain and varied food supply, it resembles a botanical weed in ability to exist under unnatural and disturbed conditions. Contrast a species such as the House Mouse with the Heather Mouse or Bog Lemming with restricted habitats and ranges and we see extremes in latitude of adaptive complexes. Some species are highly adapted to a narrow mode of existence while others fit into a wide array of living circumstances. Who is to say which is the more highly adapted? It is perhaps fortunate that we resemble the House Mouse in this respect.

The House Mouse is extremely prolific and its protected environment often makes breeding possible throughout the year. The gestation period is about three weeks or slightly less, with animals able to breed in as short a time as six weeks after birth. Four to ten constitute extremes in numbers for a litter. The House Mouse feeds upon anything that is edible and makes an excellent existence out of the waste materials of man's activities. As mentioned before, care in preventing waste is not only good economy, but limits the food resources available to such "weeds" as this.

While usually thought of as a commensal with man, House Mice are occasionally found living successfully in the wild. Probably the best example of this in the Northwest is in the Palouse grain country where they sometimes vie with the Deer Mouse and Montane Meadow Mouse in wheatfield abundance. They are encountered coming into houses mainly in the fall when the first few cold days and nights send them inside to leave their droppings and odors, as well as other depredations, that reveal their unappreciated invasions. Mousetraps baited with cheese and bacon rind usually take care of normal situations. House cats, while varying somewhat in zeal toward hunting, are excellent permanent mouse removers.

Figure 100.
House Mouse.

124

PACIFIC NORTHWEST SPECIES

ROOF RAT 15⅗-8⅔-1½-⅘ (390-216-39-20). A large, rat-like rodent with a long, nearly-naked tail. Color brownish or blackish. Similar to the Norway Rat, but has tail longer than the head and body. The different color forms of this rat were formerly considered to be subspecies, but current mammalogical thought treats them as color phases. One arrangement is as follows: (1) "Alexandrian Roof Rat," upper parts grizzled brownish, under parts grayish; (2) "Black Rat," upper parts blackish gray, tail and ears sooty, and under parts bluish gray; (3) "White-bellied Roof Rat," upper parts brownish, under parts white, rare— the author caught one in Seattle a number of years ago. RANGE and HABITAT. Occurs irregularly in the NW, mostly in the coastal areas, frequenting marshes and brushy places in and near cities and towns, around human habitats, and the edges of forests along the w. slope of the Cascades, and on various islands along salt water in Wash. and s. B.C., including the Queen Charlotte Islands.

NORWAY RAT; BROWN RAT 14¾-7½-1¼-¾ (400-190-40-18) Fig. 99. This is a large, brownish, rat-like rodent with a long, nearly-naked tail. It is similar to the Roof Rat (brown phases) but the tail is shorter than the head and body. Dark buffy or reddish brown above; dirty, grayish white below. RANGE. Occurs widely and commonly throughout the Pacific NW in and around cities, towns, and human settlements. HABITAT. Most abundant in garbage dumps and in buildings. Has taken to living in the feral state in marshes and along streams in lowlands near settlements. More effective sanitation, better storage of food and grain, and more effective control of solid wastes has reduced their numbers somewhat.

HOUSE MOUSE 6¼-3¼-⅝-⁹⁄₁₆ (160-82-16-14) Fig. 100. The common, small, brownish mouse of houses and buildings. Upper parts yellowish or buffy brown; under parts slightly lighter. Tail long and naked, with obvious, ring-like scales. A few specimens occasionally found with white bellies. RANGE and HABITAT. Occurs commensally with man wherever he exists in the Pacific NW, in and around his habitations and buildings. In grain-growing regions, such as the Palouse country of e. Wash. and n. Idaho, to be found commonly in fields and weedy fence and ditch rows. A few penetrate the woods and foothills along streams. Commonly enters houses in the fall and early winter. Often numerous in haystacks in open farmland.

JUMPING MICE

Figure 101.
Western Jumping Mouse.

The jumping mice are small-bodied, long-tailed rodents with dusky orange backs and sides and whitish under parts. Locomotion is by a series of kangaroo-like leaps which carry them rapidly through or over the dense grass and herbage of their favorite habitats. They are commonly called "kangaroo mice," but mammalogists prefer to restrict that name to members of the genus *Microdipodops* of the Great Basin desert region. The Family Dipodidae, to which our jumping mice belong, is a Holarctic one which includes the birch mice of northern and eastern Europe. The Pacific Northwest possesses three species of jumping mice, the Pacific Jumping Mouse (Cascades and western slope regions), the Western Jumping Mouse (Rockies and interior), and the Meadow Jumping Mouse (northern and central British Columbia).

The Pacific Jumping Mouse is common in wet, grassy, swampy places in the western part of the region covered by this guide. Cattail marshes, sphagnum bogs, and similar moist habitats are also favored.

Martha R. Flahaut, late curator of biology at the Washington State Museum at the University of Washington has written an interesting article on two hibernating jumping mice that she found in a bank under her home near the end of Henderson Inlet, seven miles north of Olympia, on February 24, 1939. The following quotations are from her paper in the January-April, 1939, issue of THE MURRELET.

"The nests were located about four inches apart, thirty inches below the ground level, on a stratum of harder soil, and about two feet from the face of the cut bank. While it was hard to tell positively, the indications were that the mice had entered from the face of the bank rather than from above. The nest chambers were about five inches in diameter, the entrance being approximately an inch and a half in diameter, and entering the nests slightly above the floor, in such a way that the burrow curved up and then down in a gooseneck fashion.

"One mouse had used the shredded paper from orange wrappings, the other was content with shredded newspaper, both materials having been obtainable from the basement. Both mice were completely dormant, covered by the nesting materials, and curled up in the customary manner with head tucked toward the belly and with the tail wrapped around the body. After exposure to the warmth of the house for a few hours they began to stir, but went back to sleep as soon as they were placed outside. The trip to Seattle and subsequent removal to a cage in the zoology department of the University put an end to the dormant period. They proved to be a pair, and are now, one month after capture, fully active and apparently in good condition."

To a person visiting the wet, grassy haunts of the Western Jumping Mouse, only a fleeting glimpse will be had of a beautiful white, yellow, and dusky creature. In its kangaroo-like method of hopping, it usually keeps below the tops of the grass, so that only a fast movement in the vegetation is visible. Traps set in this habitat will reveal the following morning an attractive little rodent which is dusky above with yellowish sides and creamy-white under parts, and with a long tail and large hind feet. The fur is of a delicate nature. It has always amazed the author how the jumping mouse could remain so clean and spotless in such a muddy habitat.

Primarily nocturnal, these mammals feed on insects, seeds, and berries and hibernate during the colder months of the year. In late summer, as any collector knows, jumping mice become very fat in preparation for their winter fasting. A thick layer of greasy fat forms beneath the skin and somewhat infiltrates the skin itself, making these mice difficult to prepare as specimens, as too much force in pulling the hide from the body will cause it to break. The proper procedure is not to remove all of the fat masses from inside of the skin that will not come off easily, but to stuff the specimen, even though it is greasy, and allow it to dry and become stiff in the usual manner. Then, in a method recommended by the late Dr. George Hudson of Washington State University, immerse the dried specimen in two consecutive baths of white gasoline for 24 hours each, dry it out in plenty of sawdust, and blow the sawdust out of the fur with an air jet. This technique not only removes the fat and grease but cleans the fur and kills any insect eggs that may be in it, and the air blowing fluffs up the cleaned fur nicely. In fact, all specimens should be so processed before they are incorporated into one's mammal collection. So much for our taxidermy lesson for today!

Shallow burrows or crannies under rocks or logs are used during the summer with deeper nests for hibernation. In reproduction, gestation is about 18 days with some five or six young born in a litter, and often two litters per summer season.

The Meadow Jumping Mouse occupies a more northern range, occurring in our area only in central and upper British Columbia. The three species treated here are very similar in appearance and can be separated technically more or less only by cranial analysis. For the most part, the ranges of the three Pacific Northwest species do not overlap, but where they do, the species involved seem not to interbreed, indicating some ecological or ethological separation that keeps the forms reproductively isolated. Most of the users of this guide will be content to identify jumping mice to genus only and recognize the group. Geographic range can be relied upon for species determination only outside of possible areas of sympatry. It is considered that the three species were separately isolated in three different refugia south of the continental ice sheet during the last glaciation and subsequently spread northward following the retreat of the ice to occupy their present ranges. During their isolation, they developed sufficient genetic differences to prevent their post-glacial reuniting.

(continued on page 129, following the color plates)

128

Figure 102.
Jumping mice are common in this wet, brushy bog in northern Idaho.

Northwest mountains provide a variety of mammal habitats.
Plate 1.
Though at the other ecologic extreme, desert environments often contain
the highest densities of mammals.

Broken rockslides shelter such mammals as Pikas, Mantled Ground Squirrels, Marmots, and Pack Rats.

Plate 2.

These seemingly barren lava beds harbor high concentrations of Pocket Mice.

The high mountain forest is the preferred habitat of the Marten.

Plate 3.

The marsh is home to the Muskrat and Beaver.

This boulder serves as both observation post and cover for the burrow (lower right) of a Mantled Ground Squirrel.

Plate 4.

A jackrabbit "form" under a bush. All the home this mammal possesses.

Desert mounds and burrows of the Chisel-toothed Kangaroo Rat.
Plate 5.
Mouth of a Badger den, a species that feeds on desert mammals such as
pocket gophers, ground squirrels, and mice.

Look for Pack Rat nests in caves at the bases of cliffs.
Plate 6.
Cliffs provide food and protection for Mountain Goats (Pole).

Watch for construction evidence of mammals—A Beaver dam in this photo.
Plate 7.
Stick nest of a Desert Wood Rat (sagebrush, cactus, and bones). Note rat in trap.

A Marten in a rockslide. Comparison with Fig. 168 shows the value of color photography (Pole).

Plate 8.

Raccoon tracks in the mud—evidence of the presence of a mammal.

Studying mammals of the past. Fossil work in the Juniper Forest of Eastern Washington.
Plate 9.
Fossil bones of a Pocket Gopher being uncovered by wind erosion
in the Juniper Forest.

Bunchgrass plains—home of the Long-tailed Meadow Mouse—but becoming an endangered habitat.

Plate 10.
Tunnels cut by Pennsylvania Meadow Mice in winter in the compressed turf under the snow.

Marten tracks in the snow; common evidence of mammal presence in winter.

Plate 11.

Muskrat taking grass to its bank burrow for bedding.

An unnatural mammal scene; the roadside beggar, a good mammal to avoid.

Plate 12.

An unnatural mammal scene; performing White Whale at the Vancouver, B.C., Aquarium

Watch for mammals along lake shores.
Plate 13.
Keep an eye out for mammals using game trails.

Go to the open grasslands for such species as the Pronghorn.
Plate 14.
Mule Deer in winter—a good photo (Pole).

The American Buffalo, or Bison; once down to a few hundred from an original population of 60 million.

Plate 15.

A female Bighorn harmlessly "shot" by the photographer.

Mounted skeleton exhibit in the University of Idaho's Department of Biological Sciences. Mammals can be profitably studied in museums.

Plate 16.

Measuring the color of Townsend's Pocket Gophers by electronic equipment, a technique used by the museum mammalogist.

PACIFIC NORTHWEST SPECIES

PACIFIC JUMPING MOUSE 9⅖-5⅖-1⅓-⅗ (235-135-33-15). Very similar to the other jumping mice, but larger in size and darker and brighter in color. Back dusky with buffy-tipped hairs, to form dark olive band down middle of dorsum; sides orange to ochraceous tawny, intermixed with a few blackish hairs; narrow orange or buffy line between sides and belly; under parts whitish to pale buffy white. The dark dorsal band is relatively narrower than in the other species of jumping mice and is sharply separated from the lighter sides. Ears dark brown and not conspicuously bordered with lighter color. No pale yellow stripe between dorsal band and sides. Tail sharply bicolored, grayish brown above and yellowish below. Skull broader, premolars larger, and baculum longer than in other *Zapus*. The three NW species are difficult to separate and are best distinguished by certain technical, cranial characters. Users of this book will find the ranges to be of some help along with close attention to the colors. RANGE. S.w. B.C., w. Wash. and Ore., including the Olympic and Cascade Mts. and the Coastal Range of w. Ore. HABITAT. Occurs widely and commonly in moist, grassy, weedy habitats, such as boggy meadows and streamside brush from sea level to subalpine cirques. Dense grass, forbs, and brush near water constitute the favorite haunts.

WESTERN JUMPING MOUSE 9-5⅛-1¼-¹¹⁄₁₆ (230-130-32-17) Figs. 101 and 102. A medium-sized jumping mouse with dark, blackish upper parts (black hairs mixed with buffy) to form an olive-brown appearing band down the middle of the back; yellowish sides (mixed with blackish hairs and not sharply separated from back); white or buffy white under parts; and long, bicolored tail which is light brown above and buffy gray below. The ears are conspicuously rimmed with buffy. The lateral line (between back and sides) is yellowish buff, mixed with blackish hairs. Another clear, pale buffy band between sides and belly. Skull narrower, premolars smaller, and baculum shorter than in above species, but these structures larger than in the following species. RANGE. Occurs throughout B.C., excepting the extreme s.w. and n.e. corners of the province; in the n.e., extreme e. and s.e. parts of Wash.; and in e. and s.c. Ore.; all of Idaho. HABITAT. Wet meadows, bogs, streamside brush, and moist, grassy, herbaceous places near water. Mostly in forested and subalpine areas.

MEADOW JUMPING MOUSE 8¼-5¹⁵⁄₁₆-1⅛-½ (215-127-30-13). Similar to the other species of jumping mice in the NW, but smaller. Dark dorsal band is olive brown, mixed with yellowish hairs. Sides are ochraceous, mixed with blackish. Lateral stripe pale yellow and indistinct or absent. Under parts buffy white. Tail bicolored, brownish above, white to buffy white below. Skull narrowest, premolars smallest, and tooth row shortest of the three species of *Zapus* here treated. Smaller size and more northern distribution may be of some help in identification. RANGE. C. and n. B.C., excluding the s.w. coastal region and the s.e. corner of the province. HABITAT. Moist, grassy and brushy areas, marshes, and alder and willow riparian along water.

PORCUPINES

Figure 103.
Porcupine.

The Porcupine is one of the best known and most peculiar of North American mammals. Literally a walking pincushion, it carries on its stodgy clumsy ways in the forests of the Northwest, apparently preferring the more open coniferous woods, especially the yellow pine areas. Its method of defense is unique among American mammals. Quills, which are actually modified hairs, are loosely held in the skin and a sudden flick of the heavy tail is enough to drive a number of them into the flesh of any animal bothering or attacking it. The back and sides are also covered with the spines, which being barbed on the heads, tend to penetrate farther in the body of the victim as they are worked in by the movement of the skin and muscle masses in which they are lodged. They can pose a serious threat to an animal if pushed into the lips, tongue, or palate, making it impossible for it to feed and bringing on eventual starvation. The author remembers seeing a large bull at a dude ranch in southern Idaho which had nosed into a "porkie" and had a thick fringe of quills about its muzzle. After sending a heavy wooden stanchion flying off in all directions, the bull was still in need of help, but not helpful. Finally, it was roped and thrown with all the guests piled up on its legs and body, subduing it sufficiently to allow the quills to be pulled out with a pair of pliers. Speaking of pliers, a dog which has had Porcupine quills removed with this tool will wince ever afterwards when he sees it. The thing to do, of course, is to blindfold the dog when removing the spines.

The Porcupine feeds on buds, leaves, and particularly the bark of trees, especially conifers. In the Northwest, yellow pines seem to rank highest in preference, with lodgepoles second. Firs and hemlocks are seldom used. A favorite area of foraging is in the "sugar zone," a part of the crown leader three or four feet long and a short distance below the tip. Here the stem is usually girdled, killing the crown. The proximal parts of upper branches are frequently girdled as well. Such activity damages the tree and often kills young saplings, rendering the Porcupine a serious enemy to reforestation. Porkies also damage tools, canoe paddles, auto tires, and electrical insulation.

Usually only a single young is born a year to a female after a gestation of seven months. The young are on their own after some four or five months of care by the mother. Coyotes, Bobcats, Lynxes, and Fishers feed on these animals, the usual technique of attack being to get the Porcupine off guard and to disembowel it with a rapid slash of a paw. We once found a Porcupine at the lake that had been killed by a pair of Coyotes. Only shreds of skin remained, everything else, including the viscera, had been eaten.

In spite of their built-in protection, Porcupines are shy and retiring by nature and readily climb trees or enter rocky niches if possible when pursued. The animals are largely nocturnal in habit and spend the day under cover or high in trees which they climb with apparent ease. Quills are already on the young Porcupines at birth, but the fetal membrane surrounds the entire young animal. Besides bark as mentioned above, Porcupines feed on the catkins of willow, maple, or poplars and on the foliage of quaking aspens and larch. Grasses, berries, alfalfa, and truck crops may form important parts of their food in some localities. Tree cambium is perhaps the main staple in the winter. Previously damaged trees are particularly vulnerable to further attack, usually above the old wound, as the cambium above a debarked scar may have many times more sugar than below the damaged area, and several times more than in an undamaged tree.

Porcupines serve as a food source for the larger predators, notably Mountain Lions and Fishers and occasionally for man, though in the author's experience, one has to be very hungry in order to enjoy Porcupine con gusto. Persons camping in Porcupine country should be particularly watchful that these animals do not damage the tires or electrical wiring insulation. The author was almost stranded in the back bush of British Columbia by the fondness of a certain porkie for the radiator hose of a jeep. Part of a plastic raincoat and some wire ordinarily used for mouse tails were all that got us back to civiliza-

Figure 104.
A Porcupine in the Juniper Forest preserve in eastern Washington.

Figure 105.
Porcupine damage on a lodgepole pine.

tion. A fire protection association truck was almost entirely stripped of its rubber and insulation in a couple of days when left parked near the lookout tower on Moscow Mountain near the author's home. The varnish on a new two-wheel car trailer that Larrison used to transport camping gear during a summer spent in the Owyhee mountains in southwestern Idaho seemed more than ordinarily attractive to Porcupines. If found gnawing on the trailer, they could not be permanently chased away as they would be back as soon as the owner had returned to his tent and gotten in bed.

The trails in the snow made by Porcupines are easily identified by the tracks made by the slowly plodding animal. "Swish marks" left by the tail as it is swung from side to side are also visible. Individuals frequently make well marked and deep trails from their dens to feeding areas. Foraging is done in all but the worst weather. Days may be spent aloft in trees away from the den and most feeding seems to be done at night. If some distance from the home den or caught by a winter storm, Porcupines may use certain trees as "line cabins," not returning to the den for several days.

Porcupines are commonly touted by experts on wilderness survivalship as a ready source of food for the lost person. Even in dense porkie country, they are hard to find when needed, especially in summer when there may be no tell-tale tracks. The copious supply of parasites in the animal's guts is enough to make a vegetarian out of anybody.

*   *   *

PORCUPINE   30½-8¾-4⅛-⅞ (775-220-105-22) Figs. 103, 104, and 105. This is a large, spiny rodent, blackish or yellowish in color. It is a stocky, slow-moving, clumsy animal with long quills interspersed through its long, coarse fur, especially on the back and tail. RANGE. The entire Pacific NW, excluding Vancouver and Queen Charlotte Islands. HABITAT. Mostly restricted to coniferous forests, especially the more open stands, as of such species as yellow pine. May occur in deciduous woods and occasionally some distance from timber, as in sagebrush and open tundra. Rare in the dense, dark rain forests.

NUTRIAS

Figure 106.
Nutria.

The Nutria, like certain other furry little mammals, has often been the butt of "get rich" schemes by purveyors of breeding stock with the result that a number of individuals have been released by disillusioned would-be Nutria farmers. These abandoned, or sometimes escaped, animals have developed feral populations in several parts of the Pacific Northwest. Also called the "coypu," it is a semi-aquatic form much like the Beaver or Muskrat and may place its nest in self-constructed burrows in banks or in floating lodges. Three to five young are produced in a litter after a gestation of about four to four and a half months. The Nutria feeds entirely on vegetation. Because of its round tail, it has often been called the "beaver rat."

*　　*　　*

NUTRIA　34⅓-11⅘-5½-¾ (857-295-136-19) Fig. 106. A large rodent, the size of a medium-sized Beaver, with reddish-brown fur, webbed hind feet, and a round scaly tail. Size, round tail, and semi-aquatic habits are distinctive. RANGE. Fur farm escapees have produced feral colonies in parts of Oregon and Washington, particularly in the lowlands, and in the lower Fraser River delta of British Columbia. A few records for northern and southwestern Idaho. HABITAT. Marshy shores of lakes, ponds, and slow-moving rivers.

WHALES

Figure 107.
A school of Killer Whales.

Of all the mammals, the whales have diverged the most from the ancestral form. This has been in response to adaptation for an aquatic existence and they have been so successful in taking up the life of the sea that occurrence out of the water is no longer possible. These huge mammals are completely marine in our region and are seldom seen near shore by the ordinary observer, so it is to the offshore areas of the ocean coast that he must usually go to see them. Some 23 species of whales visit Pacific Northwest waters, rarely or commonly. The dolphins and porpoises are small, reaching only a few feet in length among the lesser forms, but the large whales may attain 40 or 50 feet and many tons in weight. As these mammals deserve to be better known, diagrams of most Northwest species have been provided in the pages that follow this general account.

Whales are divided into two groups, the toothed whales and the whalebone whales. This is reflected in their systematic arrangement, though mammalogists currently differ as to whether whales should be assigned to a single order or to two different orders.

The Baird's Beaked Whale is the largest of the beaked whales and may reach a total length of 35 to 42 feet. It apparently feeds mainly on cephalopod mollusks and herring; squids, and octopuses being most common as representing the former phylum. Stomach contents of a male of this species taken off the coast of British Columbia consisted of a few soft and hard parts of small squids and a skate egg case. The food, about two gallons in volume, was accompanied by numerous nematode worms. Stomach contents of a female from the same region were made up of about two gallons of small rockfish and squid remains, along with a few nematodes. Scars along the flanks of these whales have been attributed to scratches left by the sharp beaks of the squids on which they feed. Similar scratches have been found on the heads of Sperm Whales.

Beaked whale calves have been noted in August off the coast of British Columbia. The gestation period is apparently about 10 months and the length of the single young at birth is about one-third that of the mother. These whales commonly travel in tightly-packed schools of about 20 individuals. They raise their flukes in the air when diving, reminding one of Sperm Whales. The species is said to be very alert and hard to capture. One harpooned individual dived straight downward at high speed taking almost 3,000 feet of line with it.

The economic importance of the Baird's Beaked Whale seems to be of little significance throughout its range. Scanty information on beaked whales in general indicates that they are so rare as not to have left much in the whaling literature. Studies are beginning to reveal a greater occurrence of these whales than previously thought. A few were taken annually from July to October off west-central Alaska. Over 300 individuals were captured in waters adjacent to Japan in the 1949-50 season, according to the records. Part of the problem of pinning down consumption figures of this and many whales is the matter of identification and nomenclature as well as thorough reporting.

Although the ancestors of the whales were once land mammals, their descendants have almost completely adopted an aquatic existence. The whales have discarded the hairy coat of the other mammals with the exception of a few bristles on the muzzle. To take the place of the pelt for warmth, whales have acquired a sub-surface layer of blubber which sometimes reaches thicknesses of a foot or more. This layer also protects the whale from starvation when food is scarce. The hind limbs, once used for movement on land, have completely disappeared externally, but internally, one or two bones are buried deep in the body. The front limbs act primarily as steering devices while swimming. The appearance of five toes is present in the tips of these appendages.

The Sperm Whale is the largest of the toothed whales, males averaging 60 feet with extremes of 85 feet recorded. The female is about half the male's length. The eye of the Sperm Whale is located on the side of the head about one-fourth of the body length from the tip of the snout. It has been stated that the Sperm Whale's eye position is about the location of the ear in a human. The eyeball does not rotate and the lens is permanently set at one focus. The whale, therefore, must shift its whole body to change its line of sight. It is also unable to see directly in front of its snout, due to the posterior position of the eyes on the sides of the head. A set of glands secrete an oily substance to provide the eyes with protection from contact with salt water. The pelagic habitat of the whales offers them no possibility of shelter and they must literally exist on the bosom of the deep. The Sperm Whale has been known to submerge to maximum depths of 3,000 feet and possibly farther. At such depths, the pressure may be as much as 1,400 pounds per square inch. Studies have revealed that the Sperm Whale can remain submerged for 75 minutes at a time. While man renews only 15-20 percent of his lungs' content of air on breathing, the whale renews approximately 90 percent. The Sperm Whale feeds mostly on large cuttlefishes, squids, and certain ocean fishes. It often eats the giant squid which may reach a total length, including tentacles, of over 30 feet. The cuttlefish and squid with their long, sharp beaks and suction cups on the tentacles may inflict deep wounds on the whale's body in the titanic sub-surface struggles but this does not deter the whale from subduing its prey. The Sperm Whale has teeth only in the lower jaw which are peg-like and up to eight inches in length. The number of such teeth varies from 20 to 25. The gestation period for this huge species is approximately a year and normally a single calf is born which may be 12-14 feet in length. The young animal is extruded by breech presentation and nursing begins soon after. The milk is not sucked out but actually is squirted out by the female under considerable pressure to reduce the time for milk transfer because of the need for frequent trips to the surface for breathing. After the calf reaches a length of somewhat more than 20 feet, it is weaned.

Before the discovery of petroleum and the development of its derivatives, whale oil was in great demand. It was used as fuel for lamps and in the manufacture of candles, the source of most home lighting in the early whaling days. The whalebone of baleen whales was also valuable for corset stays. At the present time, oil from whales is used in the soapmaking industry and also in the production of lard and butter substitutes. As regards the latter, approximately 95 percent of the whale oil commercially used is for the making of margarine. Whale bones also produce a fine fertilizer when ground up and applied to infertile soil. From the Sperm Whale comes the material known as *ambergris*. This is found in the intestinal tract of sick, infected, or constipated whales, but large masses of ambergris have also been found in ostensibly healthy individuals as well. Since beaks of the giant squid are commonly found embedded in the material, it may be a way that the whales have for rendering these indigestible fragments harmless. Although the basic component of ambergris, *ambrein*, has been synthesized, other substances found mixed in with the ambrein seem to be the most important for use in the perfume industry, where the ambergris is utilized as a vehicle to greatly increase the persistence of the scents and to give a peculiar velvety quality or substance to them. In the past, it was used for everything from a tonic and aphrodisiac to a repellent for ghosts. In appearance, ambergris may be brown, black, or yellow; soft and waxy or hard as a rock. Usually, it is gummy or wax-like. Several dollars an ounce is the customary price. Sperm oil, which is composed chiefly of waxes rather than fats, is still in great demand for lubricating light machinery and fine instruments, for treating leather, and in the production of facial creams, although satisfactory substitutes for whale oil have now been developed.

Actually a dolphin, the Killer Whale is the largest of the family. Most students of whales now consider the Atlantic and Pacific Killer Whales to be one species. Along the Pacific Coast, this whale is widely distributed, but most numerous in the colder Arctic waters. It is a common visitor in Puget Sound where it is often called "blackfish." It is well adapted to cold ocean conditions with its tough hide and five to eight inches of blubber beneath.

The mating of the Killer Whale occurs in December and the gestation period is about a year, resulting in the birth of a single calf which measures some seven to nine feet long and weighs about 300 pounds. The calf nurses for approximately a year from the two nipples set in grooves near the tail fluke of the female, but is able to eat meat before that time as teeth appear about six weeks after birth. The life span of a Killer Whale is estimated to be between 30 and 40 years.

The Killer Whale is seldom harvested as a commercial species, though it achieves not a little economic import through its feeding on young fur seals in the Pribilof Islands area. It is also an enemy of migrating salmon and takes great numbers when these fish mass to head inland. Residents of the Puget Sound area will remember "Namu," the Killer Whale kept in captivity at Seattle for some months and have doubtless seen other Killers housed at the Seattle Marine Aquarium at Pier 56. Several others whales are usually also on display at that place which is certainly worth a visit for it offers about the only opportunity that most persons have to view whales at close range. A number of whales of several species are on display at the very fine aquarium at Vancouver, British Columbia. These have been trained to perform stunts and the show they put on well attests their intelligence and cooperation.

The Harbor Porpoise is perhaps the most abundant of the porpoises in Northwest waters. The origin of the word "porpoise" comes from the French word combination *porc-poisson* which means "pig-fish" in that language. The word was then shortened to *porpoise*. The appropriateness of names is often difficult for later students to determine, but possibly the following explanation will offer some light. During the 10th century, the meat of the porpoise was decreed by the Catholic church to be "fish," placing a price on the head of this whale. Transmuted, thus, to a fish, porpoise meat becomes a delicacy. King Henry VIII regarded "polpess pudding" a form of porpoise meat and sugar suspension, as his favorite Lenten dish and as such was commonly used in many seaports. One early writer, however, says of the porpoise flesh that it is "of a very hard digestion, naysome to the stomach, and of a very grosse, excremental and naughty juyce." Actually, cooked with modern methods, it tastes like tough, dry beef.

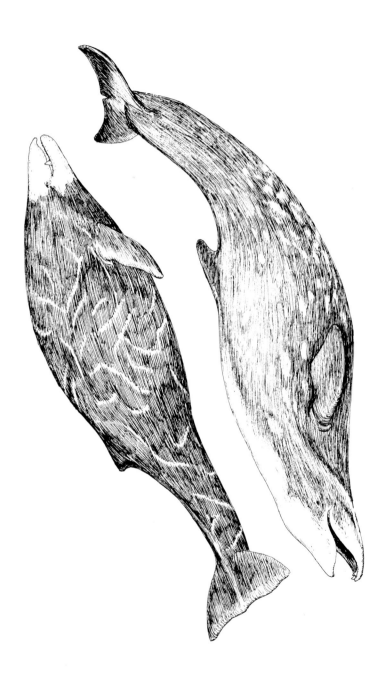

Figure 109

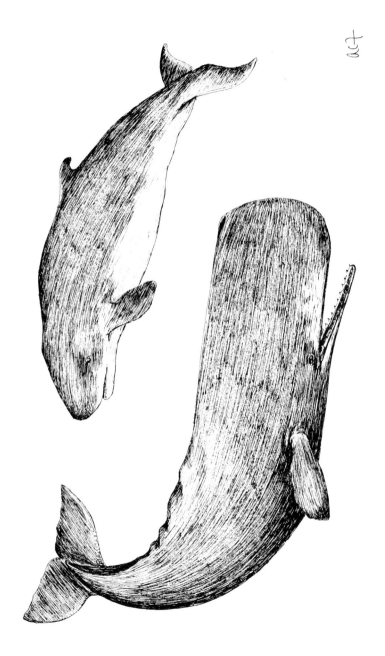

Figure 110.
Pygmy Sperm Whale (upper); Sperm Whale (lower).

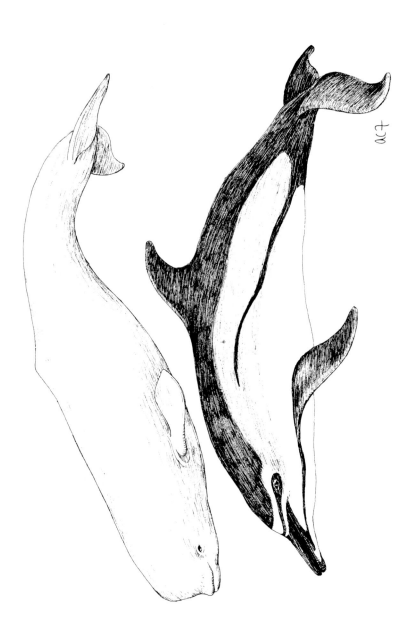

Figure 111.

Figure 112.
Northern Right-whale Dolphin (upper); Pacific White-sided Dolphin (lower).

Figure 113.

Figure 114.
False Killer Whale (upper); Risso's Dolphin (lower).

Figure 115.

146

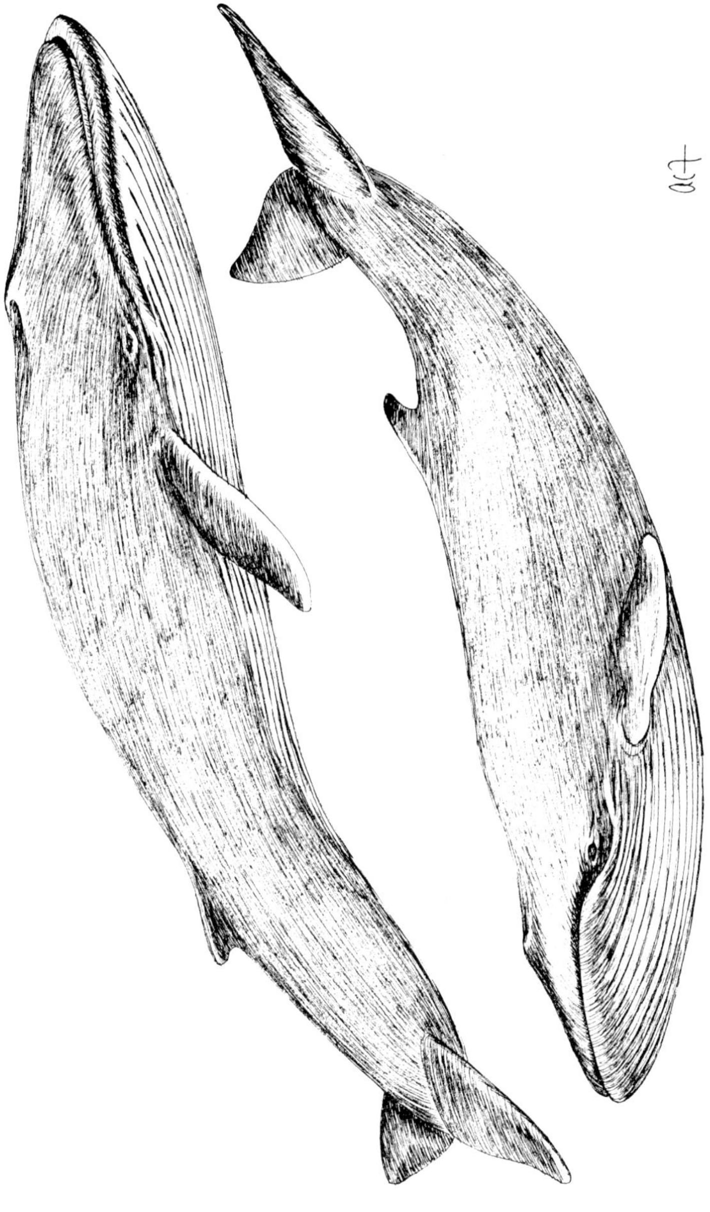

Figure 116.

Finback Whale (upper); Sei Whale (lower).

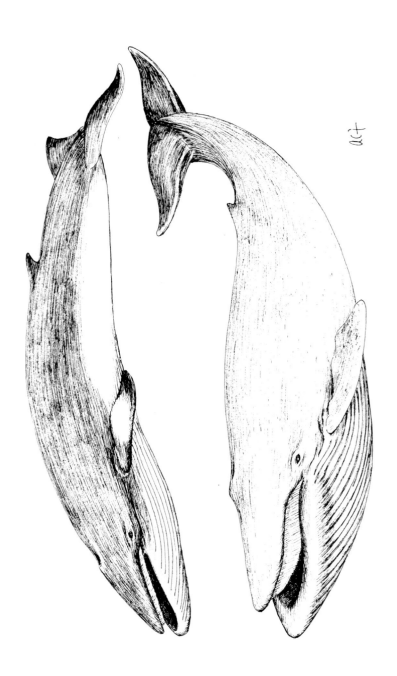

Figure 117.

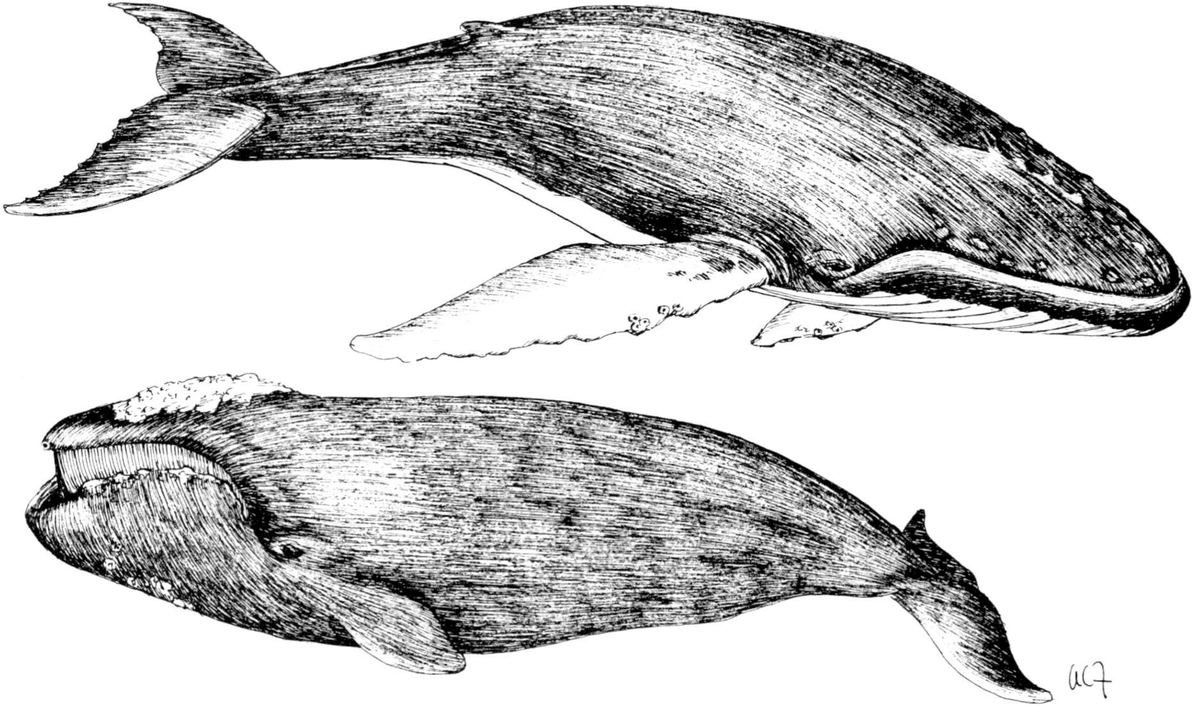

Figure 118.
Humpback Whale (upper): Right Whale (lower).

PACIFIC NORTHWEST SPECIES

BAIRD'S BEAKED WHALE   Length, 35-40 feet. Fig. 108.   Upper parts and sides black; under parts whitish or grayish. Snout is elongated into a definite beak and the dorsal fin is very small and placed far back on the body. Some individuals show white scratches on back and flanks. RANGE. Uncommon visitor along the ocean coast, mostly off shore.

STEJNEGER'S BEAKED WHALE   Length, 15-20 feet. Fig. 109.   The body is mostly blackish with white or grayish head; white streaks or scratches over the body surface. The dorsal fin is small and located two-thirds of the way back on the body from the snout. A single, large tooth on each side of lower jaw projects to the outside when the jaw is closed. RANGE. Rare visitor along ocean coast; to be occasionally seen off shore during the salmon runs.

HUBB'S BEAKED WHALE   Length, 16 feet. Totally black, except for the whitish beak and face. As in the preceding species, there is a single, massive tooth on each side of the lower jaw, some 6-8 inches long, and exposed to the outside when the mouth is closed. In the preceding species, the anterior edge of this tusk is straight, while in the present form, the anterior edge is convexly curved. RANGE. Very rare visitor along the ocean coast n. to s. B.C. Three strandings recorded along the NW beaches.

GOOSE-BEAKED WHALE   Length, 20-28 feet. Fig. 109. Though the colors are variable, individuals being black, grayish, or brownish, or even purplish with white spots on the sides, many specimens have a whitish or grayish head with the light color extending on the back as far posteriorly as the dorsal fin. This fin is re-curved and located two-thirds of the way from the snout to the tail. There is an obvious ridge on the back between the dorsal fin and the tail and there are small grooves on the throat converging toward the chin. Males have two teeth about 2 inches long projecting forward at the tip of the lower jaw. RANGE. Uncommon to rare in occurrence off the NW coast. Five strandings reported for Vancouver Island, B.C. and one for Wash.

SPERM WHALE   Lengths: males, 50-60 feet; females, 30-38 feet. Fig. 110. This is a large whale with a very large head (appears to make up one-third of the body length) and square snout. The lower jaw is small and narrow. No dorsal fin. Color of body is dark, bluish gray, though sometimes there is white on the belly and lower jaw. The spout is prolonged and projected diagonally forward over the tip of the snout. RANGE. Fairly common visitor along the NW ocean coast and rarely into the Strait of Juan de Fuca. Banfield (1974) reports over 5,000 Sperm Whales have been taken off the B.C. coast since whaling operations began in that region in 1905.

PYGMY SPERM WHALE   Length, 9-13 feet. Fig. 110.   A small whale with blackish upper parts and grayish-white belly. The dorsal fin is small, sickle-shaped, and pointing backward. The snout is bulbous, bluntly cone-shaped, and projects ahead of the narrow lower jaw. RANGE. Very rare visitor along the ocean coast of Ore. and Wash.

BLUE DOLPHIN   Length, 6-8 feet. A very small whale with black upper parts and white under parts. A narrow black band from the eye to the flipper and another black band from the eye to the vent on each side. A prominent sickle-shaped, dorsal fin. Difference between dolphins and porpoises: dolphins have short beaks, while porpoises have blunt heads. RANGE. Rare visitor along the ocean coast.

COMMON DOLPHIN   Length, 6-8 feet. Fig. 111.   A very small whale with greenish-black upper parts, yellow stripe along each flank, and a whitish belly. A black streak runs forward and upward from near tip of the tail to above the flipper on each side. Dorsal fin is prominent and re-curved. RANGE. Uncommon to rare visitor along the ocean coast, probably more numerous farther off shore.

NORTHERN RIGHT-WHALE DOLPHIN   Length, 7-8 feet. Fig. 112.   A very small whale with jet black back and sides and narrow white stripe on the belly. No dorsal fin. RANGE. Uncommon visitor along the NW ocean coast, mostly occurring several hundred miles off shore; rare inshore.

PACIFIC WHITE-SIDED DOLPHIN   Length, 8-10 feet. Fig. 112.   A small whale with greenish-black upper parts, gray stripes on sides, an a white belly. Dorsal fin is strongly recurved (almost hooked) and black in color with a white posterior edge. RANGE. Common visitor along the ocean coast, particularly in spring and fall; occurs in the Strait of Juan de Fuca, but rarely in Puget Sound.

KILLER WHALE   Lengths: males, 19-28 feet; females, 11-24 feet. Figs. 107 and 108.   A medium-sized whale with black upper parts, white under parts, and an elongated white spot below and behind the dorsal fin, which is very high, standing more or less straight up above the back and reaching a height of six feet in males. RANGE. Common visitor, often in groups, along the NW ocean coast and in the Strait of Juan de Fuca and Puget Sound. Regular and numerous in summer during the salmon and herring runs in the Strait of Georgia, Washington Sound, and Saratoga Passage off Camano Island, Wash. Spring and fall visitor in s. Puget Sound, as well as at other times of the year. Occasional in Willapa Bay and in the mouth of the Columbia R. (recorded as far upstream as Vancouver, Wash.) Probably the second most common whale in NW marine waters.

RISSO'S DOLPHIN; GRAY GRAMPUS   Length, 7-12 feet. Fig. 114.   A small, blunt-nosed whale with a grayish body (becoming light grayish on the head) and black flippers and tail flukes. Under parts paler gray to almost white. The dorsal fin is large and strongly recurved. Scratch marks on body are commonly present. RANGE. Rare visitor along and off the NW ocean coast, particularly in summer.

FALSE KILLER WHALE   Lengths: males, 13-18 feet; females, 11-15 feet. Fig. 114. A small to medium-sized whale with completely black body and small recurved dorsal fin. The snout is blunt and rounded, and the head flattened. RANGE. Very rare visitor along the ocean coast from Wash. southward.

PILOT WHALE; BLACKFISH   Length, 12-25 feet. Fig. 113. This is a medium-sized whale with a black body marked by a narrow, white, ventral stripe and a grayish saddle behind the large, strongly recurved, dorsal fin. The forehead is peculiar in that it is large and bulges forward over the short beak. RANGE. Occasionally visitor in marine waters of the NW, mostly off shore.

HARBOR PORPOISE   Length, 4-6 feet. Fig. 113.   A very small whale with blackish or brownish upper parts and a white belly. The snout is short and the dorsal fin is small and triangular in shape. RANGE. Occurs commonly and widely, often in small groups ("gams") in the marine waters of the NW. Especially numerous along the ocean coast, they frequently invade bays and harbors (except shallow, muddy areas). Has been recorded up the Columbia R. to the extent of brackish water. Common in summer in the Strait of Juan de Fuca. Possibly the most abundant whale in Wash. and Ore. salt waters.

DALL'S PORPOISE Length, 6-7 feet. Fig. 115. A small whale, black in color except for a large, white patch on each side. The snout is short and the dorsal fin is triangular in shape. RANGE. Occasional summer visitor along the NW ocean coast and in the Strait of Juan de Fuca, eastward to the San Juan Islands.

GRAY WHALE Length, 40-45 feet. Fig. 115. A medium-sized to large, but slender, blotched, grayish-black whale with 2-4 longitudinal grooves on the throat, a slight hump, no dorsal fin, and some small bumps on the dorsal side of the tail. The spout is vertical, spreading, and of short duration. RANGE. Common, regular spring and early fall migrant along the NW ocean coast and rarely in such inside waters as Puget Sound and around Vancouver and Victoria, B.C. A few as summer visitors. Most individuals are to be seen a few miles off shore along the Pacific beaches.

FINBACK WHALE Length, 70 feet. Fig. 116. A large, flat-headed whale with dark grayish-brown upper parts and whitish under parts. The under sides of the flippers and flukes are white. The dorsal fin is small and placed far back on the dorsum. The spout is high (15-20 feet), spreading near the top and accompanied by a whistling sound. RANGE. Occasional spring, summer, and fall visitor and resident along the ocean coast and in Puget Sound. Most individuals to be found well off shore in summer.

SEI WHALE Length, 40-55 feet. Fig. 116. A large, dark-blue, brownish, or dark grayish whale with a reduced amount of white on the belly and no white on insides of flippers or flukes. The dorsal fin is hooked and located two-thirds of the distance from the snout to the tail. The spout is cone-shaped and whistled. RANGE. Uncommon to at times common visitor, mostly in the spring and summer, along the ocean coast.

LITTLE PIKED WHALE; MINKE WHALE Length, 25-33 feet. Fig. 117. A medium-sized whale with bluish-gray upper parts and white under parts. A prominent white patch on each flipper; under surface of flukes is white. Dorsal fin is prominent and recurved. Spout is diffuse. RANGE. Occasional summer visitor along the NW ocean coast and in the Strait of Juan de Fuca and Puget Sound.

BLUE WHALE Length, 70-90 feet. Fig. 117. The largest of the whales, some individuals have been measured over 100 feet and a weight of up to 145 tons. The upper parts are bluish gray, and the under parts, yellowish or whitish. Occasionally there are grayish patches on the back. The dorsal fin is very small. The under side of the flippers is white. The spout is high (15-20 feet), vertical, and columnar. RANGE. Uncommon offshore visitor and migrant along the NW ocean coast.

HUMPBACK WHALE Length, 35-50 feet. Fig. 118. This is a large whale with very large flippers (amounting to some one-third of the length of the body).

The upper parts are black, while the under parts and under surfaces of the flippers and flukes are white. The colors, however, are variable. The dorsal fin is very small. The whale's spout is high and spreading. This species is much given to leaping and rolling at the surface of the sea. RANGE. Previously, a common spring and early summer visitor along the ocean coast, straits, and Puget Sound, where it was the most abundant of the large whales. Since 1964, North Pacific stocks have been drastically reduced and the species must now be considered rare in the NW region.

RIGHT WHALE   Length, 45-60 feet. Fig. 118.   A large whale with a bow-shaped mouth and an almost entirely blackish color. No dorsal fin. There is a horny growth or "bonnet" on the snout. The spout is double and spreading, to become V-shaped. RANGE. Rare offshore visitor along the NW ocean coast.

In addition to the accounts of certain early North American mammalogists appearing previously in this book, the following brief biographies of some pioneer naturalists who worked in the Pacific Northwest and contributed to our early knowledge of the region's mammals are provided. This material is based on a series of biographical footnotes in the MAMMALS AND BIRDS OF MOUNT RAINIER NATIONAL PARK by Walter P. Taylor and William T. Shaw.

John Kirk Townsend was born in Philadelphia, Pennsylvania, on October 10, 1809, and died in Washington, D.C. on February 6, 1851. A contemporary of Audubon, he was a naturalist and explorer and a member of the staff of the National Institute, a precursor of the National Museum of the Smithsonian Institution, as collector and preparator. Townsend made a trip to the Rocky Mountains and the Columbia River in 1834 and discovered the mole, warbler, solitaire, and fox sparrow that were subsequently named after him, as were numerous other mammals.

George Gibbs was born on Long Island, New York, July, 1815, and died at New Haven, Connecticut, on April 9, 1873. Eminent for his investigations in several branches of natural history, he specialized in ethnology and made valuable contributions to the knowledge of the Indians of the Northwest. During his terms of service as a collector at Astoria, Oregon, with the U. S. Government Boundary Commission, and as geologist on the Pacific railroad surveys, he did much work in the present state of Washington.

William P. Trowbridge was born in Troy, New York, in 1828 and died in New Haven, Connecticut, on August 12, 1892. In the course of scientific work for the U. S. Coast Survey along the Pacific Coast from 1853 to 1856, he made extensive collections of birds and mammals for the U. S. National Museum.

Major Charles Emil Bendire was born in the duchy of Hesse-Darmstadt, Germany, on April 27, 1836, and died in Jacksonville, Florida, on February 4, 1897. He was eminent for his field investigations in nautral history, particularly the life histories and eggs of birds. His work in constructing telegraph lines for the U. S. Army carried him to many parts of the Pacific Northwest where he collected the types of such species as the Merriam's and Bendire's Shrews.

David Douglas (1798-1834) was an eminent Scottish botanist. Employed by the London Horticultural Society as a botanical collector, he made valuable contributions to the knowledge of plants and animals in his short lifetime, particularly in British Columbia, Washington, Oregon, and California. The Douglas' Squirrel was named after him.

Robert Kennicott was born in New Orleans, Louisiana, November 13, 1835, and died near Nulato, Alaska, on May 13, 1866. He was a naturalist and leader of the Russian-American Telegraph Expedition. A protege of Baird's, Kennicott did much work in the northern part of the Northwest.

Captain Meriwether Lewis (1774-1809) was the famous American explorer who with Captain William Clark (1770-1838) crossed the continent from St. Louis to the mouth of the Columbia River and return in 1803-06. From 1807 to the time of his death, Lewis was governor of the Louisiana Territory. Clark became a brigadier general in the U. S. Army and later governor of the Missouri Territory and Superintendent of Indian Affairs. In addition to leading the famous expedition, the two made numerous collections and notes on the plants and animals encountered, both in the Rockies and in the Pacific Northwest.

Dr. William Fraser Tolmie (1812-1888) was a medical officer in the service of the Hudson's Bay Company. During 1833 and thereafter, he served at Nisqually House, southern Puget Sound, and at other points in the Pacific Northwest, making valuable contributions to the knowledge of the botany and zoology of the region.

Dr. James Graham Cooper was a pioneer naturalist on the Pacific coast. Born in New York City on June 19, 1830, he died at Hayward, California, on July 19, 1902. From 1853 to 1855, he worked principally in Washington state. He collected the type of the Cooper's race of the Townsend's Chipmunk in "Klickitat Pass" between Mounts St. Helens and Adams, during July, 1854.

In addition to these persons, a number of later workers added much to our understanding of Northwest mammals during the earlier part of the present century. Some of these are George Cantwell, Walter P. Taylor, William T. Shaw, Stanley P. Jewett, John M. Edson, William L. Finley, and Leo K. Couch. The work of the various members, past and present, of the Caurinus Club, later renamed the Pacific Northwest Bird and Mammal Society, should be mentioned here, as much of the later information on Northwest mammals has appeared in the society's journal, *The Murrelet*.

DOGS

Figure 119.
Coyote.

The family of dogs is distinguished by being digitigrade (walking on its toes), long-legged, cursorial (running), and provided with four or five front toes and four hind ones; also an elongated muzzle, and non-retractile claws. They are primarily carnivorous, but some species, notably the foxes, tend toward omnivorous habits. The long, pointed teeth are admirably suited for their snapping, slashing mode of fighting and killing.

The domestic dog, in one breed or other, is among the most familiar of mammals. The several wild species of the Pacific Northwest dogs are similar in their canid characters. One of these, the Coyote, is widespread throughout the Northwest and may frequently be heard at night in the open areas, particularly east of the Cascades. The larger Gray Wolf is much scarcer and south of British Columbia is very seldom seen or heard. The Red Fox seems to enjoy a fairly wide range in the region but keeps mainly out of human sight. The tiny Kit Fox occurs, or at least did occur, in extreme southeastern Oregon and southwestern Idaho. It apparently is rare or absent from these areas at present. The Gray Fox is to be found only in western Oregon, as regards the Northwest.

The sun had set behind Johnson Ridge and "Kingbird Lake" lay in the evening shadow. Most of the bird singing had ceased, and only the *beeship* of the nighthawks and the *per-dill-ik* of the poor-wills were to be heard. An

155

occasional tail-slap of a Beaver came from across the lake. Suddenly, a sharp, rapid, yapping followed by a falsetto peal sounded from the Aspen Spring on the other side of the Grecian Grove, to be joined by another voice. In a few seconds, more howls came from a different direction—from Coyote Canyon. The sounds, rising and falling, continued, and then a third group chimed in from Coyote Point on Johnson Ridge. We were surrounded by this canine evening chorus. After another minute all had ceased and only the calls of the nighthawk and poor-will were to be heard. What a tragedy it would be if the voice of the Coyote should be stilled in the land!

In spite of the environmental encroachments of civilization, relentless persecution, and variation in food supply, the North American Coyote has continued to maintain itself in many parts of its original continental range. One has to admire this gaunt dog, as it glides through the forest groves or sagebrush plains for its ability to survive under often adverse conditions. Food-finding is always a problem, and while fat ground squirrels are for the stalking in spring and early summer, the Coyote often has to feed on grasshoppers later in the season and in some areas consumes quantities of juniper berries during the winter to keep the stomach full. When deep snows, hoar frost, and ice bury the vegetation, when the mice are safe in their sub-surface burrows and runways, and when the tracks of many Coyotes are marked with blood from ice cuts, we have a strong feeling of sympathy for those of the wild which must exist outside in the wind and weather. In summer, the living may be easy, but winter pits the skills of existence gained through eons of evolution against the elements of nature. Truly, the Coyote is a master of survivalship.

The Coyote is both a carnivore and a carrion feeder, existing mostly on animal flesh. While stories of its voraciousness are a regular part of rangeland lore, the author has talked to a number of ranchers who feel that the animal has a positive value in the keeping down of rabbits, ground squirrels, gophers, and mice, and should consequently be protected, E. Raymond Hall, the outstanding North American mammalogist, has written an objective, but outspoken, analysis of the Coyote's economic situation in the account of the species in his classic MAMMALS OF NEVADA which is well worth the reading (as is his beautifully written description of a desert cloudburst in the same book). Nevertheless, amid 1080 stations, cyanide guns, traps, rifles, and cowboy mythology, this animal persists.

Dens are located under large boulders, in crevices or caves in rocky outcroppings, or in burrows in earthen banks. The average litter runs from two to four pups which are born in the spring or early summer. They make interesting pets, though usually by fall they respond to the call of the wild and are likely to run away. The author has always been impressed by the alertness of pet Coyotes and Bobcats in comparison with the dulled senses of their domesticated cousins. Such reduction of senses has usually been one of the principal aims of domestication.

Of all the world's mammals, probably no one has aquired such an association of dread as has the Wolf. Occurring wild throughout the northern hemisphere, it has figured widely in legend and fact, in story and poetry. And, indeed, it has been an animal to reckon with in the early days. While tales of these white-fanged hunters harrying the countryside and devouring any unprotected peasant they happened to find are probably overdrawn, the early pioneers in America's West found them enough of a problem in the growing

Figure 120.
Gray Wolf.

of stock. In fact, at one time, it was stated that they and the Grizzly Bear were so numerous in California that cattle-raising on any scale in that region could never be carried on. Little did such prophets realize the power of the incoming hordes of white men and their guns, traps, and poisons.

In spite of all the legends and stories, the Wolf is, nevertheless, a remarkable animal. The superb evolutionary development of the dog type, it is the almost perfect hunter. Intelligent, powerful, and gregarious, it still is common in the Far North, in spite of almost universal persecution. It was possibly more numerous in the southern parts of the Pacific Northwest at one time in the past, though the early records are imperfect and unreliable, with the Wolf sometimes confused with the Coyote, at least in name.

The Wolf is probably one of the least seen of the large mammals, being shy and largely nocturnal. In the wilder parts of its range, it often bands together in packs for the winter foraging on hoofed prey. Its consumption of deer in much of the Northwest is so slight, due to the paucity of Wolves, that such predation is of no importance at all and this interesting animal should be carefully and completely protected. The long, throaty howl of the Wolf is one of the great sounds of nature, the truest apotheosis of the wild, now so fast receding. The author has heard it hundreds of times (he lived for many years near a zoo), but in these days, one has to go farther and farther back in the recesses of the northern part of the continent to hear this truest call of the wild.

Unlike the Wolf, the Red Fox is widely distributed in much of the Northwest, excepting the dense forests of the coastal region. It occupies a variety of habitats from sea level to the higher mountains and feeds on a wide spectrum of

157

Figure 121.
Red Fox.

foods. Rocky areas for dens are an important need, perhaps accounting for the partiality to talus slopes in subalpine areas. Favored foods are mice, insects, rabbits, birds, as well as frogs and other herps. The breeding season of the Red Fox is in mid and late winter, usually in January and February. After a little more than 50 days, the young are born, usually in a litter of four or five pups. After two months, they are weaned, but remain near the den and are fed by the vixen and dog. The young stay with the parents, often hunting as a family unit, till the end of the summer when the pups, now almost full grown, break off on their own.

The Gray Fox, in our region, occurs in open timber and brush in the valley areas of western Oregon and at least formerly on the lower east slopes of the Cascades in that state. One of the interesting features of this species is its ability to climb trees which it commonly does when pursued closely. Dens are commonly placed among rock in slides or outcroppings or in crevices on cliffs. Six or seven young are born in the spring and cared for by the parents till almost full grown. A great variety of foods is consumed by these pretty little fellows, including a considerable amount of berries. There are as many plusses as minusses in the economic picture of the Gray Fox, its occasional depredations being easily balanced by its consumption of rodents and insects and its even greater esthetic value as a part of the wild scene.

It is a pity that the Kit Fox with its dainty ways and soft, silky fur is so rare

158

in the territory covered by this book. This is the most subterranean of our foxes. It lives in burrows which enter the ground at about a 45 degree angle and lead to a den eight to ten feet below the surface. Most dens have three entrances. Known as "desert swifts," it is believed that these are the fastest quadrupeds on the plains for short sprints, but for long distances, the Coyote could overtake them. Rodents, particularly Kangaroo Rats, make up the staple of this fox's diet. Rabbits are also a favorite, along with some insects and mice. Among the most beautiful of the plains animals, they should be strictly protected, but it is doubtful that they could ever be restored to any degree of abundance in the Pacific Northwest.

Figure 122.
Kit Fox.

Figure 123.
Gray Fox.

PACIFIC NORTHWEST SPECIES

COYOTE 51-13¾-7⅞-4⅖ (1,300-350-200-120) Figs. 119 and 126. The Coyote resembles a slender, medium-sized, domestic dog, grayish brown in color with shades of red on the legs, feet, and ears. Coyotes are smaller than wolves and have more pointed muzzles. Their large, pointed ears usually face forward, but can be moved in other directions. Coyotes have a graceful, springing gait and possess tails that are bushier than those of domestic dogs and are held down when the animals run. The general light coloration of the Coyote, causing it to blend in with most vegetation and rocks is distinctive. RANGE. Occurs throughout the NW, with the exception of coastal B.C. and Vancouver and Queen Charlotte Islands. HABITAT. Most numerous in open prairies or desert type habitats; less common, but present, in the denser forest and subalpine and alpine areas. Has become adapted to living on ranches and to visiting farmsteads and rural settlements where it may prey on the house cats at the edges of town. Well adjusted to living with man and its numbers are increasing.

GRAY WOLF 59-15-10-4 (1,500-400-250-100) Figs. 124 and 125. The Gray Wolf is the largest of the wild dogs and is larger than most domestic breeds. While variable in color, most wolves are grayish or blackish above with lighter colors on the sides and belly. The tail in light phases is buffy with a black overlay and usually carried high when the animal is running. The legs of the wolf appear noticeably proportionately longer than those of domestic dogs.

160

RANGE. Originally occurred throughout the Pacific NW, with the exception of the Queen Charlotte Islands, but now is rare or absent from most parts of the region south of the Canadian-U. S. border. A few occur in the mts. or forested areas of n. Wash. and n. and c. Idaho. Scattered records elsewhere in the NW. Not adapting well to man and his activities. HABITAT. May occur in all types of natural, terrestrial habitat.

RED FOX 39-16-7-3½ (1,000-400-175-90) Figs. 121 and 127. This species is about the bulk of a medium-sized domestic dog. Its normal color is reddish yellow with white under parts, but color variations of silver, cross, and black also occur. Silver and black phases have been most commonly seen by the author in the Cascades and mts. of Idaho. The long, bushy tail (the "brush") is tipped with white in all color phases and the feet are black. The four color phases are as follows: (1) *red*, reddish-yellow upper parts and tail (with white tip), white under parts, and black feet; (2) *silver*, black all over (upper and lower surfaces) with white sub-terminal bands on guard hairs over back, and white tip of tail; (3) *cross*, grizzled dusky or black along middle of back and across shoulders (the cross-shaped pattern) and on throat and chest and most of tail except for the white tip; sides, belly, and rump yellowish red; feet, legs, and nose grizzled black. (4) *black*, glossy black all over (upper and lower surfaces), except white tip of tail; by far the least common of these four, also occur. RANGE. Occurs throughout the Pacific NW, with the exception of the coastal region of B.C., the Olympic Peninsula, s.w. Ore., and the arid, semi-desert parts of Wash., Ore., and s. Idaho. Has been introduced into several areas, especially parts of the Puget Sound region and is extending its range into places not originally occupied, as in s. Idaho. HABITAT. Occurs in a variety of habitats, though preferring semi-open terrain, especially in the foothills and mts.

KIT FOX 28½-9⅞-4⅞-3½ (725-250-125-90) Fig. 122. The Kit Fox is a much smaller relative of the Red Fox. It is nearly buff in color, but grayer on the dorsal surface. The tip of the tail is black, and the chin, throat, and belly are white. The fur is soft and silky. RANGE. Strongly reduced in distribution and apparently now occurs in the NW at least, only sparsely and scatteringly in s.e. Ore. There are old records for s. Idaho but the species seems not to occur in that state at present. HABITAT. The open, desert areas.

GRAY FOX 40⅖-15¼-5⅝-2½ (1,030-390-145-65) Fig. 123. About the same general size as the Red Fox, or slightly smaller, this species has shorter legs and smaller ears, and more strongly curved claws (which enables it to readily climb trees). Upper parts blackish gray, with dark midline; under parts reddish brown, with white on throat and middle of belly. Black muzzle and top and tip of tail. RANGE. W. Ore., mostly in the interior valleys, and, at least formerly, along the e. base of the Cascades. HABITAT. Open timber, brush, rocks, and cliffs.

Figure 124.
Gray Wolf (black phase) running on a river bar. Note the relatively long legs.

162

Figure 125.
Three young Britts and the pelt of an Arctic wolf.

To vacationers whose annual experience with mammals occurs in some campground in July or August, it may come as a surprise that much mammal study can be done in the dead of winter. This is a time of environmental stress for the wild things—a challenge to their adaptations for existence. It may also represent a challenge to the student of mammals, which may account for the exhilaration that some of us find in studying animals at this time of year.

The needle mat of the forest floor and the thick turf of the meadow in summer seldom reveal the comings and goings of mammals and only an experienced eye can recognize the spoor in crumpled blades of grass or broken branches. Those of us fortunate to live in the snow country possess a pure white "slate" on which many of nature's creatures write a record of their activities, their foraging patterns, and their victories and defeats. Here we may see the pairs of prints of some weasel, as it hops from tussock to tussock searching for mice. There goes off in the distance the trail of two Coyotes, the second animal carefully stepping in the prints of the lead dog. The plodding trail of a Porcupine with the swish marks of its swinging trail are easily to be seen in the shallow crystals of a tracking snow. In the forest, the surface may be literally covered with the prints of a hare or two, while well-used trails lead to their brush-patch home. In a clearing or on a frozen lake, a maze of circling tracks may reveal the mating ground of Coyotes. That night, while we slept soundly in the fire-warmed cabin, a company of mammals, large and small were going about their various businesses. In the morning, they had disappeared but they left behind a record of their doings in the snow for those who could read the story.

As I sit in my camp in the forest writing this essay, I can see no weasels, nor have I so far during my stay here, but I know that they are around, for the snow last winter revealed their presence.

As I have indicated several times in this book, mammals are more difficult to find and observe than birds, but this gives added zest to their study. Occasionally, we see the individual animal itself, but more often we find only the evidence of its presence. Yet there is much we can learn from such evidence, and trailing an animal reveals to us what it was doing. First, we discover what habitat it was in. We find, for instance, that Snowshoe Hares keep strictly to the forest and do not venture out into the fields or meadows. We see that the Coyote or Wolf boldy strides in a straight line to its destination, while the fox keeps to the hollows and depressions. We find that the Martin spends much time on the snow surface in its foraging, only occasionally climbing a tree for a squirrel. Trails may lead to kills where carnivores have feasted on the unwary. Such is the way of life and little is wasted. "Recycling" it is known as nowadays. Do animals roam aimlessly through the woods or are their movements purposeful? Get on the trail of one and follow it for a day. You will learn something about that beast you didn't know before!

Figure 126.
The modern Coyote, tame and brash (Pole).

164

Figure 127.
A Red Fox with a bushy tail called the "brush" by fox hunters.

BEARS

Figure 128.
Black Bear.

Although usually listed as among the world's largest terrestrial carnivores, bears are actually highly omnivorous, eating with equal relish vegetable, flesh, or insect material. They are heavily built plantigrades (entire sole of foot placed on ground), with short tails, thick fur, large heads with powerful jaws, and strong claws. Black Bears can readily climb trees and young Grizzlies have often been seen climbing, but as the latter grow older and heavier, they cannot be coaxed to ascend a tree. Cases of bears attacking humans are rare, but such provocation is sometimes unintentional and it is wise to treat them all with considerable care. Offering food to a wild bear will occasionally lead to unhappy results.

Two species of bears are to be found in the Pacific Northwest: one, the Black Bear, is common and widespread; the other, the Grizzly, is very rare in the southern part of the region, becoming somewhat more numerous in parts of British Columbia.

The North American Black Bear is probably one of the best known mammals of the continent. It has a wide distribution through the Pacific Northwest, being absent only from the open prairie country. Bears are irregular in ocurrence, though most numerous in areas where wild berries are common. They have a tendency, also, to "thicken up" around resort and logging camp garbage dumps, where in the latter area, part of the work of the "bull cook" is to keep the local bear population away from the back door of the mess hall.

165

Figure 129.
Grizzly Bear.

Black Bears appear to be clumsy, slow-moving, and stupid. Actually, this appearance is deceiving. They are powerfully muscled animals with great strength. They can run rapidly and strike with their front feet with amazing speed. The author has looked up trees climbed by bears and seen light between the trunk and the animal's belly indicating that the trunk was literally being held between the paws with a grip firm enough to support the animal's weight.

The Black Bear's diet is controlled mostly by availability of the wide variety of items upon which it feeds. In fact, it has been said that this species is the most omnivorous of all North American mammals. Most of its animal food is small, however. Bears do show an interest in young calves and the author remembers watching an amusing episode in the Seven Devils Mountains of Idaho where a range cow chased a bear around a meadow after the bruin had tried to stalk her calf. There are verified reports from the Idaho Bitterroots of Black Bears killing young Elk calves. Some packers consider the bears to be a serious menace to the Elk in this respect.

The gestation period of Black Bears is somewhat more than 200 days, females breeding when three years old. The young (most litters consisting of twins) are born in late winter or early spring while the mother is still denned up. The young are very small, averaging some eight to ten ounces in weight. The author once observed a female and two cubs denned up in a hollow tree, the main part of which had been cut off. We could view the animals from above. The female lay on its belly in a semi-torpid condition, though it was

166

fully conscious. Its front paws and chin covered the two cubs which nursed at the breasts on the nearby chest. Later, when they would be suckling from the mother when she would be sitting upright, they would use the much lower abdominal nipples.

The Grizzly Bear is probably the most dangerous of North American mammals. Its tremendous size, powerful musculature, and fearless aggressiveness combine to produce a most formidable beast which does not fear man or any other animal, when bothered or threatened. Ordinarily, these bears avoid direct contact with man and retreat or hide when he approaches. Nevertheless, they are not to be trusted. While primarily carnivorous, the Grizzly feeds on much vegetation and is not at all above raiding garbage dumps in certain national parks. In the latter areas, a number of attacks on humans have occurred in recent years, particularly in two national parks. Some of these were the result of human carelessness, while others were voluntary on the part of the bears. Human females in the menstrual period are particularly vulnerable and would do well, when in such condition, to strictly avoid Grizzly Bear areas. Little children should be carefully shielded from bears as there may not be much difference, as far as the bear is concerned, between a two-year-old and a plump marmot.

These animals may attain a weight of half a ton, though most are in the 400-600 pound class. Though most active in early morning and particularly in early evening, Grizzlies may be found in their never-ending search for food at any time of the day or night. Most individuals hibernate during the snowy months, though the period of dormancy is shorter than that for Black Bears. The Grizzly follows a rather strict pattern of trails in its home range and where they are numerous these trails may be very evident. Mating in the Grizzly is at irregular intervals, mostly every two or three years. Two, rarely three, cubs are born in mid-winter after being bred the previous summer. As with the Black Bear, the Grizzly young are relatively tiny, compared with their parents.

Whether the "Alaska brown bear" or "big brown bear" represents a species separate from the Grizzly Bear is an undetermined question. The bears of the extreme northern coast of the Northwest approach these large forms which in their typical size inhabit the saltwater fringes from Norton Sound to the Sitka region of Alaska. C. Hart Merriam considered, in his study of the Grizzlies of North America, that some 87 species inhabited the continent. The present thought that all of the big brown and Grizzly Bears, as well as the brown bears of Europe and Asia, represent a single species is probably just as extreme a view. Renewed studies, based on a better understanding of variation, evolution, genetics, structure, and behavior in the genus *Ursus*, are desirable to sort out these interesting mammals.

Figure 130.

PACIFIC NORTHWEST SPECIES

BLACK BEAR 69-5-10-3½ (1,750-128-250-90) Fig. 128; Color Plate 12. Black Bears are the smallest of North American bears. Color phases range from blue-black through black, brown, cinnamon, blond, gray, to white. The black and brown phases are the most common, the former being more numerous in the wetter, coastal areas and the latter better represented in the drier, interior regions. The average adult individual may weigh 200-300 pounds. The fur is relatively long and shaggy. The nails are short and black and the shoulder hump found in the Grizzly Bear is lacking. RANGE. Occurs throughout the NW, though usually not found in the open, non-forested areas. HABITAT. Prefers forested or wooded habitats, as well as swamps. Black Bears commonly visit open berry patches in burns or subalpine areas when the fruit is ripe.

GRIZZLY BEAR 75-6¾-10-3 (1,912-172-255-75) Figs. 129 and 130. These bears are large, heavy-bodied mammals, sometimes reaching half a ton in weight. Colors are variable from yellowish to brown and almost black, but the hairs are tipped with whitish or buffy, giving the grizzled appearance. There is a large hump on the shoulders and the long yellow or brown claws are about four inches in length and curved. The hair is very long and shaggy. Populations of very large bears along the southern Alaskan coast are often referred to as "big brown bears" and may reach enormous size. Some of these may be present on, or stray into, the extreme northwest coast of British Columbia. RANGE. Formerly occurred throughout the NW, though shunning the dense coastal forests of Wash. and Ore., but now very rare south of the U.S.-Canadian border. A few occur in the n.e. Cascades of Wash. and the Bitterroots of n. Idaho. Widely distributed through the mts. and along the coast of B.C. HABITAT. Restricted to open or semi-open habitats, particularly subalpine forests and alpine meadows. Also occurs along the coast belt of B.C., especially at the heads of inlets.

Much of the ornithological and mammalogical work done during the period 1850 through 1880 was inspired by Spencer Fullerton Baird (born at Reading, Pennsylvania, February 3, 1823, and died at Woods Hole, Massachusetts, August 19, 1888). He had served as professor of natural history at Dickinson College and inaugurated in North America the method of field study of animals and plants used successfully by Louis Agassiz in Switzerland and later in the U.S. Baird joined the Smithsonian Institution in 1850 as Assistant Secretary, becoming its director or "Secretary" in 1878. A major emphasis in Baird's work was the assembly of collections for the institution. For this goal, he solicited the support of the U. S. Army in authorizing its field surgeons and officers to procure specimens of birds and mammals and send them to the Smithsonian. The naturalists in the surveying parties for the various railroad routes to the Pacific Coast were also under the direction of Baird. He even interested the Hudson's Bay Company to direct its employees to contribute specimens from Canadian areas. All the materials thus acquired formed the nucleus of the mammal collection of the U. S. National Museum.

PROCYONIDS

Figure 131.
Raccoon.

Members of this family, the *Procyonidae,* are small to medium-sized carnivorous mammals with soft, dense fur and long-heavily-haired tails usually characterized by a contrasting ringed color pattern. Most of the species are tropical or sub-tropical, and contain such interesting forms as the Ringtails, Raccoons of several species, the Coatis of the elevated tail, and the Kinkajous and Olingos of Central America. Two characteristics are commonly shared by this small but fascinating group, the omnivorous diet and the tendency toward arboreality. Only two species occur within the scope of the present manual.

The North American Raccoon is a brownish-colored animal easily recognized by its black face mask and ringed tail. Raccoons have a wide distribution in the Pacific Northwest except for British Columbia where they occur only in the southernmost part and on Vancouver Island. 'Coons are most abundant near water in the lowlands but may be found in the arid interior as well as along the tidewaters of the coast. Their presence is often revealed by the typical human, hand-like prints in the soft mud along the margin of a stream or lake.

Raccoons make interesting pets, though varying in degree of tameness. The author has known friends who have had considerable success in taming them and teaching the animals some simple tricks. The key to taming this, as well as most other wild mammals, is in the amount of time spent in playing and otherwise becoming familiar with them. Close association seems to establish a bond of friendship or rapport which can only be gotten through considerable effort. This should begin at the earliest possible age of the animal. Not everyone is willing to devote the necessary time to such an occupation and those persons had best keep a domestic cat or dog, or preferably no pet at all. It is no longer legal in most parts of the Northwest to own wild animals as pets. This restriction is probably wise, as seldom are the native species kept in as natural a condition as necessary for their well being. In fact, some persons are beginning to question the wisdom of the zoo collection, considering that the best experience to be had with wild animals is to meet them in their native haunts or through the medium of movie documentaries or TV shows. The author can vouch for the view that after having seen the large mammals of Africa in their natural habitats, the same species confined in a zoo leaves one with a distinct feeling of sadness. He is also of the opinion that most zoos in the Pacific Northwest are little better than animal ghettos!

Raccoons breed at one year of age and bring forth an average litter of four young, after a gestation of some 65 days. The cubs are born in a den in a hollow log or crevice under a rock. By the end of the summer, they are on their own. As mentioned previously, Raccoons are omnivorous and feed on a wide variety of foodstuffs, some of which, like ripe ears of corn and henhouse inmates, may not endear the beast to the farmer. There is a popular belief that the Raccoon always washes its food before eating it, as the specific technical name implies. Unfortunately, this is not true. The fact that it commonly forages along water and gathers much food below the surface, such as crayfish, frogs, and fresh-water mussels, with a considerable amount of handling has probably given rise to this bit of folklore. Raccoons are good swimmers and climbers and are frequently treed when being hunted, the use of hounds being the most common method. In some parts of North America, Raccoons are commonly used for food, though the practice is not at all common in the Pacific Northwest. The value of 'coon pelts has been modest in recent years, though the vagaries of fashion occasionally have catapulted this and other furbearers to considerable value. The European market has caused certain furbearers to have extremely high prices at present, a situation not entirely conducive to their population welfare in the area, though this is a highly controversial point.

The delicate little Ringtail is of limited occurrence in the Pacific Northwest and is so shy and nocturnal as to be seldom seen even when living close to man. It is not until night has completely fallen that these animals begin their foraging. Caves and rock crevices are usually preferred for dens, but they occasionally live in hollows of trees. The gentle nature of these beasts led to their being kept as pets by early settlers and miners in the West and used as "mousers." From the little bit known of these animals, three or four young seem to be the usual number in a litter. Like the Raccoon, Ringtails are highly omnivorous.

Figure 132.
Ringtail.

PACIFIC NORTHWEST SPECIES

RACCOON 35½-11-4¾-2⅜ (905-280-122-61) Fig. 131; Color Plate 8. These are medium-sized carnivores, easily recognized by their grizzled, blackish-gray upper parts; black-and-brown, striped, bushy tails; and black masks over their eyes and cheeks. The toes are long and finger-like, and the snouts and ears are pointed. RANGE. Occurs throughout Wash., Ore., and Idaho, and s. and s.w. parts of B.C., including Vancouver Island. HABITAT. Brushy or wooded areas near water and saltwater beaches along the ocean coast. Prefers lower elevations and seldom penetrates very far into the montane forests.

RINGTAIL 28-14¾-2½-1⅞ (700-370-62-48) Fig. 132. This is a slender, cat-sized animal with varying shades of buff on the upper parts and white or whitish buff on the under parts. The fur is overlaid with darker brown or black hairs. The tail is longer than the body and is prominently marked with whitish and blackish rings. Long ears and a long snout are evident and the short, straight claws are semi-retractile. RANGE. S.w. Ore. and extreme e. Idaho, near the Wyoming border (one record). HABITAT. Rocky areas with canyons and cliffs, but also in open forests and brush.

MUSTELIDS

Figure 133.
Marten.

   The weasels and their allies belong to the family Mustelidae which consists of small to medium-sized mammals with short legs and small feet. They have five toes on each foot and large paired anal scent glands which reach their peak of perfection in the skunks. Economic loss caused by this group of animals is usually the result of local conditions which favor them, since most of the species are rather shy and wary of man's habitations. Perhaps the Striped and Spotted Skunks form exceptions to this. Nevertheless, mustelids have more than compensated for their destruction of property by offering their valuable furs to the markets of man. Though the advances of civilization and

173

over-trapping have nearly extirpated certain of these animals in parts of their range, their pelts still bring fine annual profits for the trapper, varying, of course, according to fashions and consequent market values. Commercial fur farms have been developed to compensate for the diminishing wild representatives of the family and to propagate, under conditions of controlled environment, such mutant varieties as the blue and platinum mink.

Mustelids show widely divergent habitat preferences, ranging from the arid desert region of the Badger to the arboreal haunts of the Marten and the highly aquatic habitats of the River and Sea Otters, accompanied by unique structural and behavioral adaptations for the particular way of life. Wherever they occur, members of this family form a vastly interesting group and a necessary part of nature's scheme. Twelve species of mustelids are to be found in the Pacific Northwest.

The Marten is truly an arboreal weasel, foraging through the trees for Red and Flying Squirrels and small birds, though, as its winter tracks reveal, it spends considerable amounts of time on the ground where it catches and eats a variety of animal life. Trappers have often found that the local squirrel population must be decimated before Martens can be caught as these rodents will fill up the traps set for the carnivores and reduce their need to depend on trap bait. Martens are fairly easy to trap if the sets are placed along their foraging routes. These routes often extend along connecting ridges and the entire circuit may take, in the author's experience, a week or ten days to complete. Dead, halved Red Squirrels make a good bait when nailed a foot or so above the trap which is placed on an inset notch on a tree trunk with a sapling leaning from the ground into the notch. Trappers often place some ripe fish mixture in a hole bored into the tree a few inches above the trap and covered with a little wire screening.

Although Martens mate in mid or late summer, delayed implantation of the eggs delays the gestation period to about ten months, after which some three to four young are born. After three months, they are about full grown and strike out on their own.

The author and some friends were hiking up through the snow toward Kootenay Glacier Park in British Columbia one Thanksgiving Day afternoon some years ago. We had noticed the tracks of a Porcupine going up the side of the snow-filled road in the same direction we were traveling. Suddenly, we saw the trail of a Fisher come in from the side, examine the porkie tracks, and then proceed to go along those of the other animal. We hastened to follow these to see if the Fisher had made a meal of the spiny one, but fading daylight, three feet of soft snow, and a dinner engagement prevented us from recording, at least from the tracks, a typical encounter between Fisher and Porcupine.

The Fisher is larger than the Marten and darker in color. In fact, the three individuals that the author has seen in the wild reminded him of a black house cat at a distance. Unlike the Marten, the Fisher prefers heavy timber. However, it feeds much like the Marten, though including Snowshoe Hares and Porcupines, as well as carrion from larger mammals, in its diet. The foraging patterns of the Fisher are also larger, sometimes three to four times the length of the circuits of the Marten.

Delayed implantation occurs in Fishers as in Martens, lasting for some nine months, with actual gestation estimated at 15 weeks. The young are born in

Figure 134.
Mink.

late spring and are on their own in about seven months.

The delicate little Short-tailed Weasel is one of the most efficient of predators. A study of its tracks in the snow will reveal tireless searching for food—under tussocks of projecting grass, over logs, through brush and thickets, and in rock piles. The animal feeds largely on mice, though it may consume rabbits and birds, as well as cold-blooded vertebrates and some insects and larger invertebrates. It is also not above killing chickens and domestic rabbits. Breeding begins in midsummer, but, due to delayed implantation, the young are born in the spring, four to seven making up the average litter. Five or six weeks later, the little ones are weaned and rapidly become independent. This species is common, especially in the lowlands, and accounts for considerable of the predation pressure on mice. It is difficult to walk through the snow in many places in the Pacific Northwest without finding the tracks of this species.

The three common semi-aquatic mammals around lakes and ponds and along rivers are the Beaver, Muskrat, and Mink. Barring the occurrence of a River Otter or two, most of the larger mustelids are scattered in distribution and mainly erratic visitors to any particular body of water, and the Mink is the common predator in such places. It is probably more common along rivers and creeks than standing water, unless there is considerable area of marshland or swamp.

The Mink is a graceful swimmer which spends much of its time in water, although it also travels and forages on land, especially in winter. Primarily carnivorous, it feeds upon a considerable variety of aquatic life, both vertebrate and invertebrate, and is a dry land forager of some repute, its diet being controlled largely by season and local availability.

Few mammal species in North America have such an aura of myth and fable surrounding them as does the Wolverine. If one-tenth of the stories told about it were true, it would be quite an animal. However, it is nothing more than one should expect, if he took a weasel and enlarged it to Wolverine size. Moreover, not all adverse to carrion, this animal feeds on anything it can subdue, even up to deer size, as well as animals caught in traps. Powerfully built, it can, bear-like, break into cabins for food contained therein. Intelligent, aggressive, and constantly on the move, it is one of nature's more active members. In places in the North where Wolverines are common, they are animals to be reckoned with as far as the camp's food supply is concerned and the typical Northland cache, the "little cabin on stilts," is the answer to the beast. Recently, Wolverines have become attracted to the vicinity of roads and campgrounds in northern Idaho. It is hard to imagine a much more serious pest and camp moocher than this species.

The Badger is one of the most interesting of mammals with its unique flattened shape, characteristic coloration, and powerful excavating abilities. It forages mainly by digging out such rodents as ground squirrels, pocket gophers, and mice. It can easily dig itself out of sight and out-burrow two men with shovels. It is a fearsome antagonist, as some dogs have found out to their sorrow. Badgers can easily get out of under-sized steel traps if the jaws do not close far enough up on the wrist to catch behind a bony protruberance. Badgers put on considerable fat in the late summer and fall and hibernate during the winter, though the sleep is not profound and surface foraging is occasionally engaged in. However, in warm desert areas, the Badger is active throughout the year. Much surface animal life, vertebrates as well as insects, arthropods, and mollusks are used for food, as well as carrion. Burrows, other than the breeding den, are located on hillsides or on level ground in brush, with the nest some five to 20 feet from the mouth of the burrow. The average litter contains two cubs. Furred at birth, the eyes open in about a month and weaning takes place a few weeks later. Visitors to the sagebrush sections of the interior of the Northwest sometimes find many square yards of soil disturbed, literally torn up. The answer to this mystery is the Badger, searching for wild bee larvae just below the surface of the ground.

An omnivorous species, the Striped Skunk is famous as a chicken house raider, though probably a large share of its diet is devoted to insects and some plant material. Skunks breed in early spring, producing a litter of about six young after a gestation period of a little more than 60 days. The scent glands are a famous defense mechanism, and such stories as the animal's being unable to discharge when held by the tail are untrue. We have always wondered how one could safely get close enough to grip a skunk by its tail without an accident. A family of skunks with the little ones is an interesting sight and one that may occasionally be seen in the wild. However, most of the foraging by this species is done at night. In late fall, skunks retire to dens, usually burrows in the ground, where they spend the winter in shallow hibernation.

Figure 135.
Long-tailed Weasel (summer pelage).

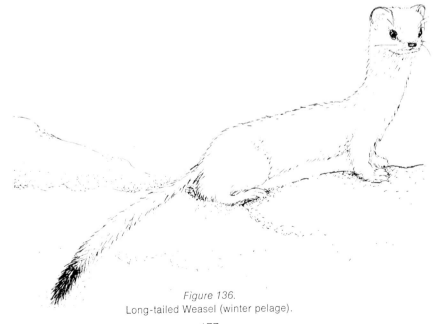

Figure 136.
Long-tailed Weasel (winter pelage).

Figure 137.
Short-tailed Weasel (winter pelage, left; summer pelage, right).

PACIFIC NORTHWEST SPECIES

MARTEN 24-6¾-3½-1⅜ (600-170-90-35) Figs. 133 and 168; Color Plates 3, 8, and 11. This is a large, weasel-like animal, brownish or reddish yellow above and slightly lighter below. A yellow or orange patch decorates the chin and throat, and the head is tinged with grayish. The soft, flufly fur is longer than that of a Mink and the tail is moderately long and bushy. RANGE. Occurs in forested, often mountainous, regions throughout the NW, shunning the arid, open, interior parts of e. Wash. and e. Ore., and s. Idaho. HABITAT. Restricted to the coniferous forests, mostly of the mts., where they frequent the ridges and the subalpine woods. On the Olympic Peninsula, uncommon at sea level and along the ocean coast where it occurs in cedar swamps.

FISHER 40-16-5⅛-1⅝ (1,000-400-130-42) Fig. 138. Similar to the Marten in appearance, the Fisher is considerably larger. Dark brown hairs, nearly black, tipped with white, give a frosted look to the animal. The under parts, as well as the rump, legs, and tail, are blackish. The legs are short, the muzzle pointed, and the tail long and bushy. RANGE. Occurs scatteringly and rarely through the forested areas of the NW, excepting the arid, non-timbered regions of Wash., Ore., and Idaho; Vancouver Island; and the n.w. corner of B.C. Probably most numerous in the Olympic Mts. of Wash. HABITAT. Undisturbed, virgin forest at low to intermediate elevations, particularly near water.

178

Figure 138.
Fisher.

SHORT-TAILED WEASEL; ERMINE males: 8⅝-2³/₁₆-1-⅝ (220-56-26-16)
females: 7⅞-2-1-⅝ (197-50-25-15)
Fig. 137. This species is separated from the similarly-colored Long-tailed Weasel by its lesser size. It is slender with a prominently-arched back. The summer pelage is brown above and pale yellow or white below. The brown tail is tipped with black. In winter, the fur turns white, except for the black tail tip, which remains. In this coat, the animal is commonly called an "ermine." RANGE. Occurs throughout the NW; uncommon or absent in the drier, desert areas of the interior. HABITAT. Occupies a variety of habitats, though usually stays close to stream bottoms, rock slides, fence rows, and brush near water.

LONG-TAILED WEASEL males: 16½-6⅛-1¹³/₁₆-1 (420-157-46-24)
females: 12⅞-5½-1½-⅞ (328-138-37-22)
Figs. 135 and 136. Similar to the Short-tailed Weasel in body proportions and color but differs from it in being much larger. In summer, brownish above and

179

yellowish below; pure white in winter, except for black tip to tail. Some low-land populations do not become completely white in winter, as in the Puget Sound area. RANGE. Occurs throughout Wash., Ore., and Idaho; and s. and c. B.C., excepting the coastal region and Vancouver Island. HABITAT. Found in a variety of haunts but prefers drier uplands of grass, forest, and rock; at all elevations from sea level to alpine.

LEAST WEASEL males: 7¹¹/₁₆-1⁵/₁₆-⅞-½ (196-34-22-13)
females: 6⅞-1-¾-⁷/₁₆ (176-25-19-12)

In summer, brown above and white below. In winter, completely white, except occasionally a few black hairs at the tip of the tail. Size and lack of conspicuous black tail tip distinctive. RANGE. N. and c. parts of B.C., except for the coastal region. Rare. HABITAT. The open to semi-wooded parklands of the interior.

MINK 21½-6⅞-2⅛-⅞ (548-175-55-22) Fig. 134. A medium-sized weasel-like carnivore, rich brown in color with white patches on the chin and throat. The moderately bushy tail is about one-half the length of the body. RANGE. Found in suitable habitat throughout the Pacific NW, except for the Queen Charlottes and other islands off the B.C. coast. HABITAT. Occurs mostly near water where the diet of Muskrats, fish, frogs, and other aquatic animals is available.

WOLVERINE 40-8¼-7¼-2¼ (1,000-210-185-32) Fig. 144. This mustelid is more bear-like than weasel-like in appearance. It is dark brownish black above and has a skunk-like pattern of yellowish stripes extending along the upper sides from the shoulders to the rump and out on the tail. Dark under parts are marked with white or yellowish throat patches. Light markings are evident on the head. RANGE. Occurs scatteringly and irregularly throughout the NW, except possibly for the arid, desert-like interior of Wash., Ore., and s. Idaho. Uncommon, but fairly regular resident and wanderer in the Cascades and Okanogan areas, the n.e. part of Wash., and Idaho. Scattered through the n. and c. parts of Ore. HABITAT. A great wanderer and likely to be seen any-where, but most records are for coniferous timbered areas, especially in mts. The recent increase in numbers of records in Wash. and Idaho may indicate a southward movement of Wolverines from Canada. Shows evidence of adapting to the proximity of man, as in forest campgrounds, which may or may not be a blessing!

BADGER 29½-4⅞-4⅛-2⅜ (750-125-105-60) Fig. 140. The Badger is a short-legged, heavy-bodied carnivore with a decidedly flattened appearance. The back is yellowish gray; a white stripe extends from the nose back across the top of the head; the cheeks are white; and a black spot is present just forward of the ear. In winter, the pelage becomes more grizzled and grayish in appearance and softer in texture. RANGE. Found in e. Wash. and Ore., including the drier parts of the Cascades and the upper Rogue River area, and s.e. B.C. HABITAT. Occurs in open to semi-open country, such as sagebrush and grassland plains, open yellow pine forests, farmlands, and parklands. Probably most numerous in sagebrush and grasslands where pocket gophers and ground squirrels abound.

SPOTTED SKUNK 16½-5½-1¾-1 (420-140-44-26) Fig. 142. The Spotted Skunk is a small carnivore with soft, short fur. White spots on the forehead and cheeks, broken white stripes on the sides and back, and a white terminal

Figure 139.
Striped Skunk.

tail tassle are in sharp contrast to the jet black background. The plantigrade
feet are equipped with long claws. RANGE. W. and s.e. Wash., all of Ore.,
most of Idaho (excepting the n. and c. parts of the Panhandle), and s.w. B.C.
HABITAT. Prefers brush, canyons, farmlands, and particularly the vicinity of
farm buildings.

STRIPED SKUNK   28-11¾-3⅛-1¹⁵⁄₁₆ (710-300-80-34) Figs. 139 and 179.
This is a familiar animal with totally black, shiny fur, contrastingly marked with
a white stripe extending from the top of the head down each side of the back
to the base of the tail. A thin white stripe extends down the center of the head
between the eyes. The long, bushy tail is black and with some intermixed white
hairs. As in the case of all skunks, make your identification at a distance.
RANGE. Occurs throughout the NW, except for Vancouver Island and the w.

181

Figure 140.
Badger.

Figure 141.
River Otter.

Figure 142.
Spotted Skunk.

part of B.C. HABITAT. To be found widely and commonly throughout its range, except for the higher, montane areas. Prefers marshes, saltwater beaches, farming land, and riparian growth along streams in the dry country. So faithful are skunks to the last-named habitat that such wooded bottoms are often known locally as "skunk hollows."

RIVER OTTER 45⅓-18⅛-5¼-¹³⁄₁₆ (1,150-460-135-21) Fig. 141. This species is a large, weasel-like carnivore with a rich brown color above and a lighter shade with a silvery sheen below. It has short ears and short legs with webbed feet. The tail is thick toward the base and tapers near the tip. A broad head and snout, prominent whiskers, and short, dense fur are distinctive. Almost always seen in or near water. RANGE. Occurs in suitable habitat throughout the NW. HABITAT. Prefers the immediate vicinity of fresh or salt water, particularly lake shores, rivers, and larger streams. Scattered in occurrence and a considerable wanderer.

SEA OTTER   60-12⅖-8⅘-¾ (1,530-310-220-19) Figs. 143 and 174.   This species varies from reddish brown to very dark brown or blackish, more or less frosted with whitish. The head and neck are usually paler in color than the rest of the body. The ears are very small and the hind feet are webbed and flattened to form flippers. The tail is thick and relatively short. The front legs are short. Commonly floats and swims on its back. Much time spent in dressing the fur. RANGE. Formerly along the ocean coast of the NW, but completely extirpated shortly after the turn of the century. Has been re-introduced at several points in recent years. HABITAT. Almost entirely marine, frequenting the kelp beds just off rocky shores. Comes to shore for occasional rest periods and to give birth to the young.

Figure 143.
Sea Otter.

Figure 144.
Wolverine.

A romantic, if dangerous and difficult, occupation is that of the fur trapper. Much of the northern Rockies and the Pacific Northwest was explored in detail, not by the prospector but by the fur trapper, during the first 75 years of the 19th century. Following closely on the heels of such early explorers as David Thompson and Lewis and Clark, these men sought the Beaver and the pelts of wild mustelids, dogs, and cats. Braving the perils of mountain winters in the more or less unknown wilderness, as well as the Indians who did not always approve of the white men's invasion of their lands, the fur trappers worked alone or in small groups, searching the streams, forests, and alpine ridges for their quarry.

Much of the trapping of Marten, weasels, Fishers, River Otters, Mink, etc., had to be done during the fall and winter when the pelts were prime. A trapper would establish a line of traps, often a number of miles long, which he would regularly traverse, removing the animals caught and re-setting the traps. Considerable study and knowledge were necessary to place the traps in the best places. Marauding Coyotes and Wolverines would frequently set off traps or damage or destroy captured animals.

Deep snows, avalanches, and sudden storms might catch the trapper out on his line and many a man failed to make it home or to the next line cabin. The work appealed, however, to the independent spirit and the loner who probably would not have exchanged his occupation for any other.

185

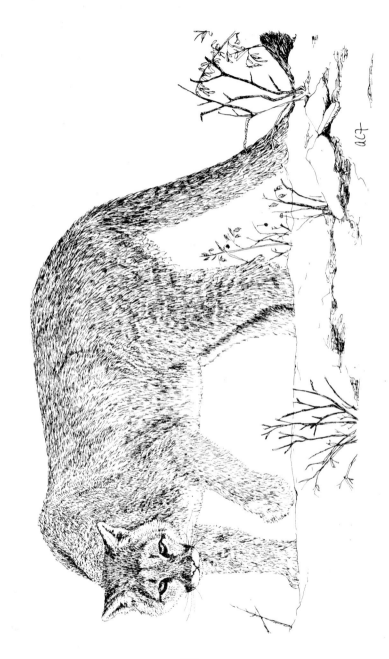

Figure 145.

CATS

The cat family contains some of the most efficient hunters among mammals. Generally, these are medium-sized to large animals with large feet and usually with long tails. The forefeet have five toes and the hind feet, four, the claws of which are sharp, curved, and retractile. The eyes are large and the medium-sized ears well developed. Long canines accompanied by broad, short jaws are well suited to the stabbing, clinging type of fighting characteristic of cats. Some of these animals have tremendous speed over short distances. The leaps of some Cougars have been measured at 30 feet on the level ground and fully 40 feet as they sped downhill. Cats stalk their prey within a few feet, then attack with several short steps and tremendous leaps. Often the weight and added inertia of the hunter on the victim's back are enough to bring about the spine-breaking death of the quarry. Cats are largely nocturnal. Their extreme wariness in the advance of man has led certain species to be driven farther and farther back into the more primitive areas until they have become uncommon or rare over their ancient ranges. Cats certainly form a fascinating part of our native fauna and much of the damage attributed to them is without feline cause, and even the existence of the Cougar is worth the price of a relatively few deer. The thrill it adds to a camper's delight or a sportsman's hunt surely merits protective measures to replenish its diminishing numbers. Three wild members of the family inhabit the Northwest.

The Cougar, or Mountain Lion as it is often called in the Rockies, has obviously all too often run afoul of man's economy. While attacks on humans are extremely rare, a few offenses have occurred on domestic stock. The biggest clamor for reduction of Cougars has come from a certain part of the sportsman element which seems to begrudge the big cat the deer it must kill for food. To illustrate the rationale of this philosophy, one of the Washington game protectors told the author of a situation some years ago in the Lake Chelan area where a shortage of deer in the early part of the hunting season caused the local nimrods to demand an investigation and removal of the Cougars in the region which, according to these persons, were eliminating the deer. The game department looked into the matter and found no Cougar, but did find that mild weather had not driven deer down to the hunting areas. This is the sort of thing that game departments continually have to put up with and it is amazing that, considering the variety of political pressures, they do as good a job as they do.

The average number of young in a litter is two, though some as large as five have been noted. The eyes open in roughly one and a half to two weeks and they are weaned in eight weeks.

The Cougar is a good climber and, when pursued by hounds, often takes to a tree where it may easily be shot. It is a noisy animal and possesses a variety of calls and screams. In 1966, the state game commission of Washington made the Cougar a game animal and set bag limits and a restricted season on it. A number of other states have done the same. Some of us even feel that it should be completely protected.

The Lynx is one of the least observed of Pacific Northwest mammals. It seems to be widely distributed in the mountain forests, even south of British Columbia, but its presence is revealed only in traps, a rare sighting, or the characteristic tracks or pug marks in winter snows. This species is one of the most graceful of mammals and has tremendous leaping abilities. In running through the woods, it rather resembles a small gray ghost flitting between the bushes and blending in well with the snow cover when such is present. It is easy to understand how the aboriginal peoples ascribed supernatural aspects to the Lynx, as well as to certain other peculiar animals.

Known also as the "Canada Lynx," this cat is a highly specialized predator, concentrating on Snowshoe Hares, with other mammal species and birds as minority foods. The construction of the cat's body, with the very large paws and long hind legs, enables it to pursue and capture hares on their own terms. Deep snows protect these rabbits from most surface enemies, but not from the Lynx.

The Lynx has a fine coat with long silky hairs. Since it has grown scarcer with the inroads of civilization, few are taken—it is protected as a furbearer in most regions—and it is doubtful they will ever increase in numbers. Only in Canada do considerable populations exist, and with the filling in of that country, especially British Columbia, the Lynx and the wolf, as well as certain other species, may show a marked decrease in number. Like the wolf, this mammal seems to retreat before the advances of civilization, while the next species to be mentioned flourishes in the broken, semi-wild areas left after logging, burning, etc.

The Bobcat is the commonest wild cat south of the U.S.-Canadian border, but has a rather restricted range north of that line. To the south, it occurs practically throughout the Northwest states, though perhaps is most numerous in logged-over land and rocky, brown areas. The animal is seldom seen except by accident as it is shy and keeps pretty well out of human sight. Just yesterday, John Weber of Pullman and the author were "birding" along upper Asotin Creek south of Clarkston, Washington, and, pausing to look at the many basaltic outcroppings along that canyon, commented on the supposition that there must be Bobcats in the area, but how rarely did one ever see one in the flesh. A pack of hounds, however, can often tree a cat and this is the common mode of capture in many places. Bobcats make interesting pets and several of the author's friends have successfully raised them. Having one of these tamed cats in one's lap is an experience. One gets the impression of the appearance of extreme alertness on the part of the animal towards such sounds as cars on nearby streets, bird calls, and human voices, responses not commonly evidenced by most house cats. Having one of these animals as a pet, like all other wild species, is a chancy thing and best not attempted.

The food of the Bobcat consists largely of rabbits, ground squirrels, mice, and birds, with other animals in lesser amounts. Small domestic animals are occasionally taken with rare attacks on larger species. The extent of utilization of mammals larger than the rabbit is not definitely known. Some indication of how such lightly-constructed mammals may subdue larger species is given in Charles Sheldon's THE WILDERNESS OF DENALI where he records a Lynx immobilizing a Dall's Sheep by leaping on its back and tearing its eyes out.

Speaking of Charles Sheldon, the reader of this guide who wishes to do more reading about mammals can hardly do better than to read that naturalist's three "wilderness" books, the aforementioned THE WILDERNESS OF DENALI, THE WILDERNESS OF THE UPPER YUKON, and THE WILDERNESS OF THE NORTH PACIFIC COAST ISLANDS. These are books that the vicarious adventurer will have a hard time putting down, once he starts reading them. Try to find the illustrated first editions in libraries, if possible, as Sheldon

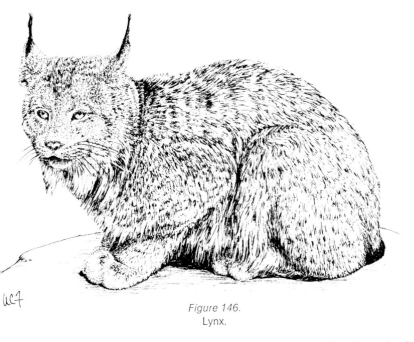

Figure 146.
Lynx.

was an expert photographer and the pictures do much to vitalize the episodes he narrates.

Charles Sheldon represented a peculiar species of outdoorsman that flourished from about the time of the Civil War to the 1930s known as the hunter-naturalist. Most of these men began their interest in wildlife as sportsmen, but gradually grew more interested in the conservation and scientific side of nature. Some became expert photographers as that art gradually developed and appropriate equipment appeared. Others took up painting and drawing. Some became accomplished mammalogists and ornithologists, while many wrote interesting and valuable books and articles about their experiences. All developed a sincere interest in the emerging fields of conservation and wildlife management, many to be leaders in these fields. Present-day environmentalists have much to thank these people for.

One of the most famous of these hunter-naturalists was George Shiras III who pioneered the art of night flashlight photography of wildlife. He wrote a number of articles and books on his experiences as an animal photographer for the National Geographic Society. One of his friends, the aforementioned Charles Sheldon, was perhaps the finest example of this outdoor "breed." Retiring early in life from a successful business career, Sheldon staged a number of expeditions to the Yukon, Alaska, and British Columbia, as well as to Mexico and the American southwest. In the north, he was particularly interested in the Dall's Sheep and the Grizzly. His previously mentioned "wilderness" books recount his adventures and studies in fascinating detail.

Sheldon's Mount McKinley book is an intriguing journal of his day-to-day experiences in that area. The prime mover in establishing Mount McKinley National Park, he campaigned to change the name of the peak back to its native "Denali." It is interesting to note that at this writing there is a strong movement to do just that.

Figure 147.
Bobcat.

PACIFIC NORTHWEST SPECIES

MOUNTAIN LION; COUGAR 78⅔-28¾-9⅞-3⅜ (2,000-730-250-85) Fig. 145. The Mountain Lion is a powerfully-built cat that may weigh as much as 180 to 200 pounds. It is tawny to grayish on the back and lighter beneath. The fur is short and the tail is long and tipped with dark brown or black. RANGE. Occurs throughout most of the NW, except n.w. and n.e. B.C. HABITAT. In the NW, prefers mt. forests and broken, semi-wooded canyon areas where its deer food is available. Greatly reduced in numbers in much of its range due largely to unwarranted persecution from portions of the hunting and ranching groups.

LYNX 36-4⅖-9-2½ (900-110-225-65) Fig. 146. This is a medium-sized bob-tailed cat. The upper parts are gray with shades of yellow; the belly is gray with faint black spots. The ears are tufted and edged with black, and prominent "sideburns" of hair are present at the jowls. The gray tail is completely surrounded at the tip with black. This feature, along with the long un-spotted legs and long, silky fur, best separates it from the Bobcat. RANGE. Throughout the NW in its favored habitat, being rare or absent from the coastal regions w. of the Cascade Mts. HABITAT. Dense coniferous forests, moving rarely in times of population expansion or starvation into the more open country.

BOBCAT 34½-6¾-6⅞-3¼ (875-170-175-82) Fig. 147. This species is similar in appearance to the Lynx, but differs from it in being smaller, having

190

spots on the body and legs, being more reddish in color, and having the black tip of the tail only over the top half and preceded by two black bars. The Bobcat's feet are small and the ear tufts and sideburns short. The fur is shorter and less silky than that of the Lynx. RANGE. Wash., Ore., and Idaho; also s. and e.c. B.C. HABITAT. Fairly common in broken, rocky areas and logged-over and forested land; also second growth timber. More adaptable to man's alteration of the environment than is the Lynx.

Early in the last century, that great genius after whom the Audubon Society is named embarked upon a program of publishing which even today boggles the mind. He would write a great treatise on the birds of North America, illustrated with life-size color paintings of all species. Then, he would write a book on the mammals of the continent, again illustrating it with his art. Next would come the amphibians and reptiles, all in color with descriptive text; and to cap all of this, a great work on the insects. The amazing thing is that much of this grandiose plan was accomplished. The bird project was completed. Audubon's notebooks contain drawings and notes on herptiles and insects. But man can only do so much. His sight almost gone and his mind failing, Audubon left the mammals to his sons and his friend, John Bachman, to complete, the first work on the mammals of North America, a truly heroic achievement.

Figure 148.
Heads of Bobcat (left) and Lynx (right).

191

Figure 149.
Northern Fur Seal.

SEALS

Like the whales, the seals and sea lions are both strongly restricted to salt water and highly adapted for an aquatic existence. The forefeet are flipper-like, small, used mostly for swimming, and of little value on land. The hind feet are fin-shaped and in many species cannot be turned forward, so must be stretched posteriorly and are of value only in swimming, which is done mainly with the hind feet. The fur is mostly short and dense. Seals are beautifully streamlined and amazingly supple in motion and agile in their watery world. One must look for them in salt water and, unless they are seen on land, only the head and shoulders usually are visible. These are carnivorous mammals and their food is largely made up of fish. Five species occur in Northwest marine waters.

The Northern Fur Seal bears one of the finer furs in the mammal group and was almost hunted to extinction for its pelt. Now, fortunately, its fur harvest is under strict international control and these animals produce a steady supply for milady's use. Like all such female clothing, however, furs are subject to the whims and vagaries of fashion. The author can well remember a period in the 1930s when every woman, his mother included, could not consider herself properly attired in public without a fur seal coat. The price went up accordingly. At present, one seldom sees coats of this fur, but the passage of a few years may completely alter the styles.

The Northern Fur Seal breeds on the Pribilof Islands in the Bering Sea where the young are born, one per litter, to cows grouped into zealously guarded harems by the large bulls. While a cow may weigh as much as 100 pounds, a bull may amount to six times that weight. During the winter migration, Northern Fur Seals pass down the North American and Asiatic coasts, often making a round trip of 6,000 miles. The principal food of these animals is non-commercial fish and squids.

Careful studies of this species have made possible the controlled harvest of pelts. The three-year-old non-breeding males are cropped in part, usually some 65,000 individuals being taken annually for a value of some six million dollars. In the processing of the fur, the coarse guard hairs are removed, to expose the dense, soft underfur which gives the pelts their value. Much credit for research on this valuable mammal should go to a prominent Pacific Northwest mammalogist, Victor B. Scheffer, a leading authority on marine mammals of the world. Anyone interested further in the Northern Fur Seal should consult the writings of Dr. Scheffer and his associates.

The Northern, or Steller's, Sea Lion lacks a coat of underfur, having only the coarse guard hairs, and thus does not figure importantly in the fur trade. It does, however, get into man's economy through its habit of preying on halibut and other fish in nets and on lines. This species bred at one time along the Pacific Coast on suitable rocky places, but their pupping grounds are now considerably reduced. Sea lions breed in colonies, usually 10-15 cows per bull. The single pup is born in May or early June. Food consists of various kinds of fish, especially herring, as well as squids. This species has been consistently persecuted by fishermen who regard it as a competitor for their catch. Since the numbers of sea lions have decreased markedly in recent years, it would appear that strict management and protection should be afforded these animals, based on proper scientific study.

The alternate common name commemorates Georg Wilhelm Steller, naturalist on Vitus Bering's expedition to Alaska in 1740-42. While at that place, Steller studied the birds and mammals, particularly the Northern Sea Lion and the Steller's Sea Cow, the latter unhappily now extinct. The Steller's Jay was named after this pioneer North Pacific Coast naturalist.

The California Sea Lion is about half the size of the Northern Sea Lion and varies in color from yellowish brown to black, usually appearing black when wet. It is the trained seal of marine land, circus, and zoo shows, and is a playful, friendly animal capable of being trained to perform numerous tricks. Unlike the previously described species, the California Sea Lion does not breed in closely maintained harems. A single young is born to the female in early summer. Most bulls do not breed until at least five years old; cows, in their third year. Food consists of squids and fish. This species has a honking bark, unlike the roar of the Northern Sea Lion. Numbers have been killed by fishermen who consider it a predator on food fish. Investigation has not revealed these seals to be more than an occasional nuisance in this respect, however.

The hot rays of the late afternoon sun blazed down on the motionless waters among the mud flats along the delta of the Stillaguamish River where it empties into Puget Sound. The three kayaks and their occupants moved slowly

Figure 150.
Northern Sea Lion.

Figure 151.
California Sea Lion.

through the heat-stricken maze toward the end of a trip from the mountains, the purpose of which was to gain first-hand information for a chapter on water for a book on Mount Pilchuck. The mouth of the river had been reorganized since our map had been published and we had come to the Sound several miles below our proposed final destination and the location of the waiting cars to take us back to Seattle. As a result, we had a long paddle to make northward through the pungent flats against an ebbing tide. Suntans were rapidly turning to sunburns. The author, having resigned his pants and shirt to a bikini-clad partner of his canoe, was sizzling to a well-done turn in a pair of swim trunks. It was in this situation that we became friends with a group of Harbor Seals. Apparently curious, they pushed their heads up above the water around us, looking us over briefly, and then submerging to change their position. Seemingly friendly and not fearing us at all, they accompanied the party practically the entire distance of our mudflat journey. As this episode demonstrated, this seal is an inshore species, being common in harbors, bays, and other protected waters and is probably the one member of the order most commonly seen by Northwest coastal people.

The Harbor Seal feeds entirely on fish, cephalopod mollusks, and crustaceans, especially crabs. Mating takes place in midsummer with usually a delayed implantation of the blastocyst with the gestation of some nine months then resulting in the birth of a single pup the following early summer. The young seal begins to catch fish within a few days after birth and is weaned after about two months.

The giant of all seals, the Northern Elephant Seal, occasionally strays north from its main haunts along the Mexican and Californian coasts to appear in more northern waters. The bull is immense, reaching a length of just under 20 feet and a weight of two and a half to as much as four tons. The female is somewhat smaller. The Elephant Seal gets its name from the trunk-like proboscis which occurs on the snout of the male. When the male is snorting, as in territorial disputes, the proboscis is enlarged and bent down into the mouth where it apparently acts as a resonating organ. Small harems are maintained by the mature bulls. A single pup is born to the female which was bred during the winter breeding season. The food consists of fish, small sharks, and squids. Although not common in coastal waters, the animal with its immense size and general light coloration should be easily identifiable.

Figure 152.
Harbor Seal.

PACIFIC NORTHWEST SPECIES

NORTHERN FUR SEAL Total lengths: males, 7-8 feet; females, 5 feet. Fig. 149. A medium-sized seal, dark brown in color (females are somewhat paler) with grayish on the shoulders and foreneck and with very fine underfur beneath coarse guard hairs. The males bear a prominent crest on the forehead and the snout is short. RANGE and HABITAT. Common in migration off the NW ocean coast in late fall and spring and occasionally in winter. Usually seen well off shore, but sometimes comes into coastal waters. Main migration approaches within about 3 miles of the Wash. coast, near the Umatilla Reef w. of Cape Alava. Immature individuals may wander into Puget Sound.

NORTHERN SEA LION Total lengths: males, 10-12 feet; females, 8-9 feet. Fig. 150. The color of this species varies from tawny through yellowish brown to dark brown. Underfur is lacking, as is a crest on the head of the male. These animals are large and a bull may weigh a ton and a female half a ton. Large size and brownish color distinctive. RANGE and HABITAT. Occurs in coastal waters along all of the Pacific NW. Certain rocks and islands, such as the Quillayute Needles off Wash. coast, used as summer and winter hauling grounds, but does not breed along Wash. coast. Breeds at several places along Ore. coast and off the Scott Islands of B.C. During winter, may enter more protected waters, even penetrating mouths of larger rivers.

CALIFORNIA SEA LION Total lengths: males, 7-8 feet; females, 5-6 feet. Fig. 151. This species varies from light brownish to dull blackish, usually appearing black when wet. The high forehead, or crest, of the bull is distinctive, as is the size and color. No underfur is present in this species. RANGE and HABITAT. Occasional visitor along ocean coasts of Ore. and Wash. up to and including the s. coast of B.C. Less numerous in the n. part of its NW range.

HARBOR SEAL Total length, 4-6 feet. Fig. 152. A small seal whose body is grayish or yellowish and covered thickly with dark grayish, brownish, or blackish spots and blotches. The shape of the head is dog-like, and the hind flippers are always extended backwards. There is no underfur, nor does the species possess external ears. RANGE and HABITAT. Occurs commonly, at least formerly, along the inshore marine waters of the Pacific NW, including Puget Sound, San Juan and Gulf Islands regions, Inner Passage, etc. Has been recorded as far up the Columbia R. as The Dalles. Numbers reduced in recent years from thousands to hundreds, according to Victor B. Scheffer (1969).

NORTHERN ELEPHANT SEAL Total lengths: males, 14-16 feet; females, 7-14 feet. Fig. 153. This very large seal is dark grayish to tannish or light brownish in color. No external ears or underfur. Male possesses a large, inflatable proboscis which has given the species its name. RANGE and HABITAT. Recorded occasionally, mostly as males, off the ocean coast of the NW, mainly in the spring and early fall. Sometimes seen from land; one record for Puget Sound. N. to the Queen Charlotte Islands.

Figure 153.
Northern Elephant Seal.

197

Figure 154.
Elk.

198

DEER

The deer of the Pacific Northwest, members of the Family Cervidae (Order Artiodactyla), comprise a group of our most popular game mammals. The amount of money spent to hunt these species runs into millions of dollars annually in this region alone. The number of hunters stalking these elusive quarries may approach a million persons. To many of us, however, these animals rate more importantly as spectacular representatives of the mammal kingdom which, being diurnal, can often be observed if visited in their native haunts. They are able swimmers and, notably the Moose and Caribou, will often take to water to elude their pursuers. Deer are chiefly browsers with the typical four-chambered stomach of the ruminants. It is because of this feeding habit that they most frequently interfere with man's economy, damaging gardens, orchards, and reforestation projects. Usually, however, this occurs in areas or seasons when the natural food has become scarce and may be aggravated by over-population. Deer, when zealously protected and not adequately harvested, have a tendency to become more numerous than their natural environment will maintain.

The forests, swamps, brushlands, and plains of the Northwest support a great number of these animals, constituting a valuable natural resource. Five species of deer occur in the region covered by this book.

The Elk is the Northwest's finest game mammal and enjoys a fairly wide distribution in the mountainous and high plateau areas. Deliberate in movement, stately in appearance, the sight of a bull is a fine reward for a hike into Elk country. The sizes of populations of Elk in the region have varied considerably in the last hundred years, mostly increasing in many areas. On their trip in the early 1800s, Lewis and Clark reported game animals of all kinds to be scarce in the Bitterroots of Idaho. The great 1910 fire, while destroying millions of acres of first-growth timber, did open up the environment making possible the establishment and luxuriant growth of browse species of vegetation, thus greatly enhancing the increase of the Elk, as well as the Mule Deer. The large Yakima Elk herd, estimated at 10,000 animals, is considered to be descended from 21 individuals brought to the central Cascades from the Rocky Mts. in the early 1900s.

The Mule Deer is the common representative of the family in the Northwest. Originally thought to be two species, studies in British Columbia have shown areas of intergradation so that the two, the "mule deer" and the "black-tailed deer" must be considered conspecific. West of the Cascade crest the name "black-tailed deer" is commonly used, while to the eastward, "mule deer" is the common one, designating as they do the two races of the species in our region, both of which are easily identifiable by the dichotomous (two-branching) antlers and the black-tipped tail.

The winter of 1968-69 brought up a number of deer management problems in northeastern Washington where Mule and White-tailed Deer were forced to congregate in yards and along highways. Many tons of hay and high-protein pellets were fed to deer by the state game department. In spite of food shortages, game protectors consider drivers on highways and domestic dogs as the greatest causes of winter deer mortality. One example of this is the number of 125 deer killed on the 30-mile stretch of highway between Colville and Chewelah. An estimated minimum of 500 deer were killed by dogs in six counties of Eastern Washington in the same winter, with 44 reported killed by

Figure 155.
Mule Deer.

dogs alone in Stevens County. Ralph Johnson, long-time game protector in Pend Oreille County, informed the author that he has found as many as a hundred head killed at night by trains in the canyon near the Chain Lakes deer yards in that county.

One of the pleasures of fishing along a stream or lake in the evening when the sun has set behind the ridge and the shadows are beginning to stretch out is the opportunity to see a deer as it slowly, step by watchful step, comes down to the margin to drink. This mammal is among nature's most graceful things and perhaps no animal gives the casual traveler or camper more of a thrill.

In Washington, the White-tailed Deer is most numerous in the northeastern part of the state. There, it prefers the wooded thickets and areas along water. The animal thrives in such places and its numbers support an active hunt in the fall and early winter, attracting thousands of nimrods. In spite of the pressure, these managed harvests permit an adequate population reserve to remain. The state game department has done a good and necessary job in handling the populations of our native game mammals, considering the pressures of complete protection from the ultra-conservationists and excessive desires for bars-down hunting from the ultra-hunters and game hogs. One can but speculate on the fact that as the Pacific Northwest's population of humans increases, very careful management will have to be extended to more and more of our wildlife, both large and small. The land acquisition program for the establishment of preserves and refuges carried on by the Washington game department should do much to alleviate the inroads of a burgeoning human population in that state, both for the consumers and non-consumers of game, and all mammals for that matter.

The White-tailed Deer is easily identified by its large white-margined tail which it waves excitedly when alarmed. Constant vigilance and alertness seem to be the necessary requirements for successful existence. Foraging is done mostly in twilight and at night. Regular trips are made to water and to salt licks. The latter are valuable means of controlling deer populations and areas occupied. Deer feed along the sides of trails which may be used for years at a time. Breeding occurs in the late fall, and after a gestation of just under 200 days the fawns (usually two) are born, often in May or June, and begin to move with the doe by mid July or early August. The young are weaned in three to four months. Male fawns may be easily distinguished from female fawns by the significantly larger spots on the hide of the former. Most does do not breed till their second year.

The Moose is the largest deer in North America, as in the world, but is represented in the Pacific Northwest only in southern British Columbia, northeastern Washington, and northern, central, and eastern Idaho. The species is unique in appearance and does not even closely resemble any other member of the deer family.

While feeding on a variety of leaves, mostly deciduous, the Moose also utilizes aquatic vegetation, frequently standing partly or almost completely submerged in the water to secure this material. It is a common sight in Moose country to observe a bull or cow standing in the water repeatedly submerging its head and shoulders while pulling up sub-surface vegetation. The Moose does not usually form herds, as does the Elk, nor does it commonly yard in large numbers like the smaller deer. Deep snows are not a problem with this

Figure 156.
White-tailed Deer.

long-legged animal and it maintains its solitude both winter and summer. The rut occurs in early fall, resulting in a gestation period for the young of some 240 days. Single calves, less frequently twins, are the rule. The young Moose at birth usually weighs about 30 to 40 pounds, but grows rapidly, reaching a weight of as much as 600 pounds by the end of the first year. The characteristic antlers are shed during the winter, new ones beginning growth the following summer to reach maturity by late summer.

The Caribou, which is represented by the woodland race in the Pacific Northwest, is distributed in the far northern region around the North Pole, both in the Old and New Worlds. It is a wonderfully adapted animal, with large feet to enable it to progress rapidly over soft spongy tundra as well as snow, and the digestive system to handle the various lichens and mosses on which it feeds. Antlers are present in both sexes, a unique feature for North American deer.

For centuries, the Caribou formed an important part of the food supply of the Eskimos and northern Indians. In fact, in many places in the barren grounds, life would have been impossible without the presence of this animal. There is some doubt in the author's mind as to what the future of the Caribou will be. The numbers seem to be decreasing strongly across the North, due not only to more effective hunting techniques, but to the obliteration of much habitat, especially by fire. It has been fashionable for hunters and some so-called experts to blame the Wolves for all this, but we must remember that the Wolf and the Caribou lived together for ages. Ecological change would seem to be the enemy of this species, along with increased hunting pressure by white sportsmen, the numbers of which are growing at an amazing rate in the once "forbidden" North. The opening up of this region, much of which has taken place since World War II, is nothing less than spectacular and places that 40 to 50 years ago could be reached only by well-equipped expeditions are now merely stops on sight-seeing tours for recreationists. Careful evaluation of the animal populations and their environments, accompanied by careful management and interest in the permanence of our resources—not just the use of them to lure a few easy bucks for today—backed up by rigorous action of dedicated conservationists will be necessary to preserve this species, as well as many others of the northern part of the continent. It is to be hoped that the plight of the Caribou in the northern regions will be an object lesson to us in the Pacific Northwest, where the Caribou of British Columbia will be adequately cared for. Unfortunately, the Caribou population in northeastern Washington and extreme northern Idaho is very small, almost a token one.

Caribou feed principally on lichens, a fact strongly restricting their distribution. Poor of eyesight, but with good senses of hearing and smell, they are both curious and shy. They are strongly gregarious and are most often seen in herds, ranging from family groups to the many thousands that assemble for migration in the tundra areas of the far North. The rut occurs in the fall with a gestation period of 240 days, producing usually a single fawn. After a few months, small antlers appear in both male and female.

Figure 157.
Moose.

204

PACIFIC NORTHWEST SPECIES

ELK 87-4-22-8¼ (2,200-100-550-210) Fig. 154. The Elk is a large deer-like animal with brown or reddish-brown body and a large yellow rump patch. The males have chestnut-brown manes and, in the late summer and fall, widely-spreading antlers. Elk tails are yellow with no dark markings and their 4½-5 foot body lengths are distinctive. RANGE. Occurs in suitable habitat throughout the NW, with the exception of w.c. and n.w. B.C. Found on Vancouver Island. HABITAT. To be found irregularly, mostly as protected or introduced, in mt. and foothill regions, preferring the semi-open forests, particularly sub-alpine country in summer. The coastal race (Roosevelt, or Olympic, Elk) may occur down to sea level in certain areas. In winter, protected "yards" in river bottoms and canyons are frequented.

MULE DEER 64-5-20½-9 (1,700-130-510-225) Figs. 155, 159, and 173; Color Plate 14. A medium-sized deer standing 3½-4 feet in height and averaging 200 pounds in weight. In winter, the color of the back is grayish and in summer it becomes reddish or buff. There are white throat and rump patches and the tail may be white, tipped with black ("mule deer") or solidly black ("black-tailed deer"). The large ears give the animal one of its names. The antlers are typically two-branched and not with the tines branching from a main beam as in the White-tailed Deer. Runs with a bounding "bouncing ball" gait, with all four feet coming down together, with the forefeet before the hind feet. RANGE. Throughout the NW, in suitable habitat. HABITAT. W. of the Cascade crest, prefers dense woods and coniferous forests; e. of the crest, frequents mostly rocky, brushy areas and open meadows, yellow pine forests, and extensive burns, but denser growth in some places. Occasionally found in scattered coniferous groves in open desert country.

WHITE-TAILED DEER 64-10-19-4¾ (1,700-225-475-120) Figs. 156 and 160. This species is reddish to tan in summer and bluish-gray in winter. The bushy tail is white underneath and is carried as a distinctive flag when the animal runs. The buck's antlers are in the form of single right and left beams with the tines branching therefrom. Gallops by means of a "rocking-horse" gait in which the hind feet are placed ahead of the forefeet. RANGE. Occurs irregu-larly e. of the Cascades in s. B.C. and in Wash. (except for islands and river bank areas of the Columbia R. in Wahkiakum Co.). Found in proper habitat in Ore., except for the s.e. desert area and in Idaho, except for s. desert region. HABITAT. Dense forests, deciduous woods, and extensive brushy places of low to intermediate elevations, as well as marshy areas near water. Seeks more thickly vegetated habitats than does the Mule Deer and shows a marked tendency to occur near water.

MOOSE males: 120-3-30-10 (3,000-75-775-250) Figs. 157, 160, and 185; Color Plate 13. This large deer stands 7 or more feet tall at the shoulders. Adults weigh 900 to 1,000 pounds and are similar in size to horses. Cows are about 3/4 the size of bulls. Moose are blackish brown in color with a protu-berant, rounded snout; short tail; and a "bell" or flap of skin hanging under-neath the throat. The males have massive palmate antlers with the tines pro-jecting from the edges. RANGE. B.C. (except for the s.w. and Vancouver Island areas), n.e. Wash., and n. and e. Idaho. Also Okanogan Highlands of Wash. Increases significantly with adequate protection (especially against

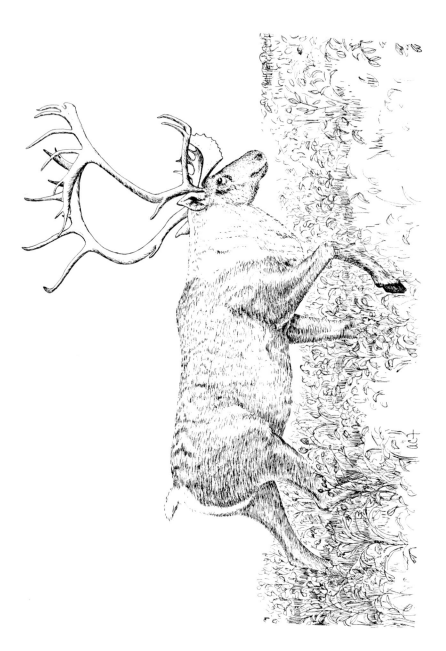

Figure 158.

Figure 159.
Mule Deer with antlers in the velvet (Pole).

poaching). HABITAT. Prefers shrubby, mixed coniferous and deciduous forests, particularly near water. Commonly found in immediate vicinity of lakes, both montane and alpine, where it feeds on submerged aquatic vegetation. Also in marshy or swampy areas along streams and rivers.

CARIBOU 96-8-24-6⅔ (2,400-200-600-165) Fig. 158. A medium-sized deer with semi-palmate antlers occurring in both sexes, although those of the female are somewhat smaller than the male racks and are occasionally lacking. The animals are blackish brown or umber colored, darkening to nearly black on the lower legs. The neck, belly, rump, and under side of the tail are grayish white. The head and neck are darker in the more southern populations. The hooves are heavy and wide, serving as snowshoes. RANGE. Occurs in extreme n. Idaho and n.e. Wash. and the n., w.c., and s. (except extreme s.e. tip) portions of B.C. The isolated race in the Queen Charlotte Islands (*R. t. dawsoni*) is now, regrettably, extinct. All the Caribou in the NW are the "Woodland Caribou" (*R. t. caribou*). The population in s.e. B.C. and the remnants in n.e. Wash. and n. Idaho are sometimes referred to as the "Mountain Caribou (*R. t. montanus*)." They are, at least, a subdivision (deme) of the Woodland Caribou type. HABITAT. Prefers montane and subalpine areas of mts., especially where lichen food of the proper type may be obtainable.

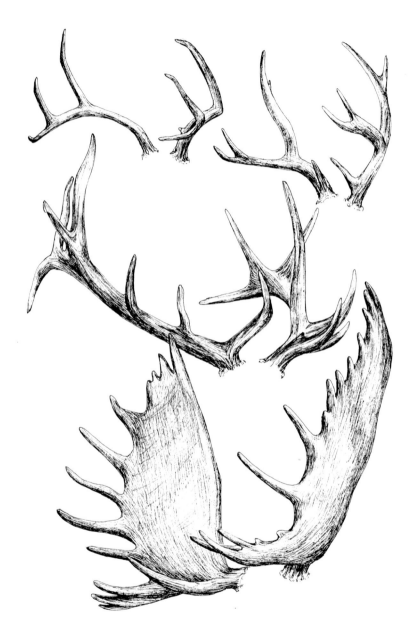

Figure 160.
Antlers. White-tailed Deer (upper left); Mule Deer (upper right); Elk (center); Moose (lower).

As regards the conservation of mammals in the Pacific Northwest, they are well protected by laws regulating their hunting or trapping. Wildlife managers have developed techniques for population analysis, birth and mortality evaluation, and hunter harvest measurement, with the result that season and bag limits reflect the amount of consumption that each game and furbearing species can stand. Preservationists might object to any hunting, but we must remember that natural resources have many uses and that species can be over-protected, such that their numbers may exceed the carrying capacity of their habitat. One has only to see the condition of the trees and shrubs in Tsavo National Park in Africa to experience a case of over-protection, of elephants in that case.

The non-game mammals are coming under protection, too, as many states now have legal provision for their safeguarding and they no longer can be indiscriminantly destroyed. Rightfully so. We remember an excellent editorial in the *Lewiston* (Idaho) *Tribune* regarding the right of an animal to live. We like to talk about our rights, but we are far from being the only animals on this planet. The greatest danger to wild animals, of course, is the destruction of their native habitats.

Many of us who have lived for 50 or more years in the Pacific Northwest have seen many environmental changes in that region. The Columbia Basin project converted thousands of acres of sagebrush and grassland into irrigated farms. Cities have greatly increased in size and rural acreage plots have spread far beyond corporate city limits. Thousands of miles of roads have eliminated great areas of natural habitat. Higher crop prices have increased farming intensity, removing the hedgerows and field corner brush patches in the Palouse, to the detriment of pheasants, quail, and Brewer's sparrows. Great tracts of forest have fallen before chain saws. It is true that much logged land has been replanted but many of us—foresters and laymen alike—often (conveniently) overlook the permanent destruction of the forest floor habitats and niches as well as microfaunas that take place in clear cutting.

An increasing concern to wild land managers is the expanding numbers of visitors to the natural areas. We are literally "loving" our wilderness to death. A few visitors to an alpine lake and surrounding meadow per year probably caused little disruption of that habitat but a weekend invasion of a hundred-person-strong hiking club may well set that lake and meadow back a number of years.

Increased hiking and camping activities in the national forests and parks are an unfortunate spinoff of the current interest in the environment—one that, if not quickly and properly managed, may defeat much of our effort to preserve those very natural areas.

The growing need for more energy may rephrase the statement from "which source—hydroelectric, fossil fuel, or nuclear—should be utilized" to "whether all three, developed to their utmost limits, will be enough?".

It seems most likely that 50 or 100 years from now, all the natural, wild land will have to be protected in preserves of some kind—in state or national parks, wildlife refuges, natural areas, and national forest wilderness and primitive areas. National forests are subject to logging, so are only semi-satisfactory as nature preserves. It behooves us to put as much wild land in permanent protection as possible.

Figure 161.
Pronghorn.

210

PRONGHORNS

The Pronghorn, or "antelope" as it is more commonly but less correctly called, is a unique mammal, both in the Pacific Northwest and North America. The sole surviving species of a once proud group, the Pronghorn represents the very embodiment of the open, wind-swept plains.

The following quotations of Pronghorn peculiarities are from a rare and very interesting book, FIFTEEN YEARS' SPORT AND LIFE IN THE HUNTING GROUNDS OF WESTERN AMERICA AND BRITISH COLUMBIA by the British sportsman and "empire builder," William A. Baillie-Grohman.

"In the Old days, when one struck a country where little hunting has been done, the once much-talked-of "flagging" of antelopes gave fair sport. By displaying on the top of any rising ground a red handkerchief tied to a stick, so that it should flutter in the breeze, it was easy to decoy a band, particularly during the rutting time, up to short rifle range, for the antelope in its primitive condition exhibits extraordinary curiosity. The shooting itself on such occasions was, of course, a very tame proceeding, but the animal's amusing tactics were interesting to watch. Now approaching at a trot the fluttering rag that had aroused their insatiable curiosity, then circling to one side, or turning back altogether but looking over their shoulders, till they stopped and again faced the flag, angry stamping of the forefeet betokening their impatience; then resuming their progress towards the flag at a mincing gait, they would finally, if the wind did not betray the hidden watcher, come up quite close. . . .

"Much has been written about the fleetness of the antelope, no animal, not even the fleetest greyhound, being able, so it is said, to overtake it. That this is not always true I can state with some positiveness, for I know occasionally one strikes bands of antelope that can be overtaken on a moderately fast horse. I have done so on several occasions, killing one or two out of the band with my six-shooter. Another circumstance for which it is difficult to offer a reasonable explanation is the obstinacy they evince in continuing their course in a straight line, irrespective of the obvious danger into which it takes them. . . . In one instance, I distinctly remember, a four-horse wagon followed our party at an interval of not more than 150 yds. or, at the most, 200 yds. A band of antelope, numbering between twenty and thirty head, actually crossed the trail in this gap without evincing much fear, and as if nothing could turn them from the line they had once decided upon."

Bucks form harems of up to 15 does during the mating season and no little fighting is done between rival males. Gestation amounts to 230-240 days with the kids being born in May, usually one per female at first and then the does have twins in subsequent years. The young Pronghorn weighs only a few pounds at birth, but grows rapidly and can outrun a man by its fourth day of life. The young usually remain with the female for a year or so, except when new kids are being born. As a result, does are usually seen in company of yearlings and just-born infants.

*   *   *

PRONGHORN 58-4-17-6½ (1,350-100-430-165) Figs. 161 and 162; Color Plate 14. The Pronghorn stands about three feet high at the shoulders and weighs 100 to 125 pounds when mature. It is a slim hoofed animal with tan or yellow upper parts and a white belly and rump. The short, heavy horns are curved slightly backward and have a forward-projecting prong. RANGE.

Figure 162.
Buck Pronghorn in typical grassland habitat (Pole).

Occurs in restricted areas in e.c. and s.e. Ore., s. Idaho, and the Yakima Firing Range area of e. Wash. HABITAT. Prefers the open sagebrush and grassland plains. Much reduced from its former post-glacial range.

A number of families like that of the Pronghorn are down to a single species and some may well become completely extinct in a few hundred years. Man should not share the sole responsibility for extinction, as it is a natural process and thousands of forms have disappeared from the earth long before man evolved. Even at the present time, certain forces or environmental conditions may be acting against some animals. Ecological changes too rapid for particular animals to keep up with, sudden catastrophic upheavals, droughts of severe intensity, glacial advances, rapid cooling or heating up of climates—all of these and many more have rendered life untenable for certain species. During the last glaciation, a number of giant animals, such as the cave bear, woolly mammoth, dire wolf, giant buffalo, and the great, bear-sized beaver flourished and then completely disappeared, some of these within the last few thousand years. Perhaps the big Alaska brown bear is one of the last of these Pleistocene giants. Their origins and extinctions remain mysteries—all the more exciting because these animals lived in our very Northwest region.

BOVIDS

Members of the bovid, or cattle, family are distinguished by having true horns consisting of horny sheathes covering bony cores. These structures may be present in both sexes. Lateral toes are incomplete and sometimes lacking as are the upper canines. Though the Buffalo will never re-extend its range from which it has been extirpated, it is, through rigid control, regaining a foothold and may some day become again a familiar sight in at least part of our plains country. Its very size, however, may prevent it from becoming a "convenient" neighbor as the land is more densely settled, except in such preserves as the national parks. Studies have and are being made continually on the management of the Mountain Goat and the Mountain Sheep in the hopes of allowing more extensive hunting of these elusive beasts. Though the Mountain Sheep, or Bighorn as it is commonly called in the Rockies region, has been pushed into the wilderness by the crowding of man, its present numbers are substantial and the remoteness of its haunts promises to allow continued population growth. Only the largest predators, including the eagles, are natural enemies of our bovids and their greatest mortality is due to hazards of their perilous habitats, as in the case of the sheep and goats. Rock slides account for a number each year, and heavy snows and ice, besides making them more vulnerable to predators, cover their food supply, causing the death of the weakened or less resourceful individuals. One can well say that this group includes animals the sight of which in the wild is a moment to be remembered.

The Buffalo, or Bison as is the official name at present, were and are inhabitants of non-forested grasslands. Though once found nearly coast to coast through the United States and in the interior of the Pacific Northwest, over the grassy plains, they are now restricted to small sites established by man. They feed primarily on grasses, but when these are hidden under snow or otherwise unavailable, the animals turn to sagebrush or other browse. This species is polygamous, a single bull supporting and defending his harem from encroaching males. Breeding takes place from July to October and the gestation period lasts for nine months. Cows are able to produce until they are at least 28 years old. Usually a single offspring is born, but twins are not uncommon.

Once highly sought after for meat and hides, Buffalo at present offer little more than esthetic value, due to their scarcity. They are difficult to maintain in the wild unless rigidly protected, as they now are in North America. It is believed that the horse had at least as much to do as the rifle in the near extinction of the Buffalo and that before the introduction of the horse early in the 18th century, the plains Indians did little to threaten the numbers then extant. Nothing, however, could withstand the White hide hunter. The one-time population has been estimated at 60 million in this continent, but by 1889, they had been reduced to less than 1,000. They have since increased and are no longer in danger of complete annihilation.

It was long the practice of the ancients, as well as of primitive peoples, to select certain animal species as representing the apotheosis of some natural phenomenon, trait, or extreme. Following this practice, we might select the Mountain Goat as the master or spirit of the high places, representing in itself all the mystique of sheer cliff and frightening pinnacle. Romanticism aside, the Mountain Goat is an amazing animal, so well adapted is it in structure and behavior for its fated existence. Its white coat makes it appear, when viewed

Figure 163.

from a distance, like a small patch of snow, a whitened and weathered stump, or a granite boulder. Its hooves enable it to gain purchase on narrow shelves and ledges and its wonderful sense of balance makes possible leaps and steps that would challenge the surest-footed alpinist.

Mountain Goats are fairly common in the Cascades and Olympics of Washington and many of the ranges of British Columbia, and no hiking adventure is complete without the sighting of these most expert of climbers. They may commonly be seen in Mount Rainier National Park, as well as in many other high places in the region covered by this manual. For some years, goats have been observed along some of the lower cliffs on Mount Si from a location just north of the city of North Bend, Washington. There is a place on the Lochsa River of northern Idaho where goats are commonly visible and which is conspicuously marked by road signs.

After a gestation rate of some 147 to 178 days, a single kid is born, although twinning has been reported. The new-born offspring measures only about a foot in height and weighs about seven pounds. A female is two and a half years old before breeding and may bear young only every other year.

One of the finest stories about Mountain Goats is related in THE MAMMALS AND BIRDS OF MOUNT RAINIER NATIONAL PARK by Walter P. Taylor and William T. Shaw. The John B. Flett referred to was long a ranger and student of Mount Rainier's animals and plants. The quotation follows:

"Flett relates an incident from his wealth of experience with goats which well illustrates their curiosity where any unusual object is concerned. His party on coming down the north slope of Puyallup Glacier after a strenuous hike from Indian Henrys suddenly encountered 25 goats feeding as usual on the tender grass and sedges above timberline. The goats scurried off across the slope and into the upper timberline meadows. Camp was established about three-fourths of a mile beyond them. After supper and a little rest Flett and a young man named Phillips took kodaks and went in pursuit. The goats first caught sight of Flett, who was approaching them from in front, while Phillips was drawing in on them from the rear. A big billy on a knoll centered all his attention on Flett. As the man crawled in a zigzag course closer and closer the goat became more interested than ever. By this time Flett was now only 150 feet from the goat; Phillips, meantime, had approached him from behind to within 30 feet. The billy became uneasy, shaking his head in a threatening manner. Flett tucked his handkerchief under his shirt collar and let it hang down to a point resembling a goat's beard. Then he confidently crept along over the snow toward the goat. The latter began to stamp his feet, shake his head, and throw up his hind quarters. Phillips, meantime, had assumed an erect position not far from the goat. Flett attempted to imitate the goat's actions, spatting the snow with his hands and throwing his legs in the air. The goat's curiosity was aroused to the highest pitch. When Flett uttered an imitation *em ba-ah* Phillips laughed. The billy turned and, seeing Phillips standing alongside, gave a leap into the air, hitting the earth with a bound at a much reduced altitude toward the glacier, and soon disappearing over the crag. Flett followed his tracks until it became too dangerous to go further, the cliff at this point being about 2,000 feet high. In five or ten minutes the goats were seen crossing the glacier, led by the big billy. They headed for a precipitous bluff on the opposite side and proceeded to climb to the summit."

Another characteristic mammal of the high mountains, the Mountain Sheep

Figure 164.
Mountain Goat.

or Bighorn, is very scarce in most parts of the Northwest, particularly south of the U.S.-Canadian border. Small nuclei have been re-introduced into a number of mountainous places and it is to be hoped that this species may increase in numbers, as the appearance of a ram silhouetted against the sky on some prominent rocky buttress is one of the finest of all nature's sights.

Our North American Bighorns belong to a great group of such animals of several species whose range swings through Asia, as has been so interestingly described by James Clark in his THE GREAT ARC OF THE WILD SHEEP. Some biologists consider our sheep to be conspecific with the Old World populations, either in whole or in part, emphasizing again the close relationships that many American mammals, especially those of the Pacific Northwest, have with similar forms in Asia. Other species falling into this pattern are the Elk and Caribou.

The rutting period of the Mountain Sheep is in early winter with the single young (less commonly twins) produced in early summer after a gestation of 180 days. The lambs are born in an advanced state of development and are able to follow along behind the mother shortly after birth. Grass and succulent foliage are the preferred fare but a wide variety of plants are eaten during unfavorable times. Feeding occurs in the morning and afternoon until late at night, between which times the animals rest either by sunning themselves or, at night, by sleeping near the crest of a ridge, often with a natural protection behind them. During the rut, the rams will move from herd to herd to breed and duels over certain females may result in the death of the loser, though more commonly the vanquished individual merely moves on, leaving the favored ewe to the victor.

The finest of all animal stories is KRAG, THE KOOTENAY RAM written by that master of storytellers, Ernest Thompson Seton. No student of the wilds can really appreciate the Mountain Sheep without reading this beautiful tale which is based to a certain extent on actual facts. A photograph and additional information on this ram and old Scotty MacDougall who killed it are to be found in the book by Baillie-Grohman referred to in the chapter on the Pronghorn.

The Dall's, or Thin-horn, Sheep occurs in only the northern-most part of the Pacific Northwest, but two color races are present. The Dall's, in its typical form, is pure white. Most of the sheep in northern British Columbia are the dark Stone's Sheep. Two of Charles Sheldon's books, those of the wildernesses of the upper Yukon and Denali (Mount McKinley) deal extensively with his studies of *Ovis dalli* and are well worth the reading. The author of this manual has visited a number of the places in McKinley Park where Sheldon studied and collected his sheep specimens and can only marvel at the stamina that this man had as exhibited in his field work. The species was named for the naturalist who made such extensive studies in Alaska in the early days, William Healey Dall. This most remarkable man, in his 82 years of life, endured frightening hardships and amazing adventures to unearth and record facts about the fauna of the ocean and the far north. He was nearly 70 when he published his monumental biography of his friend, Spencer Fullerton Baird, founder of the natural history work of the Smithsonian Institution. Your author considers himself most fortunate to be the proud owner of Dall's personal copy of this book. Associations of this kind add much to the memories of the white sheep of the northern mountains!

217

Figure 165.
Mountain Sheep, or Bighorn.

218

Figure 166.
The Stone's race of the Dall's Sheep, photographed in northern British Columbia.

PACIFIC NORTHWEST SPECIES

BUFFALO; BISON bulls: 136-24-25 (3,400-600-620); cows: 96-16-20 (2,400-400-500) Figs. 163 and 186; Color Plate 15. This is a massive animal standing 5 to 6 feet high, and weighing from 800 to 2,200 pounds. It is easily distinguished by its size, dark brown color, massive head, shaggy mane, shoulder hump, and weak hindquarters. Horns, short and black, are found in both sexes. RANGE. Now extinct in all of the Pacific NW, except for stragglers in the extreme e. portion of Idaho adjacent to Yellowstone National Park from which they stray. Some have been introduced to certain Canadian Rocky Mountain Parks. HABITAT. Open grasslands, though also found in open woods and brushy areas.

MOUNTAIN GOAT billies: 64-7-14 (1,600-175-340); nannies: 10-20 per cent smaller. Figs. 164 and 184; Color Plate 6. The Mountain Goat stands 3 to 3½ feet high and weighs 125-300 pounds. It is a large, goat-like animal with long, entirely-white fur. The hooves and the slightly backward-curving horns are shiny black in contrast to the remainder of the animal. RANGE. Occurs in the Cascades, Olympics, and n.e. mts. of Wash.; n. and c. Idaho; and w. and s.e. B.C. To be found in the most rugged of mountainous terrain, particularly steep cliffs and high ridges above timberline; often descending into forested areas in the winter.

BIGHORN SHEEP; MOUNTAIN SHEEP rams: 60-5-15 (1,500-120-400); ewes: somewhat smaller. Fig. 165; Color Plate 15. The Bighorn is a large sheep-like animal with short, grayish to brownish-gray fur on the back and sides and white fur on the belly, muzzle, and rump. The male has large horns, thick at

219

Figure 167.
Dall's Sheep (upper); Stone's Sheep (lower).

220

the base, spiraling back, down, and forward to form an arc or complete curl or loop in the older animals. The horns on the ewes are short and curve backward. RANGE. Occurs in scattered localities in s. B.C. and in Okanogan Co. in n. Wash., c. Idaho, and e. Ore. Most populations s. of the U.S.-Canadian border are from re-introduced stock. HABITAT. Formerly common on the open prairies of the Great Plains, this species is now restricted largely to the open, alpine meadows and grassy slopes near cliffs and rocky ridges in the mts. Sheep often move downward in winter.

DALL'S SHEEP; THIN-HORN SHEEP   rams: $55\frac{5}{8}$-$3\frac{7}{8}$-$15\frac{3}{8}$-$2\frac{7}{8}$ (1,420-100-400-74); ewes: $53\frac{11}{16}$-$3\frac{3}{4}$-$14\frac{7}{8}$-$2\frac{13}{14}$ (1,370-98-380-72).   These measurements for the white "Dall's Sheep"; the dark "Stone's Sheep" measure about 14 per cent larger in body size. Figs. 166 and 167.   Horns thinner and more flaring than in the Bighorn Sheep. Otherwise, separable by geographic distribution from that species. Northern race (*O. dalli dalli*), almost entirely creamy white; southern race (*O. dalli stonei*), grayish brown, except for white rump, inside of legs, and face. RANGE. Occurs only in extreme n. B.C. (excepting the n.e. corner). Sheep of the extreme n.w. tip of the province are the Dall's race, while those farther east are the Stone's sheep, with considerable intergradation between the two. HABITAT. Occurs in high, alpine tundra in summer, moving down to lower south-facing slopes in winter.

Those of us interested in natural history and the wild things are otfen asked by our friends as to what we see in animals, plants, rocks, the weather, etc. In other words, what do we *do* with them? Often these are hard questions to answer; many of us take our interests for granted.

First, of course, is the thrill of *finding* things—mammals in the context of this book—and mammals can be more of a challenge than the more abundant birds. Unless, of course, one is standing in the middle of Africa's Serengeti Plain! In this guide, we have discussed many ways and places to look for mammals. Experienced students are aware of a whole, unseen world of furry beasts that often lives in close proximity to ourselves, but one has to know how to enter that world!

Then, there is the matter of *identification*. That problem may also be solved in the Northwest by the use of this guide. Mammals are not as numerous in kinds as fish or birds and there are fewer thematic variations.

Our friends might then ask us, what do you do with the mammal when you have found and identified it? Many of us find sufficient pleasure and joy in merely observing the animal, appreciating its beauty of color and contour, its alert awareness of the surrounding environment, its intelligent reaction to stimuli, and its grace of movement, and most of all the fact that here is a living thing like ourselves, with many of our problems to meet and to solve.

It is easy to explain the use some "beast watchers" make of animals, the finding, the listing, the photographing, or the painting, but the pure and simple contemplation of a living thing is more difficult to describe. The esthetic appreciation of life in its myriad variety reveals the truest interest in the wild things.

CHECKLIST OF NORTHWEST MAMMALS

Order MARSUPIALIA

Family DIDELPHIDAE Opossums

American Opossum—*Didelphis virginiana*

Order INSECTIVORA

Family SORICIDAE Shrews

Cinereous Shrew—*Sorex cinereus*
Preble's Shrew—*Sorex preblei*
Vagrant Shrew—*Sorex vagrans*
Dusky Shrew—*Sorex obscurus*
Pacific Shrew—*Sorex pacificus*
Ornate Shrew—*Sorex ornatus*
Water Shrew—*Sorex palustris*
Marsh Shrew—*Sorex bendirei*
Arctic Shrew—*Sorex arcticus*
Trowbridge's Shrew—*Sorex trowbridgei*
Merriam's Shrew—*Sorex merriami*
Pygmy Shrew—*Microsorex hoyi*

Family TALPIDAE Moles

Shrew-mole—*Neurotrichus gibbsi*
Townsend's Mole—*Scapanus townsendi*
Coast Mole—*Scapanus orarius*
Broad-footed Mole—*Scapanus latimanus*

Order CHIROPTERA

Family VESPERTILIONIDAE Evening Bats

Little Brown Bat—*Myotis lucifugus*
Yuma Brown Bat—*Myotis yumanensis*
Keen's Brown Bat—*Myotis keeni*
Long-eared Brown Bat—*Myotis evotis*
Fringed Brown Bat—*Myotis thysanodes*
Long-legged Brown Bat—*Myotis volans*
California Brown Bat—*Myotis californicus*
Small-footed Brown Bat—*Myotis subulatus*
Silver-haired Bat—*Lasionycteris noctivagans*
Western Pipistrel—*Pipistrellus hesperus*
Big Brown Bat—*Eptesicus fuscus*
Red Bat—*Lasiurus borealis*
Hoary Bat—*Lasiurus cinereus*
Spotted Bat—*Euderma maculatum*
Townsend's Big-eared Bat—*Plecotus townsendi*
Pallid Bat—*Antrozous pallidus*

Family MOLOSSIDAE Free-tailed Bats

Brazilian Free-tailed Bat—*Tadarida brasiliensis*
Big Free-tailed Bat—*Tadarida macrotis*

Order LAGOMORPHA

Family OCHOTONIDAE Pikas
 Collared Pika—*Ochotona collaris*
 Common Pika—*Ochotona princeps*

Family LEPORIDAE Rabbits and Hares
 Pygmy Rabbit—*Brachylagus idahoensis*
 Brush Rabbit—*Sylvilagus bachmani*
 Eastern Cottontail—*Sylvilagus floridanus*
 Nuttall's Cottontail—*Sylvilagus nuttalli*
 Snowshoe Hare—*Lepus americanus*
 White-tailed Jackrabbit—*Lepus townsendi*
 Black-tailed Jackrabbit—*Lepus californicus*
 European Rabbit—*Oryctolagus cuniculus*

Order RODENTIA

Family APLODONTIDAE Mountain Beavers
 Mountain Beaver—*Aplodontia rufa*

Family SCIURIDAE Squirrels
 Least Chipmunk—*Eutamias minimus*
 Yellow Pine Chipmunk—*Eutamias amoenus*
 Townsend's Chipmunk—*Eutamias townsendi*
 Cliff Chipmunk—*Eutamias dorsalis*
 Red-tailed Chipmunk—*Eutamias ruficaudus*
 Uinta Chipmunk—*Eutamias umbrinus*
 Eastern Woodchuck—*Marmota monax*
 Yellow-bellied Marmot—*Marmota flaviventris*
 Hoary Marmot—*Marmota caligata*
 Vancouver Marmot—*Marmota vancouverensis*
 Olympic Marmot—*Marmota olympus*
 White-tailed Antelope Squirrel—*Ammospermophilus leucurus*
 Townsend's Ground Squirrel—*Spermophilus townsendi*
 Washington Ground Squirrel—*Spermophilus washingtoni*
 Idaho Ground Squirrel—*Spermophilus brunneus*
 Richardson's Ground Squirrel—*Spermophilus richardsoni*
 Uinta Ground Squirrel—*Spermophilus armatus*
 Belding's Ground Squirrel—*Spermophilus beldingi*
 Columbian Ground Squirrel—*Spermophilus columbianus*
 Arctic Ground Squirrel—*Spermophilus parryi*
 California Ground Squirrel—*Spermophilus beecheyi*
 Golden-mantled Ground Squirrel—*Spermophilus lateralis*
 Eastern Gray Squirrel—*Sciurus carolinensis*
 Western Gray Squirrel—*Sciurus griseus*
 Fox Squirrel—*Sciurus niger*
 Red Squirrel—*Tamiasciurus hudsonicus*
 Douglas' Squirrel—*Tamiasciurus douglasi*
 Northern Flying Squirrel—*Glaucomys sabrinus*

Family GEOMYIDAE Pocket Gophers
  Southern Pocket Gopher—*Thomomys umbrinus*
  Townsend's Pocket Gopher—*Thomomys townsendi*
  Northern Pocket Gopher—*Thomomys talpoides*
  Idaho Pocket Gopher—*Thomomys idahoensis*
  Mazama Pocket Gopher—*Thomomys mazama*
  Camas Pocket Gopher—*Thomomys bulbivorus*

Family HETEROMYIDAE Pocket Mice and Kangaroo Rats
  Little Pocket Mouse—*Perognathus longimembris*
  Great Basin Pocket Mouse—*Perognathus parvus*
  Dark Kangaroo Mouse—*Microdipodops megacephalus*
  Ord's Kangaroo Rat—*Dipodomys ordi*
  Chisel-toothed Kangaroo Rat—*Dipodomys microps*
  Heermann's Kangaroo Rat—*Dipodomys heermanni*

Family CASTORIDAE Beavers
  Beaver—*Castor fiber*

Family CRICETIDAE Cricetid Mice and Rats
  Western Harvest Mouse—*Reithrodontomys megalotis*
  Canyon Mouse—*Peromyscus crinitus*
  Common Deer Mouse—*Peromyscus maniculatus*
  Mountain Deer Mouse—*Peromyscus oreas*
  Sitka Deer Mouse—*Peromyscus sitkensis*
  Pinyon Mouse—*Peromyscus truei*
  Northern Grasshopper Mouse—*Onychomys leucogaster*
  Desert Wood Rat—*Neotoma lepida*
  Dusky-footed Wood Rat—*Neotoma fuscipes*
  Bushy-tailed Wood Rat—*Neotoma cinerea*

Family MICROTIDAE Voles
  Northern Red-backed Mouse—*Clethrionomys rutilus*
  Gapper's Red-backed Mouse—*Clethrionomys gapperi*
  Western Red-backed Mouse—*Clethrionomys occidentalis*
  Heather Mouse—*Phenacomys intermedius*
  White-footed Tree Mouse—*Arborimus albipes*
  Red Tree Mouse—*Arborimus longicaudus*
  Singing Meadow Mouse—*Microtus miurus*
  Pennsylvania Meadow Mouse—*Microtus pennsylvanicus*
  Montane Meadow Mouse—*Microtus montanus*
  Gray-tailed Meadow Mouse—*Microtus canicaudus*
  California Meadow Mouse—*Microtus californicus*
  Townsend's Meadow Mouse—*Microtus townsendi*
  Tundra Meadow Mouse—*Microtus oeconomus*
  Long-tailed Meadow Mouse—*Microtus longicaudus*
  Creeping Meadow Mouse—*Microtus oregoni*
  Richardson's Water Vole—*Arvicola richardsoni*
  Sagebrush Vole—*Lagurus curtatus*
  Brown Lemming—*Lemmus sibiricus*
  Northern Bog Lemming—*Synaptomys borealis*
  Muskrat—*Ondatra zibethicus*

Family MURIDAE Old World Rats and Mice
  Roof Rat—*Rattus rattus*
  Norway Rat—*Rattus norvegicus*
  House Mouse—*Mus musculus*

Family DIPODIDAE Jumping Mice
  Pacific Jumping Mouse—*Zapus trinotatus*
  Western Jumping Mouse—*Zapus princeps*
  Meadow Jumping Mouse—*Zapus hudsonius*

Family ERETHIZONTIDAE Porcupines
  Porcupine—*Erethizon dorsatum*

Family CAPROMYIDAE Nutrias
  Nutria—*Myocastor coypus*

Order CETACEA
Suborder ODONTOCETI Toothed Whales
  Baird's Beaked Whale—*Berardius bairdi*
  Stejneger's Beaked Whale—*Mesoplodon stejnegeri*
  Hubb's Beaked Whale—*Mesoplodon carlhubbsi*
  Goose-beaked Whale—*Ziphius cavirostris*
  Sperm Whale—*Physeter catodon*
  Pygmy Sperm Whale—*Kogia breviceps*
  Blue Dolphin—*Stenella caeruleoalba*
  Common Dolphin—*Delphinus delphis*
  Northern Right-whale Dolphin—*Lissodelphis borealis*
  Pacific White-sided Dolphin—*Lagenorhynchus obliquidens*
  Killer Whale—*Orcinus orca*
  Risso's Dolphin—*Grampus griseus*
  False Killer Whale—*Pseudorca crassidens*
  Pilot Whale—*Globicephala melaena*
  Harbor Porpoise—*Phocoena phocoena*
  Dall's Porpoise—*Phocoenoides dalli*

Suborder MYSTICETI Whalebone Whales
  Gray Whale—*Eschrichtius robustus*
  Finback Whale—*Balaenoptera physalus*
  Sei Whale—*Balaenoptera borealis*
  Little Piked Whale—*Balaenoptera acutorostrata*
  Blue Whale—*Balaenoptera musculus*
  Humpback Whale—*Megaptera novaeangliae*
  Right Whale—*Balaena glacialis*

Order CARNIVORA
Family CANIDAE Dogs
  Coyote—*Canis latrans*
  Gray Wolf—*Canis lupus*
  Red Fox—*Vulpes vulpes*
  Kit Fox—*Vulpes velox*
  Gray Fox—*Urocyon cinereoargenteus*

Family URSIDAE Bears
  Black Bear—*Ursus americanus*
  Grizzly Bear—*Ursus arctos*
Family PROCYONIDAE Procyonids
  Raccoon—*Procyon lotor*
  Ringtail—*Bassariscus astutus*
Family MUSTELIDAE Mustelids
  Marten—*Martes americana*
  Fisher—*Martes pennanti*
  Short-tailed Weasel—*Mustela erminea*
  Long-tailed Weasel—*Mustela frenata*
  Least Weasel—*Mustela nivalis*
  Mink—*Lutreola lutreola*
  Wolverine—*Gulo gulo*
  Badger—*Taxidea taxus*
  Spotted Skunk—*Spilogale putorius*
  Striped Skunk—*Mephitis mephitis*
  River Otter—*Lontra canadensis*
  Sea Otter—*Enhydra lutris*
Family FELIDAE Cats
  Mountain Lion—*Felis concolor*
  Lynx—*Lynx lynx*
  Bobcat—*Lynx rufus*

Order PINNIPEDIA

Family PHOCIDAE Seals and Sea Lions
  Northern Fur Seal—*Callorhinus ursinus*
  Northern Sea Lion—*Eumetopias jubata*
  California Sea Lion—*Zalophus californianus*
  Harbor Seal—*Phoca vitulina*
  Northern Elephant Seal—*Mirounga angustirostris*

Order ARTIODACTYLA

Family CERVIDAE Deer
  Elk—*Cervus elaphus*
  Mule Deer—*Odocoileus hemionus*
  White-tailed Deer—*Odocoileus virginianus*
  Moose—*Alces alces*
  Caribou—*Rangifer tarandus*
Family ANTILOCAPRIDAE Pronghorns
  Pronghorn—*Antilocapra americana*
Family BOVIDAE Cattle
  Buffalo—*Bison bison*
  Mountain Goat—*Oreamnos americanus*
  Bighorn Sheep—*Ovis canadensis*
  Dall's Sheep—*Ovis dalli*

The arrangement of species in this book represents what the author believes to be the best system as known at present. Some mammalogists may disagree with certain decisions, but differences of opinion which lead to further collection of data and study and ultimate solution are the seeds of progress. In certain cases, it is felt that not enough is yet known about the status of the species in question to warrant any change. The situation with the marmots and pikas is a case in point.

We need to know much more about the whole matter of pre-, as well as post-, Pleistocene mammal movement back and forth between Asia and North America, as well as the history of boreal North American stocks during the ice age.

We seem to be in the age of lumpers where one way to solve a difficult systematic problem, the identity of a particular species, is to eliminate the problem by lumping the offending species with something else. Excessive merging of species produces an error in the system, that of eliminating needed contrasts between taxa, that is, the understanding of the fact that species A does have differences from species B. Just as excessive splitting damages our understanding of relationships, so can excessive amalgamation reduce our comprehension of differences.

Several recent studies have indicated that evolutionary changes in anatomy and way of life can, and have, proceeded independently of protein and karyotype evolution, such that molecular analyses as now applied are not particularly valid in systematics. Organismal evolution may proceed through differential modification of the genotype much more rapidly than protein evolution. How then do we classify animals? The author prefers the organismal characters of morphology and anatomy and, almost more importantly, the niche or biotype the form occupies—its way of life to which it has become adapted.

FINDING MAMMALS

Most mammals tend to be hidden from our eyes, except, of course, for the ubiquitous, diurnal squirrels. As a consequence, we must often search spe- cially for them. Some species are rare and seldom seen, even by the mam- malogist, so don't go rushing out looking for a Pygmy Shrew, expecting to find it. Many small, nocturnal mammals are acquired only by trapping. While the trap generally used by the collector has been the snap trap that kills the animal, more and more work is being done with live traps. The non-profes- sional can make use of this means for finding and studying many species that would otherwise be unavailable to him. The Havahart brand live traps are excellent and come in a variety of sizes. Not only are they a trap, but they can be used as a cage, being made essentially of strong hardware cloth. It is doubtful whether the lay person would wish to keep the live animal for more than a few minutes, or a few hours at most, after capture—just long enough to identify and study the beast, so that a live trap can be used to good advantage. Just let the animal go, when you are finished with it, preferably where you made the capture, and it should be little the worse for wear. As many small mammals are now protected by the non-game division of game departments, it would be well to check with them on your live trapping activities.

A number of baits have been used to capture mammals. Probably the most popular are dry rolled oats and peanut butter. These will attract most of the rodents and shrews. Apples or prunes may work for Flying Squirrels and pikas and lettuce and willow leaves have been used successfully for the latter species. Sunflower seeds attract squirrels and chipmunks. Carnivores must have meat, so if you are setting a live trap for a weasel, chicken heads are suggested. Dangling some chicken heads from the low branch of a tree may provide some interesting and amusing displays of mustelid frustration and problem solving. Do not keep the trapped animal for any length of time, as most wild mammals do not make good pets. Providing the proper food for a captive is a problem and they are much healthier and happier living free in their native haunts.

Since most mammals have particular ecological preferences, as should now be clear if you have read this book carefully, you must go to where they are if you would find them. In most cases, this means traveling to natural, wild areas. Some squirrels will be in city parks and backyards and Coyotes and cottontails may occasionally be found in agricultural lands, but the forests, deserts, mountains, and grasslands are where most of the mammals live.

Shrews are widely distributed in forests, marshes, and weedy fields. Some, like the Water Shrew, may occasionally be found early or late in the day going about their business along the edges of mountain streams. Many mammals, for that matter, may be found in the twilight hours of early morning or early evening. Deer and Elk browsing out in meadows, visiting salt licks, or coming down to water to drink; Snowshoe Hares feeding on green vegetation by the edges of mountain roads; meadow and jumping mice stirring in the grass— just a few examples of crepuscular animals.

The presence of moles and pocket gophers is revealed by their earth mounds. Deer will advertise their presence by groups of droppings or tracks in the dust or snow. De-barked branches or leaders of trees will denote the presence of a Porcupine in the vicinity.

Bats are almost impossible to identify in flight, but occasionally may be found roosting in attics, under eaves of buildings, or in caves. Because some of them have been shown to carry rabies, it is best not to handle bats.

Pikas may be found and observed in mountain rock slides, as can marmots and mantled ground squirrels. Rabbits are either diurnal or crepuscular and are usually not too difficult to locate. Chipmunks, mantled ground squirrels, and Red and Douglas' Squirrels are often abundant around forest service and national park campgrounds and are always in the mood for mooching peanuts. Plain-backed ground squirrels may be common by highways, country roads, or old corrals in the dry country in spring and early summer. Beavers may be observed easily in the early evening on their ponds. Wood rats are to be found in old buildings and forest cabins, and may find you, or at least some of your belongings, if you are not careful.

National parks are excellent places to find many mammals, especially the larger species. Because of their protected status, park animals are usually very tame. But don't get too close to any of them, particularly the bears. The finest park for animals in the Northwest is Yellowstone National Park where this guide will be very helpful.

Mice, the lesser among beasts, are often hard to find, though they are common in most natural habitats. Here the small live trap may be of real value. Needless to say, you have to travel on or by salt water to see the whales. Porpoises and Pilot Whales may regularly be found in certain places in Puget Sound, as in the tidal discontinuity off Port Casey. Coyotes are common in many parts of the Northwest, especially in the interior. They often howl just at sunup and sunset and at times during the night. They are not too difficult to see if you do enough driving in the eastern parts of the Pacific Northwest. Foxes are sneaky things, but occasionally you get a glimpse of one as he attempts to flee to cover. If you need bears, you might try the mountain berry patches in late summer or apple trees in old, abandoned farms. The weasel tribe are usually seen by accident, although a curious one may come out in plain sight to give you the once over. Keep an eye out for Badgers when you are driving through desert country.

In summary, to find mammals, go to their preferred haunts, be a quiet stalker, and above all, keep your eyes open.

TRACKING MAMMALS

As mentioned in an earlier essay, much can be learned about the activities of mammals in winter by studying their tracks and trails in the snow. To a limited extent, the same analysis can be used in summer by searching for tracks in the dust of a dirt road or in the soft mud by the shore of a pond or stream. The experienced observer always keeps an eye on such places, as they may give him the only clue to the presence of certain species. The author remembers with amusement a bird walk in the Shimba Hills south of Mombasa in East Africa, in which the bird watchers got quite a shock when the leader pointed out the leopard tracks in the dust of the road we were following.

The next few pages contain diagrams of the tracks of a number of different Northwest mammals, showing both the individual footprint and a sample stretch of trail. Identification of mammals by their tracks, while possible, has certain difficulties associated with it. The actual appearance of the track and trail may vary considerably, depending on the medium in which they were made. Animals will leave little, if anything, in the way of tracks in hard, crusted snow. For that reason, mammal tracking is difficult to do in the late winter or early spring when the snow surface softens to "corn snow" during the day and freezes hard at night. Conversely, deep powdery snow will cause the animal to sink down into it and all you may find for any but the lightest of beasts will be holes or sitzmarks in the surface. The ideal snow for trailing is the "tracking snow" of the woodsman, an inch or so of soft powder on top of a hard crust so that each toenail and pad of a paw will show. The conditions of the snow will likewise vary the size of the print, a track in deep snow being much larger than that left by the same paw in shallower snow. When dealing with a trail made in deep snow, you may have to observe more carefully the spacing of the individual footprints, that is, the distance between right and left paw marks and the distance between fore and hind prints.

Pay attention to small details in identifying tracks. Note the differences in curvature of right and left nails of a deer's hoof. Observe the strongly curved crescents of the Caribou, the lesser curves of the Moose, and the almost cattle-like prints of the Elk. Most of the weasel tribe leave paired prints in the snow and one has to rely on the size of the indentation, the distance between right and left paw marks, and the leap distance between pairs of prints. You will find the study of tracks and trailing of animals a thrilling and informative hobby. Try it when next the snow flies!

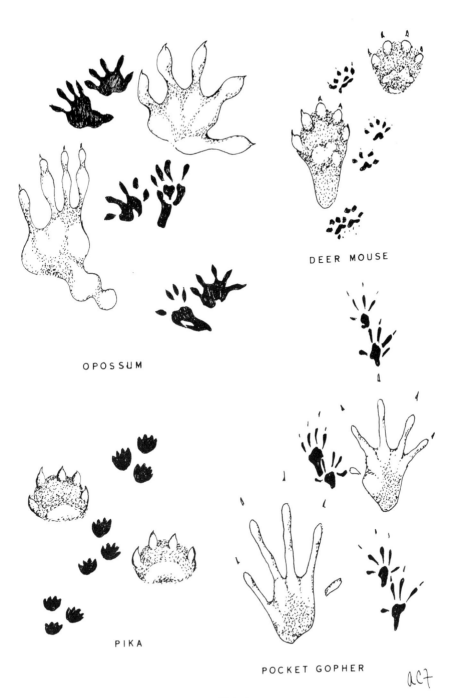

DEER MOUSE

OPOSSUM

PIKA

POCKET GOPHER

Plate I.

231

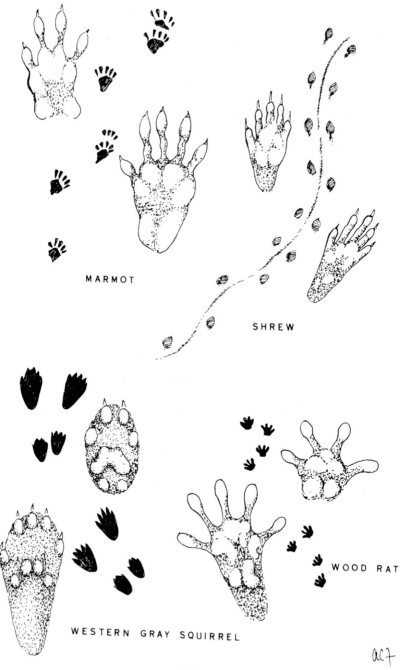

MARMOT

SHREW

WESTERN GRAY SQUIRREL

WOOD RAT

Plate II.

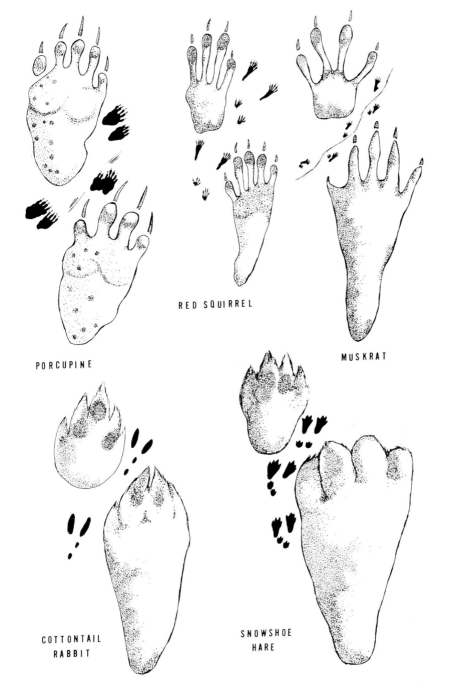

RED SQUIRREL

PORCUPINE

MUSKRAT

COTTONTAIL
RABBIT

SNOWSHOE
HARE

Plate III.

233

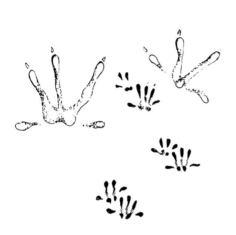

NORWAY RAT

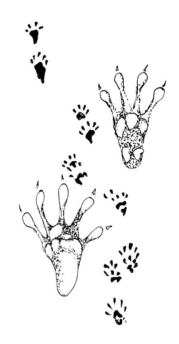

GROUND SQUIRREL

KANGAROO RAT

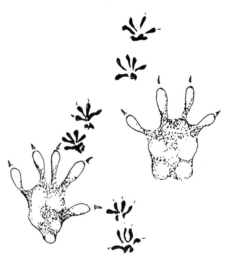

MEADOW MOUSE   ac7

Plate IV.

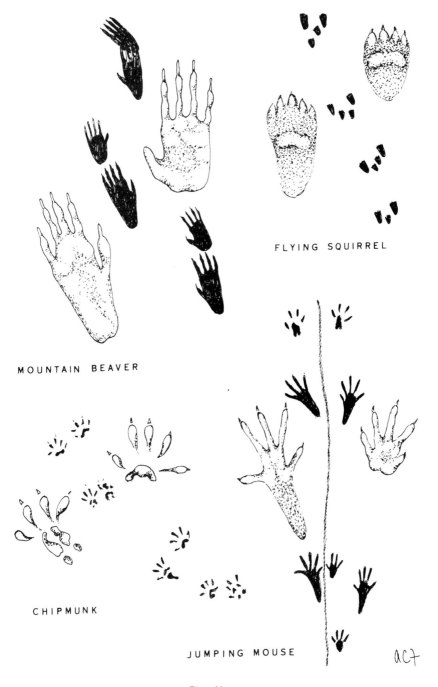

MOUNTAIN BEAVER

FLYING SQUIRREL

CHIPMUNK

JUMPING MOUSE

Plate V.

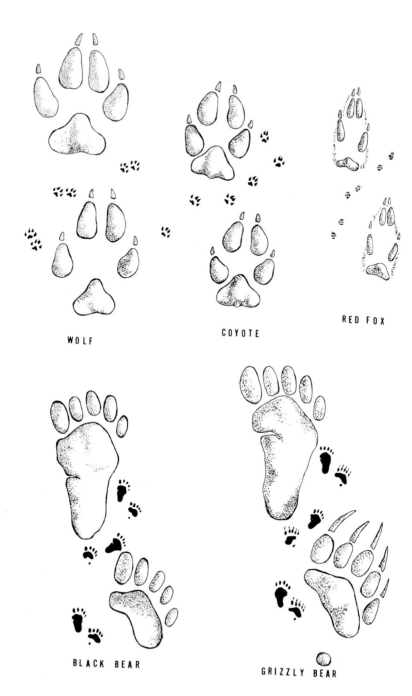

WOLF

COYOTE

RED FOX

BLACK BEAR

GRIZZLY BEAR

Plate VI.

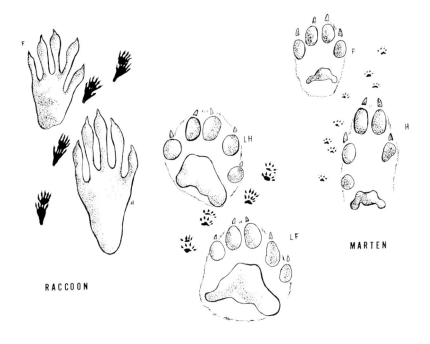

RACCOON

FISHER

MARTEN

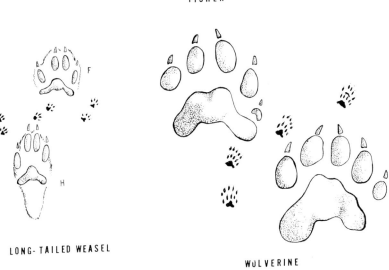

LONG-TAILED WEASEL

WOLVERINE

Plate VII.

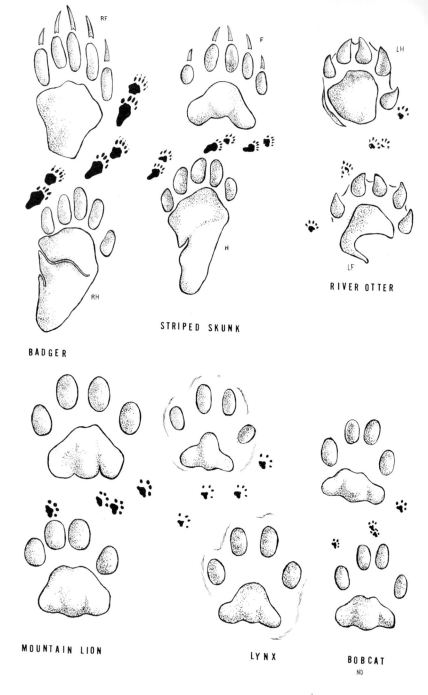

RF

F

LH

RIVER OTTER

LF

RH

BADGER

STRIPED SKUNK

H

MOUNTAIN LION

LYNX

BOBCAT
ND

Plate VIII.

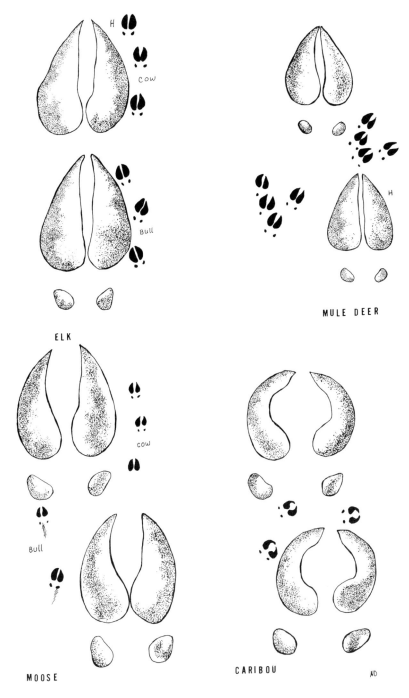

H COW

Bull

MULE DEER

ELK

COW

Bull

MOOSE

CARIBOU

ND

Plate IX.

239

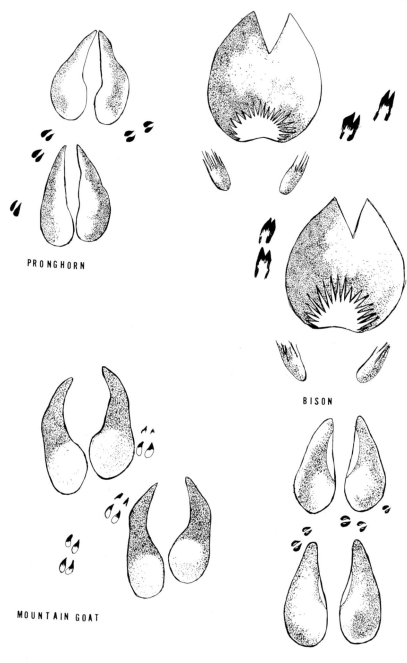

PRONGHORN

BISON

MOUNTAIN GOAT

BIGHORN SHEEP

Plate X.

PHOTOGRAPHING MAMMALS

Mammals make interesting photographic studies and the "trophies" leave the victim alive and healthy. Certain large species, such as Moose and Elk, can be photographed with comparative ease in some of our national parks, but the shyer carnivores and the host of rodents and shrews present real challenges to the ingenious camera buff.

Unlike the professional mammal photographer who works with a variety of cameras—particularly the macro and movie types—and an array of color and black and white films, the amateur photographer will most likely restrict himself to 35 mm color transparencies for projection in the home.

Recent improvement in films and cameras have changed somewhat the techniques of mammal photography. We now have an excellent, fine grain color film with very fast speed. I am referring to the Kodak High Speed Ektachrome which may be exposed at ASA 400 with subsequent special processing. This has made possible the hand-holding of a lightweight 35 mm camera and telephoto. Your author has found the 300 mm non-zoom telephoto lens to be the most usable under various field conditions. He recently took 1,600 color photographs on an African safari using an Olympus OM-1 camera with an Olympus 300 mm F 4.5 telephoto lens. The high speed of the film and strong available light made it possible to shoot most of the pictures at 1/1,000 of a second, effectively stopping any motion of the subject or camera. The equipment was hand held or rested on the sill of a vehicle window, since using a tripod in a minibus or land rover is impossible. The results were excellent.

A single lens reflex camera with "through the lens" light metering is to be recommended, as this system automatically takes care of the need for correcting the diaphragm adjustment when using supplementary lenses. A fast telephoto is desirable, one preferably opening up to at least F 4.5. While the zoom lens has some uses, most shooting will be done at its highest power. This fact, coupled with the slightly poorer quality of picture from a zoom and its higher price, makes the fixed focus telephoto more desirable. For power, 300 or 400 mm will be best. Less than 300 will not give sufficient magnification and price, impracticality of hand holding, and heat waves render a lens stronger than 400 of little value.

A lightweight metal case with foam padding, cut to fit the pieces of equipment carried, is recommended. Include a squeeze bulb cleaning brush and an extra battery for the light meter of the camera. If you travel by plane, route the camera case around the hijack monitoring frame, rather than through it, in spite of what the attendant tells you. He will make you open the case to inspect the equipment then, but the delay is minimal. Take all photographic equipment on board as carry-on luggage to avoid rough handling and excessive vibration.

Experience is the best teacher in photography, but much can be learned from studying the work of experts. Good luck!

Figure 168.
An album of mammal photography on this and the following pages. A Marten in the Selway-Bitterroot Wilderness of northern Idaho (Pole).

242

Figure 169.
Hoary Marmot, photographed on a rockslide after a careful stalk by Greg Pole.

Figure 170.
Camera with remote control for photographing chipmunks at a feeding tray.

Figure 171.
A block of cattle salt may be used to attract deer for observation and photography.

Figure 172.
Trail of a Wolverine on Galena Summit, Idaho.

244

Figure 173.
Curiosity may help the photographer (Pole).

Figure 174.
Zoos may provide the mammal photographer with good shots,
as this Sea Otter demonstrated.

245

Figure 175.
Three students (left to right: Eugene Williams, Bob Randall, and Jerry Ferrara) making
mammal studies in the Juniper Forest sand dunes in south-central Washington.

Figure 176.
A haunt of the Beaver makes an interesting scenic photo.

246

Figure 177.
A large Beaver lodge by the side of a lake in northeastern Washington.

Figure 178.
Young mammals are often curious and make good shots, as did this Hoary Marmot.

247

Figure 179.
Photographers must not approach some mammals too closely.

Figure 180.
Activity photo: burrow mouth and excavated soil of a Columbian Ground Squirrel.

248

Figure 181.
Activity photo: tracks of Black Bear, Coyote, Red Squirrel, and human in the dust of a forest road.

Figure 182.
Activity photo: Deer Mouse trail in the snow.

Figure 183.
Activity photo: tracks of a Marten in British Columbia.

Figure 184.
A rare shot of a sleeping Mountain Goat (Pole).

Figure 185.
There's a Moose in camp! Some mammals are adjusting well to their human neighbors.

Figure 186.
Buffaloes make interesting camera portraits, but don't get too close (Pole).

251

Figure 187.
The author recording the results of some mammal trapping studies.

READING ABOUT MAMMALS

Anderson, Rudolph M., METHODS OF COLLECTING AND PRESERVING VERTEBRATE ANIMALS, 4th ed. National Museum of Canada, Bulletin No. 69, Ottawa, Ontario, 1965. Thorough, detailed account of the methods of collecting and preserving mammal specimens.

Banfield, A. W. F., THE MAMMALS OF CANADA. University of Toronto Press, 1974. An interesting, well-written, and well-illustrated treatment of the mammals of Canada.

Bourliere, Francois, THE NATURAL HISTORY OF MAMMALS, 3rd ed. Knopf, New York, 1964. A good, non-technical textbook on mammalogy.

Burt, William H. and Richard P. Grossenheider, A FIELD GUIDE TO THE MAMMALS, 2nd ed. Houghton Mifflin Company, Boston, 1964. Excellent, up-to-date field guide to the mammals of North America with descriptions, brief treatment of habits, ranges, and maps. Well illustrated. A volume in the famous Peterson Field Guide Series.

Cahalane, Victor H., MAMMALS OF NORTH AMERICA. Macmillan Company, New York, 1947. A good general review of the mammals of the continent, dealing mostly with their general habits.

Cowan, Ian McT. and Charles Guiguet, THE MAMMALS OF BRITISH CO-LUMBIA, 3rd ed. B.C. Provincial Museum Handbook No. 11, Victoria, B.C., 1965. An excellent guide to the mammals of British Columbia. Contains mainly descriptions and ranges of species and subspecies. Well illustrated.

Grosvenor, Melville B. (ed.), WILD ANIMALS OF NORTH AMERICA. National Geographic Society, Washington, D.C., 1960. Primarily a picture book. A number of good color photographs and paintings of mammals.

Hall, E. Raymond and Keith R. Kelson, THE MAMMALS OF NORTH AMERICA. Ronald Press, New York, 1959. A comprehensive catalog of the orders, families, genera, species, and subspecies of North American mammals with descriptions and keys down through the species level. Many distribution maps. Thorough to time of publication. Primarily for the specialist, but much of interest to the lay person. A new edition is being prepared.

Hamilton, William J., AMERICAN MAMMALS. McGraw-Hill Publishing Company, New York, 1939. A pioneer mammalogy text, but still very useful for its information on the habits of many species of mammals.

Ingles, Lloyd G., MAMMALS OF THE PACIFIC STATES; CALIFORNIA, ORE-GON, WASHINGTON. Stanford University Press, Stanford, 1965. Excellent manual on the mammals of the Pacific Coast. Much information on characters of species and distribution. Well illustrated with very fine black and white photos, especially of the small mammals.

Jaeger, Ellsworth, TRACKS AND TRAILCRAFT. Macmillan Company, New York, 1948. Well illustrated with much informational text. Much valuable material on the art of tracking. Long out of print, but available in some libraries.

Larrison, Earl J., GUIDE TO IDAHO MAMMALS. *Journal of the Idaho Academy of Science,* Vol. VI: 1-166. Available from the Idaho Academy of Science,

Ricks College, Rexburg, Idaho, 1967. Review of the mammals of Idaho with detailed keys to their identification and discussion of mammal ecology in the state.

Larrison, Earl J., WASHINGTON MAMMALS; THEIR HABITS, IDENTIFICATION AND DISTRIBUTION. Seattle Audubon Society, Seattle, 1970. Detailed habits, descriptions, and distributions of Washington mammals with treatment of subspecies. Keys to specimens and skulls. Out of print but in many Northwest libraries.

Lawrence, M. J. and R. W. Brown, MAMMALS OF BRITAIN; THEIR TRACKS, TRAILS AND SIGNS. Blandford Press, London, 1973. An exceptionally well-illustrated manual, dealing with many different ways to determine the presence of mammals. Bone identification, skulls, teeth. Some ultra-modern illustrative techniques. A book of this kind for North America would be most useful.

Morris, Desmond, THE MAMMALS; A GUIDE TO THE LIVING SPECIES. Harper and Row, New York, 1965. Not a field guide, but a good, general account of many of the world's mammals.

Murie, Olaus J., A FIELD GUIDE TO ANIMAL TRACKS, 2nd ed. Houghton Mifflin Company, Boston, 1974. Detailed, well illustrated guide to animal (mostly mammal) tracks and scats. Much excellent natural history information by a master field naturalist. Another volume in the Peterson Field Guide Series.

Orr, Robert T., MAMMALS OF NORTH AMERICA. Doubleday and Company, New York, 1970. Brief, but thorough, treatment of the various groups and major species of North American mammals, with excellent photographs in color and black and white. Deals mainly with habits and life histories. Introductory in approach, but much valuable information.

Palmer, Ralph S., THE MAMMAL GUIDE. Doubleday, New York, 1954. A usable guide to the mammals of the continent with some life history material.

Seton, Ernest T., THE LIVES OF GAME ANIMALS. Charles T. Brandford Company, Boston, 1928. The classic monograph on the larger mammals of North America with much life history material and copious illustrations. Now mainly of historical value. Many anecdotes of the author's field experiences. Out of print, but in many libraries.

Taylor, Walter P. and William T. Shaw, MAMMALS AND BIRDS OF MOUNT RAINIER NATIONAL PARK. Government Printing Office, Washington, D.C., 1927. Basically a report on the 1919 exploration of the fauna of the mountain by a group of ornithologists and mammalogists, but contains much useful information on identification and habits of the wildlife of the park written in a very interesting manner. A number of good photographs.

Van Gelder, Richard G., BIOLOGY OF MAMMALS. Scribner's, New York, 1969. A brief, general introduction to mammals.

Walker, Ernest P., MAMMALS OF THE WORLD, 3rd ed. Johns Hopkins Press, Baltimore, 2 vols., 1975. Treats, with photographic illustrations, all of the genera of world mammals with mention of the principal species. Considerable material on habits and distribution. The best thing of its kind and a good introduction to the various kinds of mammals on this planet.

INDEX

INDEX

INDEX

9499